Emerging-Economy State and International Policy Studies

This is the first series to highlight research into the processes and impacts of the state building and economic development of developing countries in the non-Western World that have recently come to influence global economy and governance. It offers a broad and interactive forum for discussions about the challenges of these countries and the responses of other countries to their rise. The term 'emerging-economy state,' a part of the series title, or its shorthand 'emerging states,' is intended to promote dialogues between economists who have discussed policy problems faced by 'emerging-market economies' and scholars in political science and international relations who have discussed 'modern state formation.' Many emerging states are still in the middle-income status and not immune from the risk of falling into the middle-income trap. The manner of their external engagement is different from that of the high-income countries. Their rise has increased the uncertainty surrounding the world. To reduce the uncertainty, good understanding of their purpose of politics and state capacity as well as their economies and societies would be required. Although the emerging states are far from homogenous, viewing them as a type of countries would force us into understand better the similarity and differences among the emerging states and those between them and the high-income countries, which would in turn to help countries to ensure peace and prosperity. The series welcomes policy studies of empirical, historical, or theoretical nature from a micro, macro, or global point of view. It accepts, but does not call for, interdisciplinary studies. Instead, it aims to promote transdisciplinary dialogues among a variety of disciplines, including but not limited to area studies, economics, history, international relations, and political science. Relevant topics include emerging states' economic policies, social policies, and politics, their external engagement, ensuing policy reactions of other countries, ensuing social changes in different parts of the world, and cooperation between the emerging states and other countries to achieve the Sustainable Development Goals (SDGs). The series welcomes both monographs and edited volumes that are accessible to academics and interested general readers.

More information about this series at http://www.springer.com/series/16114

Yusuke Takagi · Veerayooth Kanchoochat
Tetsushi Sonobe
Editors

Developmental State Building

The Politics of Emerging Economies

Springer Open

Editors
Yusuke Takagi
Graduate School of Policy Science
National Graduate Institute for Policy Studies
Tokyo, Japan

Tetsushi Sonobe
Graduate School of Policy Science
National Graduate Institute for Policy Studies
Tokyo, Japan

Veerayooth Kanchoochat
Graduate School of Policy Science
National Graduate Institute for Policy Studies
Tokyo, Japan

ISSN 2524-5023 ISSN 2524-5031 (electronic)
Emerging-Economy State and International Policy Studies
ISBN 978-981-13-2903-6 ISBN 978-981-13-2904-3 (eBook)
https://doi.org/10.1007/978-981-13-2904-3

Library of Congress Control Number: 2018957653

This Springer imprint is published by the registered company Springer Nature Singapore Pte Ltd.
The registered company address is: 152 Beach Road, #21-01/04 Gateway East, Singapore 189721, Singapore

Preface

The late Chalmers Johnson coined the term "developmental state" to capture the features of institutional and policy configurations of the hitherto fast-growing Japanese economy, which followed neither state socialism nor Anglo-Saxon capitalism. South Korea, Taiwan, Hong Kong, and Singapore soon formed the club of Asian Tigers or the newly industrialized countries. These phenomena inspired a bunch of researchers to explore the region and have driven the vibrant research programs on the developmental state.

However, a prism of two distinct approaches is evident. While a group of economists write a sequel, the East Asian Miracle, focusing on economic policies and strategies, political scientists are concentrated on state capacity and origins of the developmental state, as exemplified in the concept of embedded autonomy. Subsequently, many countries in Southeast Asia, South Asia, and Africa in this chronological order joined the club of intermediate states, which are somewhere between developmental states and predatory or failed states, and some are getting close to the developmental state status. The increase in the number of observations has been expected to promote deeper understanding of the developmental state. Nonetheless, economists' version of sequel and that of political scientists has never crossed.

This volume is a transdisciplinary dialogue among economists, historians, and political scientists to understand the dynamics of emerging states with rapid economic growth. Throughout discussion, we realized that we have studied same or similar societies with different sets of jargons. We often met the same persons as key informants in the fields or faced similar difficulties to collect (or correct) data in the same building. We stayed in the same city without direct communication. This research project has paved the way and provided a platform for broader discussion beyond traditional disciplines. We now hope that we could cultivate the lands for more collaborative research on dynamic politics and economy of emerging states in the near future.

Without active participation by emerging and inspiring scholars, we could not have reached at the stage of publishing the book. It is always easier said than done to carry out transdisciplinary research project. We especially appreciate actual contribution and inspiration given by Caroline Sy Hau, Peter Katzenstein, Takashi Shiraishi, Keiichi Tsunekawa, Pasuk Phongpaichit, Chris Baker, and John Page among others. We are also grateful for administrative supports provided by Yasuko Takano, Akiko Ishikawa, Eriko Kimura, Miori Maeda, Yu Ito, and Ritsuko Fukuma.

Finally, we acknowledge the generous financial supports from the Japan Society for Promotion of Science (JSPS) KAKENHI Grant Nos. 25101001, 25101002, 251004, 251005, 251006, and 15K21728. The support from KAKENHI Grant No. 25101002 made the Open Access publication of this volume possible.

Tokyo, Japan

Yusuke Takagi
Veerayooth Kanchoochat
Tetsushi Sonobe

The original version of the book was revised: The print ISSN has been updated in copyright page. The correction to the book is available at https://doi.org/10.1007/978-981-13-2904-3_10

Contents

Editors and Contributors

About the Editors

Yusuke Takagi is Assistant Professor at the National Graduate Institute for Policy Studies (GRIPS). He received his S.J.D. from Keio University and taught international politics and comparative politics at De La Salle University, Manila, before joining GRIPS. He worked at the Embassy of Japan in the Philippines as advisor/researcher. He is the author of *Central Banking as State Building: Filipino Policymakers and their Nationalism, 1933–1964* (Quezon City: Ateneo de Manila University Press, Singapore; National University of Singapore Press, Kyoto: Kyoto University Press, 2016, Ohira Masayoshi Memorial Prize). His recent publications include "Economic nationalism and its legacy," in Mark R. Thompson and Eric Vincent C. Batalla eds. *Routledge Handbook of the Contemporary Philippines* (Routlege, 2018), "*Touchi* (Governance)," in Yamamoto Nobuto eds. *Tounan Ajia chiiki nyuumon: Seiji* (Introduction to Southeast Asian Area Studies: Politics) (Tokyo: Keio University Press, 2017), and "Policy coalitions and ambitious politicians: A case study on the Philippine social policy reform," (*Philippine Political Science Journal*, 2017).

Veerayooth Kanchoochat is Associate Professor of Political Economy at the National Graduate Institute for Policy Studies (GRIPS). He holds an M.Phil. and Ph. D. from the University of Cambridge, UK, and has taught at GRIPS since 2013. His research interests range from the history of state formation to varieties of capitalism and reform politics, with a focus on newly industrializing economies in East and Southeast Asia. He is a co-editor of *Military, Monarchy and Repression: Assessing Thailand's Authoritarian Turn* (Routledge, 2017). His recent publications include "The Middle-income Trap and East Asian Miracle Lessons" (United Nations, 2015), "Reign-seeking and the Rise of the Unelected in Thailand" (*Journal of Contemporary Asia*, 2016), and "Thailand Trapped: Catch-up Legacies and Contemporary Malaise" (*TRaNS: Trans-Regional and -National Studies of Southeast Asia*, 2018).

Tetsushi Sonobe is Vice President of National Graduate Institute for Policy Studies (GRIPS) and a development economist. His scholarship has contributed to a deeper understanding of industrial clusters, business management, public service delivery, and industrial development in developing countries based on a number of case studies conducted in Asia and Africa. Before joining GRIPS, he was a Professor of Economics at Tokyo Metropolitan University and a senior researcher at the Foundation for Advanced Studies on International Development. He received his Ph.D. in economics from Yale University. He is a co-author of *Cluster-based industrial development: an East Asian model* (Palgrave Macmillan, 2006), *Cluster-based industrial development: a comparative study of Asia and Africa* (Palgrave Macmillan, 2011), and *Cluster-based industrial development: kaizen management for MSE growth in developing countries* (Palgrave Macmillan, 2014). He is a co-editor of *Applying the kaizen in Africa: a new avenue for industrial development* (Palgrave Macmillan, 2018). He is a recipient of the Nikkei Prize for Outstanding Book Publication and the Ohira Masayoshi Memorial Prize.

Contributors

Veerayooth Kanchoochat National Graduate Institute for Policy Studies (GRIPS), Tokyo, Japan

Boo Teik Khoo National Graduate Institute for Policy Studies (GRIPS), Tokyo, Japan

Toshihiro Kudo National Graduate Institute for Policy Studies (GRIPS), Tokyo, Japan

Satoru Kumagai Institute of Developing Economies, Japan External Trade Organization (JETRO), Chiba, Japan

Tomoya Matsumoto Otaru University of Commerce, Otaru, Japan

Tetsuji Okazaki Faculty of Economics, Graduate School of Economics, University of Tokyo, Tokyo, Japan

Yuri Sato Institute of Developing Economies (IDE), Japan External Trade Organization (JETRO), Chiba, Japan

Tetsushi Sonobe National Graduate Institute for Policy Studies (GRIPS), Tokyo, Japan

Yusuke Takagi National Graduate Institute for Policy Studies (GRIPS), Tokyo, Japan

Shinichi Takeuchi African Studies Center, Tokyo University of Foreign Studies, Fuchu, Japan

List of Figures

List of Tables

Chapter 1
Introduction: The Nexus of Developmental Policy and State Building

Yusuke Takagi, Veerayooth Kanchoochat and Tetsushi Sonobe

1.1 Introduction: Is the Developmental State Still Relevant?

Life of the "developmental state" concept has its ups and downs. Its heyday had lasted from the mid-1980s until the Asian financial crisis broke out in the late 1990s. Many analysts considered that it would face almost certain death following that crisis, during which the term "developmental state" seemed to connote "crony capitalism". Nonetheless, its flagging fortune has been revived again in the wake of the global financial crisis of 2007–08, as the so-called Washington Consensus, with an opposing emphasis on deregulation and liberalization, is subject to growing criticisms (Helleiner 2010; Birdsall and Fukuyama 2011). Meanwhile, the Beijing Consensus, reminding most observers of the developmental state concept, has attracted increasing attention worldwide (Halper 2010). More fundamentally, however, renewed interest in the developmental state is due to the fact that the debate itself focuses on questions that are unlikely to easily fade into insignificance, that is, the relationship between the state, the market and civil society as well as the political and institutional foundations for long-term economic development (Hayami and Aoki 2001; Haggard 2015).

Of course, the traditional understanding of the developmental state had already become obsolete. Early studies were seriously problematic not only in their state-centric view and *post hoc ergo propter hoc* reasoning but also their samples which were small in number and limited or biased toward Asian economies (more on this below). Moreover, international and domestic contexts have changed considerably. While the wider process of globalization has increasingly reduced the latitude of policy choice for developing countries, the democratization process has rationalized the demands of domestic voters for income redistribution and public provision as well as the elimination of intolerable inefficiencies and injustice. As a result, unlike the

Y. Takagi (✉) · V. Kanchoochat · T. Sonobe
National Graduate Institute for Policy Studies (GRIPS), Tokyo, Japan
e-mail: y-takagi@grips.ac.jp

Y. Takagi et al. (eds.), *Developmental State Building*, Emerging-Economy State and International Policy Studies, https://doi.org/10.1007/978-981-13-2904-3_1

developmental state of the Cold War era, which in the twenty first century is forced to rethink state intervention and cannot secure political legitimacy by achieving economic growth alone.

All these analytical limitations and evolving contexts provide an opportunity for us to reconsider more thoroughly the role of the state in economic development and offer deeper reflections on development strategies for emerging economies. More specifically, this volume makes enquiries into the bled of technocracy and democracy delivering economic growth with equity, national and regional security and stability (Shiraishi 2018). It also explores those factors which lead to particular mixes of technocracy and democracy, presumably including state capabilities, geopolitical location, and ethnic diversity. Through these enquiries, the volume aims at relativizing and redefining the developmental state perspective so that the concept can treat successful and failed attempts to build developmental states in the remote and recent past in a coherent way. It also intends to draw policy implications relevant to the current and future emerging states.

This chapter proposes a framework to modify and revitalize the developmental state approach. Since the end of the Cold War, accompanied by the US declining support for the Third World (see Jackson 1990), an increasing number of developing country governments have changed their attitudes to the development of their own economies from near indifference to willingness and even to strong commitment. Meanwhile, rapid globalization has increased the opportunity cost of the remaining underdeveloped and non-industrialized. Growth "miracles" in East Asia in the past five decades have recast doubt about the principle of *laissez faire* among people in the other parts of the developing world.[1] This awareness, together with the progress of democratization, has prompted policymakers in these countries to discover when and how far economic policies should deviate from *laissez faire*, what brings effective policy designs and implementation toward economic development, what prevents political leaders and state institutions from being captured by vested interests (the so-called "state capture"), and what induces them to drive economic development.

To meet this demand for knowledge, the developmental state approach can impart its insights into development policies and institutional arrangements for planning, deciding, and implementing the policies. For this purpose, this chapter points to the importance of making developmental state argument reflect the recent globalization and democratization and the recent progresses in social sciences. Among the progresses in social sciences, we think the following are particularly relevant to the developmental state. The first is the increased availability or accumulation of case studies of successes and failures in economic development. Singapore, for example, shared somewhat similar policies toward economic development with the Northeast Asian developmental states, while Thailand did to a much lesser degree. More recently examples are Botswana and Ethiopia, which have their own versions of "Look East" policy following the lead of Singapore and Malaysia. We propose international comparisons of regimes, institutions, policies, and growth performance

[1] Skepticism about *laissez faire* has had a long tradition, with roots tracing back at least to the work of Alexander Hamilton and Friedrich List in the eighteenth and nineteenth centuries.

among these developing countries, which were impossible for earlier researchers whose observations were limited to developmental experiences in Northeast Asian and the Western world[2].

Second, new insights into the interaction of political and economic institutions and into state capture should be incorporated into the development state argument. Third, the developmental state argument should embrace the policy implications of the new trade theory and the new economic geography (or spatial economics), which explain why orthodox policies are not necessarily desirable from the national welfare point of view. Fourth and similarly, the implications of social capital and coordination failures should be taken into account. These concepts have been used extensively in recent studies to explore the determinants of the capabilities of people, firms, public offices, and their society. Depending on such capabilities, public policies that work well in one country may not work in another. The fifth is the rapid growth in the literature on social network and global value chains (or commodity chain). As globalization proceeds, global value chains extend to a broader range of the developing world, and the roles and advantages of diaspora networks have been changing. The developmental state argument should incorporate insights from these bodies of literature.

The remaining discussion proceeds in the following way. The second section traces the evolution of the debate over the developmental state to demonstrate both its relevance for the twenty-first century and its major shortcomings. The third section considers the implications of the deeper process of globalization and democratization as well as recent developments in social science studies on the developmental state. The fourth section proposes our new approach to the study of developmental states. The fifth section briefly summarizes the chapters ahead.

1.2 Evolution of the Debate: Relevance and Shortcomings

The developmental state is one of a handful of concepts that have arisen from the empirical grounds outside the Western world but have gained global currency and provoked worldwide debate across scholarly and policymaking communities, signified in the launch and aftermath of the *East Asian Miracle Report* (World Bank 1993). At least prior to the 1997 Asian financial crisis, the eight highly performing Asian economies (HPAEs)[3] were considered to be the developmental models from which other developing countries should draw institutional and policy lessons to "replicate" their highly performing economies.

---

[2]Singh provides a good collection of case studies (Singh and Ovadia 2018).

[3]HPAEs included: Japan, Korea, Taiwan, Singapore, Hong Kong, Indonesia, Malaysia and Thailand.

1.2.1 From MITI to Embedded Autonomy

Chalmers Johnson is among the trailblazers in the field, with his *MITI and the Japanese Miracle* (1982) paving the way for the later generation of the developmental state literature that examined historical origins of East Asia's staggering growth through a typological framework. It is worth reminding the context of Johnson's study. He coined the term "developmental state" in the era of Cold War when most people could think of only two possibilities of political economy regime, that is, either socialism or capitalism. In this context, he argued that we should study Japan not within this dichotomy, but with a new framework, which is a *capitalist developmental state*. In other words, the developmental state is a concept to make a typology differentiating Japan from the US and USSR. While Johnson explained the changing nature of government–business relations from 1925 to 1975, he highlighted the bureaucracy as the key entity given enough authority to guide the country's economy and to implement its policy efficiently. He emphasized the role of administrative guidance and the Ministry of International Trade and Industry (MITI), as a pilot organization (Johnson 1982: Chap. 9). He even stressed that "Japan's [model] is a system of bureaucratic rule" (Johnson 1982: 320).

The work of Johnson inspired a group of scholars to expand their empirical analyses to newly industrializing economies in the late 1980s and the early 1990s, with a focus on selective industrial policy. Alice Amsden (1989) argued that South Korea succeeded in export-oriented industrialization by "getting the prices wrong", while Robert Wade (1990) summarized the key strategy that fostered Taiwan's extraordinary rate of economic growth as "governing the market". Stephan Haggard (1990) compared the internal political dynamics that allowed Hong Kong, Singapore, South Korea and Taiwan to move from an import-substitution strategy to an export-oriented industrializing strategy. When the debate proceeded to the search for the more general lessons that can be drawn from these East Asian economies, Peter Evans (1995) brought the concept of "embedded autonomy" to the fore. In addition to being autonomous and capable, a bureaucracy needs to develop close and productive ties to the business communities to formulate and implement effective industrial and trade policies. Otherwise the state would fall into the predatory state, where political elites exploit national resources without providing social welfare to the people in general, or an intermediate type.

In sum, the rising tide of the developmental state concept in this early debate has moved from the impressive, yet specific, role of MITI in the early 1980s to the more generalized lesson of embedded autonomy in the mid-1990s. While we consider that the categorization of state type as Evans (1995) made is still of use, especially in the analysis on contemporary African economies, we maintain that the interpretation of the developmental state based on a *specific set of policy instruments* or *economic performance* is misleading. The development state should be defined in terms of the shared intentions among the leaders and policymakers, as Johnson (1982) originally perceived.

1.2.2 Fatal Flaws that Require Remedies

Despite the profound insights offered by the existing studies of the developmental state, they suffer from three major drawbacks, that is: overly structural explanations; state-centric unit of analysis; and East Asian empirical bias.

First of all, structural explanations have dominated the developmental states literature. All dominant explanations for the origins of developmental states have been made from the structuralist perspective, considering developmental state as being a product of the colonial legacies (Kohli 2004), the Cold War conditions (Woo-Cumings 1998), resource constraints (Rasiah 2003), or systemic and severe threats (Doner et al. 2005). While these structural factors are relevant, a mere focus on them results in the failure to account for the role of human agency in the complicated process of design, formation and maintenance of related policies and institutions, and contingency including timing of policy implementation (Hau 2017).

The fundamental issues of structure–agency should be dealt with in a more balanced manner. A better understanding of effective developmental strategies and states requires an analysis that compares and contrasts the interactions of leaders and leading actors across countries and regions (Leftwich 2010). A good example of such leaders is Noorul Quader, a bureaucrat-turned-businessman, whose foresight laid the foundation for the rapid and sustained development of the export-oriented garment industry in Bangladesh. This industry did not exist forty years ago, but it has led the high economic growth of the country for the last three decades by growing into the second largest garment exporter in the world (Easterly 2002; Mottaleb and Sonobe 2011).

The example of the entrepreneur in Bangladesh reminds us of the second flaws in the existing literature, which is so-called East Asian bias. In this volume, we call for a study that goes beyond the East Asian bias prevalent in the existing literature and investigate more thoroughly emerging states such as those in Southeast Asia and Africa. Even though we can hardly find a full-fledged developmental state in Southeast Asia, several scholars consider many Southeast Asian economies as possessing the intermediate states in which we can find certain parts of the *pockets of efficacy* (e.g. Doner et al. 2005). As above mentioned, we can still find pockets of efficacy in one of the latest members of the middle income country such as Bangladesh. It is interesting, analytically and empirically, to explore how the "intermediate states" have fared after the two financial crises. Even more interesting is the "developmental state experiment in Africa" (Ayee 2013). In the past decade there have been attempts to "emulate" the economic successes of East Asia, with the concept of developmental states being increasingly employed in the continent. For example, the African National Congress (ANC) in South Africa used the concept explicitly in its electoral campaign material, while the late Ethiopian Prime Minister Meles Zenawi promoted the model as the way forward to African Finance Ministers (Routley 2014). This volume aims to shed new light on the developmental state literature by going beyond the East Asian boundary to examine various aspects of economic development in newly emerging economies.

Third, the traditional developmental state approach suffers from its tendency to pay too much attention to political institutions and its relative neglect of the private sector. It is farmers, businesses, and their workers in the private sector who play the central roles in economic development. Bureaucrats and politicians are auxiliary players. The latter, however, exert enormous influences on the central players, reminding us the importance of looking at both types of players and examining their relationship carefully. Existing empirical analyses demonstrate the association among delegation, bureaucratic reform, and economic take-off, but they do not establish the underlying causal connections. Nor do they examine under what conditions political institutions lead the private sector, not the other way around. A possible hypothesis is that political institutions guide the private sector when and where the former are superior to the latter in information gathering and processing, knowledge, and foresight, and *vice versa*. In our view, such capabilities are composed of human capital as emphasized by Schultz (1961) and Becker (1964), social capital as emphasized by Putnam (1993) and Arrow (1998), and the ability to coordinate as studied by game theoretic experimenters such as Cooper et al. (1992) and Brandts et al. (2014) among others.

Going back to the example from the garment industry in Bangladesh, Quader sent 130 highly educated Bangladeshi employees to South Korea to receive intensive training for eight months at a Korean leading garment firm. These trainees would become the cadre of the subsequent industrial development (Rhee 1990). As soon as completing the training, they went back to Quader's newly established factory to produce and export their products to developed country markets. To do this successfully, they needed new government policies and regulations related to export financing and bonded warehouses. As the government had no expertise in making such arrangements necessary for the then new industry, it was Quader's firm and the Korean firm that took the initiative in making them.[4] Generally, while government services are essential for a country to achieve economic development, it is not an easy task for the government to achieve embeddedness. Even with embeddedness and good policies, however, economic development could not be achieved if the private sector was too weak. This is why this volume pays much attention to the government's capability and its intention to assist economic development and to the private sector's capability as well as government policies toward strengthening it.

1.2.3 A Redefinition of Developmental States

Following the Asian financial crisis in 1997–8, a number of critics underscored the risks associated with industrial policy and restated the case for market-oriented

[4]In contrast, the development of the generic drug industry, which has been another leading industry of Bangladesh for the last decade, was boosted by a drastic and surprising industrial policy designed by an expert committee under the head of the army who had just seized power through a bloodless coup in 1982 (Amin and Sonobe 2014).

reform. At that time such terms as "booty capitalism" and "crony capitalism" came to replace the developmental state, leading Wong (2004: 345) to summarize that: "In the end, it seemed that the most severe and lasting casualty of the 1997 crisis was the East Asian developmental state model itself."

Nevertheless, the view that the Asian financial crisis was the death knell for the developmental state is an unfounded claim, as it rests on the misleading presumption that defines the developmental state in terms of a *fixed set of policy instruments*. In fact, industrial policy of the East Asian states was not all about the promotion of "national champions" via heavy-handed credit control. Although that orientation was pursued by South Korea, Taiwan was rather characterized by its state support for small-to-medium-sized enterprises via a variety of policy means, whereas Singapore has lent a great weight to the role of state-own enterprises. As pointed out by Thurbon (2014, 4–6), the developmental state is better conceptualized in ideational term—rather than equating it with specific policy approaches that freeze the concept in space and time. Going back to the original work of Johnson (1982), his contribution was not only describing the key features of developmental states, but, more importantly, specifying what sets them apart from other state varieties. In there, Johnson distinguishes the "plan-rationality" character of the developmental state from both the "market-rational" (concerned with the rules of economic activity than substantive outcomes as in the US) and the "plan ideological" (bureaucratic planning is valued as an end in itself as in the Soviet Union) types. The pursuit of techno-industrial transformation and competitiveness of developmental states is a political-economic project that places priority on national economic growth:

> Johnson's original conceptualization of the [developmental state] placed primary emphasis on the *shared goals* or *ambitions* of the policymaking elite (i.e. national industrial transformation and competitiveness) as well as shared ideas about *how these goals might best be achieved* (i.e. via strategic intervention in the market). In this sense, Johnson's conception of developmentalism has a distinctive ideational element: it is as much a political-economic philosophy…[that is]…a set of ideas regarding the primary purpose of economic activity, the central goals of the state and the appropriate role of the state in achieving those goals – as it is a set of institutional arrangements and policy expressions. (Thurbon 2014, 6, original emphasis)

An ideationally-informed conceptualization of the developmental state not only helps us understand more fully about the evolution of East Asian states but also provides an analytical framework through which we can explore the variation among the emerging states in different regions. In addition to the three types by Johnson, we can add the type of "market-ideological" after learning the series of failures in Asia, Russia, and Eastern Europe caused by the abrupt changes triggered by the policy prescription prepared by those who believed in Washington Consensus (Stiglitz 2002).

What, then, differentiates a developmental state from other kinds of growth strategy? It is further argued here that a developmental state is one that focuses on productivity improvements rather than relying upon its market size or resources as a driving engine for economic growth. This is because, we are interested not in simple economic growth but more in transformation of political economy in particular states.

As discussed in detail in Tsunekawa (2018), if developing countries are assessed based on their catch-up speed (increase in GDP per capita) and economic size (share in global economy), there are 29 countries which could be counted as "emerging states". More interestingly, these emerging states do not take the same trajectory toward economic success. There is a significant variation in terms of advantage factor among them. Certain countries such as Russia, Chile and Nigeria recorded high growth rates thanks to their abundant natural resources. Some other countries, such as China, Brazil and India, benefit greatly from large domestic markets. The remaining emerging states are those that become dominant because of their productivity improvements, e.g. Singapore, Turkey, Thailand, the Philippines, Malaysia, Indonesia and Taiwan.[5] This third group is the focus of our volume. This is because the success of this group is mainly attributed to productivity improvements, a man-made phenomenon that can be replicated more easily than resource abundance and large domestic markets that are rather the given initial conditions.

In sum, we depart from a conventional wisdom that considers the developmental state based on a fixed set of policy instruments. The developmental state is used here as an analytical concept and redefined to underline the shared commitments of leaders and policymakers, with an emphasis on a country's productivity improvements that facilitate a process of transformation of a country's productive structure.

1.3 Democratization, Globalization and Policymaking in New Developmental States

In addition to remedying the three analytical flaws as discussed above, this volume aims to incorporate the issues of how the contexts conducive to economic growth that have differ the challenges of developmental states in the twenty-first century from the previous one.

1.3.1 Democratization and Conducive Contexts

The prime examples of developmental states, particularly South Korea and Taiwan from the 1970s to the late 1980s, were typically seen as ones governed by authoritarian regimes. As a result, many observers consider that the democratization process, which has taken place in most of the developing world since the 1990s, would hinder the possibility of developmental state building in the twenty-first century.

However, the contexts conducive to developmental state building should be considered beyond the dichotomy of democracy versus dictatorship. Political contexts

[5]Note that the advantage factor used here is not mutually exclusive. Some countries enjoy more than one advantage factor (to a different degree) such as Turkey and Indonesia that possess both large market sizes and productivity.

in which all East Asian developmental states could rather be conceptualized as a "shared growth" model, designed to achieve economic prosperity together with relatively equitable distribution of wealth and income. As Evans (1995) argues, the developmental state is the polar opposite of the predatory state. Accordingly, the more relevant questions than democracy/dictatorship are: How do the developmental states face social pressure? Why did they share the fruits of growth with the nation at least to some extent? What are the mechanisms to induce such a shared growth?

Based on the East Asian experience, scholars have considered *social policymaking* as an essential part of developmental regime making (*Tokyo Daigaku Shakai Kagaku Kenkyujo*, hereafter, *Shaken*, 1998; also see Chibber 2003). They argue that the developmental regimes aimed at establishing national economy based not on individualistic or sectoral interests but on national interests. Land reform might expand the domestic market, accelerating industrialization. In Japan and Korea, moreover, social policy could be seen through the "corporate welfare" system, including not just the lifetime employment but also health provision or educational subsidies for the employees' children. In sum, social policy can play a far more crucial role than providing a safety net and therefore significantly contribute to economic development in East Asia. For example, cost-effective public provision of health and education can bring about improvements in labor force quality that can, in turn, raise efficiency and enhance productivity. Interestingly, a comparative study of social policy regimes in East Asia, Eastern Europe, and Latin America reveals that the regime in East Asia is biased for education rather than universal social services or labor protection (Haggard and Kaufman 2008).

Social welfare also reduces tensions and enhances the legitimacy of the political system, thus providing a more stable environment for long-term investments (Chang 2002). This is another lesson we should draw from the East Asian miracle, especially when taken into account the rising expectation of people amid the democratization process (Naim 2013; Shiraishi 2016). Meanwhile, scholars working on African countries have criticized limitations of a sudden introduction of elections without a sufficient prepared process (e.g., Collier 2007, Chap. 3). Young electoral democracies have often failed to consolidate its new "game in town". This volume aims to address social pressure and its politico-economic consequences.

Even Evans has broadened his concept of embedded autonomy between states and businesses to link with civil society in his recent work on developmental states (Evans and Heller 2015). In this work, he and his coauthor point out that the government should be embedded not only in private businesses but also in civil society. In a same vein, this volume aims to examine the broader political coalitions that hinder or foster the developmental state.[6]

---

[6]Social policy or safety nets would be provided by grass-root institutions to varying degrees, depending on the initial conditions and process of state building and economic development in the past. In a country where both public and private provision of safety nets are far from sufficient, the government may lose legitimacy, which will make its development policy more likely to fail. This difficulty is an issue to be covered by Volume IV, but our chapter should at least mention it and can try to discuss a developmental state providing social services as much as needed.

1.3.2 Globalization and Developmental States

In our view, globalization is not necessarily conducive to economic growth but it opens many windows of opportunity. Economic growth has long been recognized to have two major engines: the expansion of external and internal trade and the progress of technology (e.g., Mokyr 2017). Globalization is a synonym of the expansion of international trade and investment. The latter is to some extent a result of technological progress in navigation, transportation, and communication, which have drastically reduced costs of transporting goods and exchanging ideas across the world. It is also a result of the initiatives and efforts of policy makers and international communities to harmonize institutional arrangements for international business and financial transactions and settlement as well as freer trade and investment agreements (e.g., Helleiner 1994, Chap. 4). Globalization is also associated with the diffusion of advanced technologies through technology transfers between trading partners, by multinational firms, and through foreign aids. Thus, although globalization has resulted from technological progress and expanded international commerce and finance, it has also fueled these two engines to boost further economic growth.

In addition, globalization has increasingly encouraged individuals to work abroad and resulting in the evolved idea about development finance and implications for economic development. Naim (2013, 60) reveals that remittances made by the migrant workers are now five-time more than that of total international aid and more than a total of annual inflows of foreign direct investment (FDI) to developing countries. Increasing remittances and rapid urbanization also generate huge domestic markets for service industry. The recent Philippine economy, for example, depends almost 10 percent of its GNP on remittances from abroad, enjoys rapid development of service sectors and paid less attention to the manufacturing than before (Raquiza 2014).

While globalization opens many windows of growth opportunity, it is not always beneficial or conducive to economic growth. It could aggravate fluctuations and risks due to bubbles, panics, and asset-price overshooting, which might devastate developing and emerging economies as the Asian financial crisis did toward the end of the 1990s. It could also increase the occurrence of brain drain or outmigration of special human resources to high-salary-paying countries, and that of land grabbing and resource acquisition in developing countries by foreign firms through illegal means that take advantage of foreign investment liberalization. Thus, it is little wonder that few countries have wholeheartedly accepted globalization. Rather the governments paradoxically introduce more regulations when they accelerate liberalization (Vogel 1996).

Nonetheless, some developing economies have recently emerged by selectively accepting and taking advantage of some aspects of globalization. Taiwan has become a powerhouse exporter of high-tech, high-precision goods. Thailand has become a center of automobile production in Southeast Asia by joining Japanese auto supply chains. The Philippines and India have been successful as providers of offshore outsourcing service. These emerging states have neither followed a laissez-faire strategy nor accepted every aspect of globalization, but they have embraced international supply chains and ardently made bilateral and multilateral free trade agreements. These facts must have put pressure on policymakers in developing countries to adopt wise policies to take advantage of globalization in order to achieve high economic growth. Thus, in our view, globalization will increase rather than decrease the number of countries that turn into developmental states in future (also see Baldwin 2016).

1.4 Developmental Strategy and Regime in Emerging States

To alleviate the analytical and empirical problems of the traditional developmental state literature, this book sets out to move beyond growth obsession and structural explanations to appreciate the dynamics of, and variation among, the emerging states. In doing so, we focus on both the developmental strategy and regime.

1.4.1 Developmental Strategy in Emerging States

Most scholarship in the developmental state tradition seems to evaluate the state's strength purely in terms of outcomes, usually economic growth. As Amyx (2004) puts it, those who praise Japan as a developmental state do not consider Japan's economic lost decades in their analysis (Amyx 2004). Even in the case of Southeast Asia, during the periods of rapid growth, the Thai and Malaysian states were deemed to be highly effective and any weaknesses were addressed only in footnotes. Yet the claim was reversed in crisis times. This is misleading because the impressive economic performance may result from a few state agencies or from particular economic policies without the overall effectiveness of the state changing. More importantly, it overlooks the unevenness in state capacities and the fact that the state's capacity may be high but is used for another purpose other than economic development. In order to appreciate the more dynamic nature of the developmental state, we should go beyond the developmental state as a typology of state and study the process of state transformation and their outcomes.

Revisiting Johnson's work (1982), we realize that there is a gap between his theoretical explanation in the chapter one and his historical narratives in the succeeding chapters. In the historical narratives on Japan's political economy, he revealed a process of policymaking and highlighted the roles of individuals and ideologies. For example, he paid much attention to a story of innovative bureaucrat Shinji Yoshino who elaborated on policy tools to suppress cut-throat competition in Meiji Japan (Johnson 1982, Chap. 2). A historical inquiry reminds us that a study on policymaking led by Alexander Hamilton, US Treasury Secretary, inspired Friedrich List to found German historical school of economics (Chang 2003). Historical analysis to trace the process of politico-economic transformation in a country provides us with a grip to go beyond overly static typology of countries.

Policymakers can be practitioners of grand strategy when they consider developmental policy with a big picture in order to transform existing socio-economic structure. Grand strategy is a set of policies to achieve larger policy goals beyond the control of a particular department of the government. In the case of foreign policy, for instance, policymakers led by the president work for the grand strategy combining security policy with economic diplomacy (Brands 2014). Grand strategy studies suggest that we examine a process of policymaking in addition to a specific policy and its outcome. A leading scholar in the field quotes US President Dwight Eisenhower saying, "[t]he plans are nothing, but the planning is everything" (Brands 2014, 195). As scholars working on the grand strategy of the US foreign policy scrutinize discussion and debates in the National Security Council instead of the State Department, scholars on developmental strategy should analyze deliberations for policymaking at the highest level.

Not a few scholars have already mentioned the linkage between the emergence of a developmental state and security issues (Doner et al. 2005). They argue that the systemic vulnerability composed of domestic and external threats and budget constraints compels policymakers to transform their political economy through economic development in Northeast Asia. They fail to explain, however, why similar attempts by the policymakers in Southeast Asia did not result into full-fledged developmental states. The Southeast Asian policymakers attempted to transform its regime to achieve peace and prosperity in the countries. In order to grasp the changes from the standpoint of actual political leaders, we should examine such initiatives made by individual political leaders rather than merely focusing on institutions shaping political behaviors.

By paying special attention to the role of ideas and discursive struggle, we can shed new light on the debate over the making and evolution of developmental strategy. This is because, insufficient attention has been paid to the role of human agency, ideational struggle, and discursive power. The extent to which ideas and discourses account for the dynamics of catching-up, as well as the ebb and flow of authoritarianism and democratization in emerging countries, are also the key puzzles of the book. In this way we can make a further contribution to the state transformation debate, rather than reinforcing the typological framework.

1.4.2 Developmental Regimes in Emerging States

Needless to say, we should study both will and capability of policymakers, which might be reflected in a regime composed of public and private sectors. In empirical terms, we call for a study that goes beyond the East Asian bias prevalent in the existing literature and investigate more thoroughly emerging states in Southeast Asia and Africa. Even though we can hardly find a full-fledged developmental state in Southeast Asia, several scholars consider many Southeast Asian economies as possessing the intermediate states in which we can find certain parts of the pockets of efficacy (e.g. Doner et al. 2005; *Shaken* 1998). Some agencies can be understood as "islands of state strength" in intermediate states. Skocpol and Finegold (1982) argue that the American state is not as strong as its European counterparts but is still able to effectively direct economic activities by making use of key several agencies or departments, equivalent to the islands of state strength. Evans (1995) further elaborates on the concept and finds out that the islands of state strength should be embedded in productive private sectors so that the state can move toward a developmental orientation through such pockets of efficacy. In sum, these studies make the case for the developmental regime sustained by autonomous, technocratic agencies to be embedded in a network of business organizations to facilitate and direct economic policies effectively. It is of the interest of this volume to explore how these technocratic agencies, or more broadly speaking, developmental regimes, adapt under the process of democratization. This exploration is done particularly in Chaps. 4, 5, and 6.

Meanwhile in Africa, there are several countries intending to follow the developmental state-building mission (Routley 2014). While globalization puts pressures on African states as to the fierce competition in the global markets, globalization also provides great opportunities for them to negotiate with international aid agencies. As we have touched upon in the section III, the African National Conference Party (ANC) of South Africa advocated the "democratic developmental state" in its electoral campaign. Late Prime Minister Meles of Ethiopia had a clear intention to establish a developmental state in his country and his successors are still working for it. Is it the same specter which once haunted several ambitious political leaders with gigantic but prohibitively inefficient projects for heavy industrialization? If not, what kinds of difference can be found between the old concept of industrialization and developmental state building? The study on developmental strategy and regime in Africa can therefore shed new light on state transformation in the age of globalization.

In a nutshell, the development of developing economies is a complicated process that involves a wide range of structural (e.g. state structures and bureaucracy) and agency (e.g. political leaders and policymaker) factors. This volume focuses on the developmental state as an analytical framework that facilitates the study of the politics of growth. We have redefined the developmental state to underline the shared commitments of leaders and policymakers, with an emphasis on a country's productivity improvements. Moreover, in contrast to an overemphasis on external factors and macro institutions in early literature, the volume underscores as much on the role of incentive structures as the dynamics of private sectors and political coalitions.

1.5 Developmental State Building in Asia and Africa

The Chap. 2 revisits the Japan's experience of industrial policy making at the time of the transition from middle income country to high income country. Okazaki carefully traces the process of industrial upgrading and nurturing in Japan's trajectory of escaping the middle-income trap. There have been heated debates over the role of Japanese industrial policy. Some highlight the role of the Ministry of International

Trade and Industry (MITI), others emphasize the entrepreneurship by the Japanese private businesses. Against this backdrop, this chapter argues that MITI played a pivotal role both in upgrading existing industry and in promoting new leading industries such as automobile. It attributes the successful industrial policy making not solely to the MITI but to the interaction among the MITI, private businesses, and international organizations.

In the Chap. 3, Kanchoochat revisits the second generation of developmental states such as South Korea, Taiwan and Singapore and examines one critical aspect of the catch-up process missing in the literature, that is, conflict. To understand successful catch-up more fully, the process of developmental state building should not simply be seen as a story about effective economic policies implemented by capable states. An equally important, but far less explored, dimension is how East Asian states managed the socio-political conflicts that accompanied their rapid economic transformation. The chapter argues that the characteristics of growth-led conflict vary across countries, and the diversity within the East Asian development models is the key to understanding the multiplicity of these conflicts and their paths to settlement. South Korea depended on big business complex, chaebols, creating a sharp division between the winners and losers and ending up with a series of contentious settlements. Taiwan pursued a more inclusive strategy, supporting small-and-medium-sized enterprises, paving the way for a smoother process of political opening with the relatively stable party system. Singapore aggressively invited FDI while maintaining state-owned enterprises in several key sectors, and carefully crafted social policies for new middle classes, which eventually prevented political opposition from cultivating its social base.

In the Chap. 4, Sato points out continuity and change of the development state project in Indonesia before and after its democratization in 1998. She compares the post-oil boom development program under the authoritarian Sueharto regime with the post-commodity boom developmental program under democratic regimes. She painstakingly reveals the two different cliques of economic statecrafts in developmental state building in Indonesia; one is technocracy responsible for macro-economic management, another is technologue working for industrialization with visible hands of the government. Besides, it finds out that the politicians with business background play bigger roles in policymaking in democratic developmental state.

In the Chap. 5, Takagi and Khoo begin its analysis with a story about the political leaders facing international financial institutions in their efforts to build developmental states in Malaysia and Ethiopia. Prime Ministers Mahathir Muhammad of Malaysia and Meles Zenawi of Ethiopia clashed with the IMF that opposed economic policy management coincidentally in the same year of 1997. For Malaysia, the IMF attempted to keep opening the foreign exchange market in the midst of capital flight after the Asian financial crisis. Mahathir declined the IMF's policy prescription and carried out exchange controls which eventually worked well. Meanwhile, Meles did not swallow the IMF's policy prescription to open financial market and then gradually prepare a plan to build a developmental state in Ethiopia. By examining the foundation of the leadership, the chapter eventually reveals the political process underpinning economic growth in multi-ethnic societies where some politicians tend to politicize ethnic divides of society and to add fuel to the fire of the politics of ethnicity.

In the Chap. 6, Takeuchi provides a case study of developmental state-building from a Sub-Saharan African perspective, with a focus on Rwanda. Examining the efforts of the Rwandan government to achieve rapid economic growth after traumatic genocide in the 1990s, the chapter points demonstrates how Rwanda's development strategy, which uses liberalization and state intervention. It also examines the political power structure of the government that steered rapid economic growth and highlights the vulnerability of economic development that depends more on fragile political settlements rather than vibrant private sectors. The chapter thus offers a balanced account of Rwanda's development and relates it to political factors and policy strategies.

The chapter by Kudo unpacks the (hidden) policy making process under the military rule in Myanmar. While most of conventional knowledge underestimates economic policymaking by the military junta, this chapter scrutinizes several efforts to make industrial policy. For example, Senior General Than Shwe had attempted to follow in Soeharto's footsteps to be a successful developmental authoritarian regime. However, Than Shwe's pursuit of FDI-led growth strategy faced a series of economic sanction by the US, which did not support his military regime, especially after the end of the Cold War. The Myanmar's case reminds us of the significant role played by international politics that mediates between the incentive of the government and the real implementation. The chapter also makes a contribution by offering fresh and systemic analysis of development strategy of Myanmar which considers regional imbalance of country's economic development.

The chapter by Matsumoto examines the challenges of developmental state-building after the end of the Cold War and the aftermath of the decades of structural adjustments in Africa using the case of Kennya. By scrutinizing district level data, the chapter finds an unequal economic performance among several regions in Kennya which enjoyed rapid economic growth after democratization. The findings help us understand more fully about the dissatisfaction of several ethnic groups in the country which enjoyed relatively smooth democratic transition followed by the troublesome period of consolidation. The role of leaders as well as the influence of regional characteristics has been examined carefully—leading to a number of fresh results, as the existing studies offer no rigorous evaluation on the impact of such decentralization.

Lastly, in the concluding remarks, Sonobe summarizes the findings and sets up several agenda for the future researches.

References

Amin M, Sonobe T (2014) Success of industrial development policy in the pharmaceutical industry in Bangladesh. In: Otsuka K, Shiraishi T (eds) State building and development. Routledge, London, pp 196–216

Amsden A (1989) Asia's next giant: South Korea and late industrialization. Oxford University Press, New York

Amyx JA (2004) Japan's financial crisis: institutional rigidity and reluctant change. Princeton University Press, Princeton

Arrow KJ (1998) What has economics to say about racial discrimination? J Econ Perspect 12(2):91–100

Ayee J (2013) The developmental state experiment in Africa: the experiences of Ghana and South Africa. Round Table Commonwealth J Int Aff 102(3):259–280

Baldwin R (2016) The great convergence: Information technology and the new globalization. Harvard University Press, Cambridge

Becker G (1964) Human capital. Columbia University Press, New York

Birdsall N, Fukuyama F (2011) Post-Washington consensus-development after the crisis. Foreign Affairs 90(2):45–53

Brands H (2014) What good is grand strategy?: Power and purpose in American statecraft from Harry S. Truman to George W. Bush. Cornell University Press, Ithaca

Brandts J, Cooper DJ, Weber RA (2014) Legitimacy, communication, and leadership in the turnaround game. Manage Sci 61(11):2627–2645

Chang HJ (2002) The role of social policy in economic development: Some theoretical reflections and lessons from East Asia. Background paper for the UNRISD Project

Chang HJ (2003) Kicking away the ladder: development strategy in historical perspective. Anthem Press, London

Chibber V (2003) Locked in place: state-building and late industrialization in India. Princeton University Press, Princeton

Collier P (2007) The bottom billion: why the poorest countries are failing and what can be done about it. Oxford University Press, Oxford

Cooper R, DeJong D, Forsythe R, Ross T (1992) Communication in coordination games. Q J Econ 739–771

Doner RF, Ritchie BK, Slater D (2005) Systemic vulnerability and the origins of developmental states: Northeast and Southeast Asia in comparative perspective. Int Org 59(2):327–361

Easterly W (2002) The elusive quest for growth: economists' adventures and misadventures in the tropics. MIT Press, Massachusetts

Evans P (1995) Embedded autonomy: states and industrial transformation. Princeton University Press, Princeton

Evans P, Heller P (2015) Human development, state transformation, and the politics of the developmental state. In: Leibfried S, Huber E, Lange M, Levy J, Nullmeier F, Stephens J (eds) The Oxford handbook of transformations of the state. Oxford University Press, Oxford, pp 691–713

Haggard S (1990) Pathways from the periphery: the politics of growth in the newly industrializing countries. Cornell University Press, Ithaca

Haggard S (2015) The developmental state is dead: long live the developmental state! In: Mahoney J, Thelen K (eds) Advances in comparative-historical analysis. Cambridge University Press, New York

Haggard S, Kaufman RR (2008) Development, democracy, and welfare states: Latin America, East Asia, and Eastern Europe. Princeton University Press, Princeton

Halper S (2010) The Beijing consensus: How China's authoritarian model will dominate the twenty-first century. Basic Books, New York

Hau C (2017) Elites and ilustrados in Philippine culture. Ateneo de Manila University Press, Quezon City

Hayami Y, Aoki M (2001) Communities and markets in economic development. Oxford University Press, Oxford
Helleiner E (1994) States and the reemergence of global finance: from Bretton Woods to the 1990s. Cornell University Press, Ithaca
Helleiner E (2010) A Bretton Woods moment? The 2007–2008 crisis and the future of global finance. Int Aff 86(3):619–636
Jackson RH (1990) Quasi-states: sovereignty, international relations and the third world. Cambridge University Press, Cambridge
Johnson C (1982) MITI and the Japanese miracle: the growth of industrial policy, 1925-1975. Stanford University Press, CA
Kohli A (2004) State-directed development: political power and industrialization in the global periphery. Cambridge University Press, Cambridge
Leftwich A (2010) Beyond institutions: rethinking the role of leaders, elites and coalitions in the institutional formation of developmental states and strategies. Forum Dev Stud 37(1):93–111
Mokyr J (2017) A culture of growth: the origins of the modern economy. Princeton University Press, Princeton
Mottaleb KA, Sonobe T (2011) An inquiry into the rapid growth of the garment industry in Bangladesh. Econ Dev Cult Change 60(1):67–89
Naim M (2013) The end of power: From boardrooms to battlefields and church to states, why Being in charge, isn't it used to be. Basic Books, New York
Putnam R (1993) The prosperous community. Am Prospect 4(13):35–42
Raquiza AR (2014) Changing configuration of Philippine capitalism. Philippine Polit Sci J 35(2):225–250
Rasiah R (2003) Manufacturing export growth in Indonesia, Malaysia and Thailand. In: Jomo KS (ed) Southeast Asian paper tigers? From miracle to debacle and beyond. Routledge Curzon, London
Rhee YW (1990) The catalyst model of development: lessons from Bangladesh's success with garment exports. World Dev 18(2):333–346
Routley L (2014) Developmental states in Africa? A review of ongoing debates and buzzwords. Dev Policy Rev 32(2):159–177
Schultz TW (1961) Investment in human capital. Am Econ Rev 51(1):1–17
Shiraishi T (2016) Kaiyo Ajia vs tairiku Ajia: Nihon no kokka senryaku wo kangaeru. (Maritime Asia vs. land Asia: thinking about Japan's grand strategy). Minerva Shobo, Tokyo
Shiraishi T (2018) Emerging states and economies in Asia: a historical and comparative perspective In T Shiraishi and T Sonobe (eds) Emerging states and economies: their origins, drivers, and challenges ahead. Springer, Berlin
Singh JN, Ovadia JS (2018) Special issue: Developmental states beyond East Asia. Third World Q 39(6):1033–1055
Skocpol T, Finegold K (1982) State capacity and economic intervention in the early New Deal. Polit Sci Q 97(2):255–278
Stiglitz JE (2002) Globalization and its discontents. W.W. Norton & Company, New York
Thurbon E (2014) The resurgence of the developmental state: a conceptual defence. Critique Internationale 63(2):59–75
Tokyo Daigaku Shakai Kagaku Kenkyujyo. (Institute of Social Science, The University of Tokyo) (ed) (1998) 20 Seiki shisutemu 4: Kaihatsu shugi. (The 20th century global system 4: Developmentalism). Tokyo University Press, Tokyo
Tsunekawa K (2018) Globalization and the emerging state: past advance and future challenges. In T Shiraishi, T Sonobe (eds) Emerging states and economies: their origins, drivers, and challenges ahead. Springer, Berlin
Vogel SK (1996) Freer markets, more rules: regulatory reform in advanced industrial countries. Cornell University Press, Ithaca
Wade R (1990) Governing the market: economic theory and the role of government in East Asian industrialization. Princeton University Press, Princeton

Wong J (2004) The adaptive developmental state in East Asia. J East Asian Stud 4(3):345–362
Woo-Cumings M (1998) National security and the rise of the developmental state in South Korea and Taiwan. In: Rowen H (ed) Behind East Asian growth. Routledge, London
World Bank (1993) The East Asian miracle: economic growth and public policy. Oxford University Press, Washington

Chapter 2
Development State Evolving: Japan's Graduation from a Middle Income Country

Tetsuji Okazaki

2.1 Introduction

This chapter reexamines the industrial policy in postwar Japan from perspectives of new strands of literature. The first strand is the studies on a development state. As discussed in the introductory chapter of this volume (Takagi et al. 2018), the concept of development state (Johnson 1982) has been newly attracting interests in the context of the present emerging states, facing globalization and democratization. Recent literature, including Takagi et al. (2018), focuses on the dynamic nature of the development state. Indeed, as we will see in this chapter, the industrial policy regime in postwar Japan, from which Johnson (1982) derived the concept of developmental state, is not characterized by a static set of policies, but it evolved over time.

In the period from just after the war to the 1970s, we can identify at least three distinctive phases of policy regime, which are characterized by direct government control (the late 1940s), extensive government intervention through foreign exchange allocation (the 1950s), and deregulation (the 1960s and 1970s), respectively. In this sense, the industrial policy in postwar Japan was dynamic and flexible, which arguably enabled the Japanese economy to continue high growth in the changing environment. This view is echoed with Douglas North's idea of "adaptive efficiency," i.e. "a condition in which the society continues to modify or create new institutions as problems evolve (North 2005, 169). Interestingly, North mentioned the Japanese economy after the 1990s as a typical case where institutions could not adapt successfully (ibid., 125). This chapter describes how the industrial policy regime changed over time adapting to the changes in the environment from the 1950s to 1960s.

Second, this chapter is motivated by the literature on a "middle income trap". Since Gill and Kharas (2007), extensive academic and practical discourses have

T. Okazaki (✉)
Graduate School of Economics, Faculty of Economics, University of Tokyo, 7-3-1 Hongo, Bunkyo-ku, Tokyo 113-0033, Japan
e-mail: okazaki@e.u-tokyo.ac.jp

Y. Takagi et al. (eds.), *Developmental State Building*, Emerging-Economy State and International Policy Studies, https://doi.org/10.1007/978-981-13-2904-3_2

developed on the "middle income trap". The basic notion behind this concept is that "middle-income countries have grown less rapidly than either rich or poor countries, and this accounts for the lack of convergence in the twentieth century" (Gill and Kharas 2007, 5). Empirical evidence on this notion is mixed (Eichengreen et al. 2011; Im and Rosenblatt 2015; Bulman et al. 2017), but many researchers consider that middle income countries need growth patterns and policies different from those for low income countries, for such reasons as drain of underemployed rural labor, rise of wage and decline in availability of technologies to be adopted (Agenor and Canuto 2012; Bulman et al. 2017). As we will see in the next section, Japan transited from a middle income country to a high income country in the period from the 1950s to the 1970s. In this period, the comparative advantage of the Japanese economy changed substantially, and the Japanese economy experienced a large structural change. This chapter discusses the role of the industrial policy in the transition.

This chapter is organized as follows. In Sect. 2.2, I overview Japan's transition to a middle income country to a high income country, focusing on the structural change. Section 2.3 describes the industrial policy under the regime of foreign exchange allocation. Section 2.4 focuses on the change in the industrial policy regime in the 1960s. Section 2.5 concludes.

2.2 From a Middle Income Country to a High Income Country: An Overview

Japan's transition to a high income country can be seen as a part of a long global history of the "Great Divergence" and the "Great Convergence" (Fig. 2.1). In 1870, just after Japan established a modern state, its per capita GDP was just 23% of the United Kingdom, according to the historical estimation of GDP by Angus Maddison.[1] However, from the late nineteenth century, the per capita GDP of Japan grew steadily. Its average annual growth rate from 1870 to 1940 was 2.8%, and it became 42% of that of U.K. (Fig. 2.1).

Felipe (2012) defines the threshold levels of per capita GDP from low-income to lower middle-income, from lower middle-income to higher middle-income, and higher middle-income to high-income, as $2000, $7250 and $11,750, at 1990 PPP dollars, based on Maddison's estimation. According to the definition, Japan transited to a lower middle- income country from a low-income country in 1929. After that, however, Japan experienced huge economic, political and military turbulence, such as the Great Depression, Sino-Japanese War, World War II. From an economic standpoint, the defeat at the World War II had the most serious negative impact on the Japanese economy. While per capita GDP of Japan was $2659 in 1944, it declined to be $1346 in 1945, and remained 1444 in 1946. In other words, Japan returned to a low-income country just after the war (Fig. 2.2).

[1]The Maddison-Project, http://www.ggdc.net/maddison/maddison-project/home.htm, 2013 version.

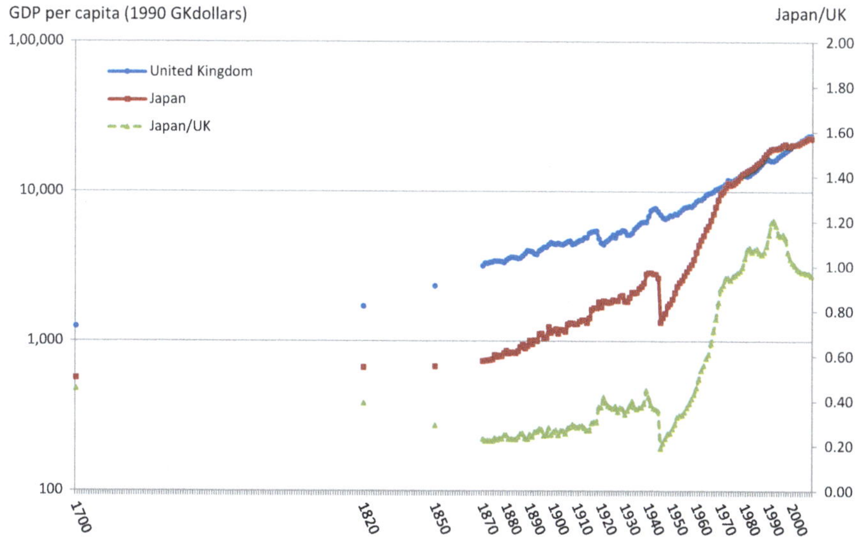

Fig. 2.1 "Great Divergence" and "Great Convergence". *Source* The Maddison-Project, http://www.ggdc.net/maddison/maddison-project/home.htm, 2013 version

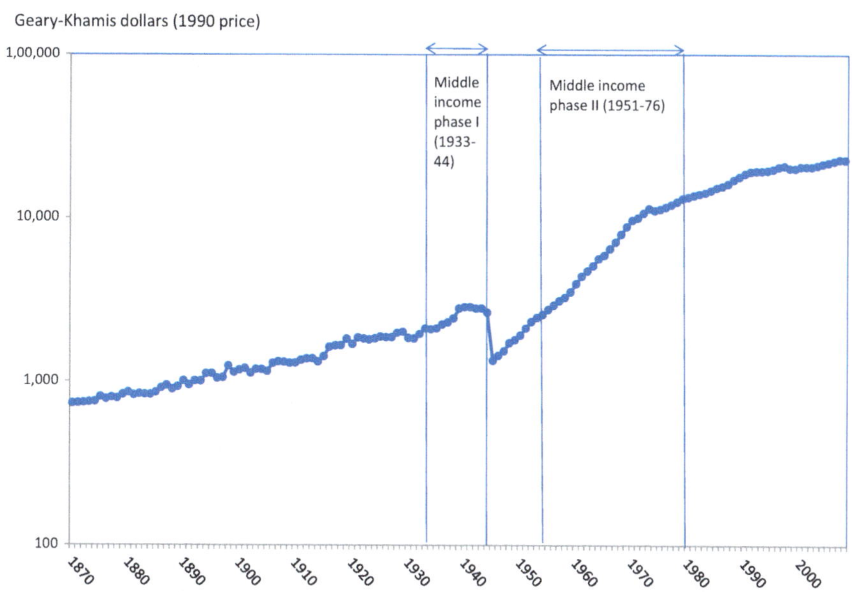

Fig. 2.2 Middle income phases in the Japanese economic growth. *Source* The Maddison-Project, http://www.ggdc.net/maddison/maddison-project/home.htm, 2013 version; Felipe (2012)

Nevertheless, the recovery of the Japanese economy after the war was very swift. As early as in 1951, per capita GDP recovered to be a prewar (1934–36 average) level and became over $2000, the threshold from low-income country to lower middle-income country. The average annual growth rate of real GDP was 9.9% in this recovery period. The Japanese government thought that this high growth was because the Japanese economy was in the process of the recovery from the war damage, and that after the recovery was completed, it would be difficult to continue high growth. The oft-cited sentence of the *Annual Economic Report* (*Keizai Hakusho*) for 1956, "the "post-war" period is over" was not an optimistic declaration of the accomplishment of economic recovery, but the warning about the end of the "growth through recovery". At the same, the Report stressed that the growth after that would be achieved only through "modernization". Here "modernization" covered not only technologies, but also economic and social structure (Economic Planning Agency 1956, 42). Indeed, as we will see below, Japan achieved the high growth, through upgrade of industrial technologies and reallocation of resources across industries.

From the middle of the 1950s to the early 1970s, when the first Oil Shock occurred, the Japanese economy continued high growth around 10% per year, while the annual growth rate of per capita GDP was around 8%. After the Oil Shock, the economic growth slowed down, but the annual growth rate of GDP remained 4–5% until the early 1990s, when the asset "bubble" burst. The 1970s was an epoch in the modern history of the Japanese economy. In this period, Japan finally caught up with the U.K. in terms of per capita GDP (1979), and also it transited to a high income country (1977) (Fig. 2.2).

The growth of the Japanese economy in the postwar period was accompanied by substantial structural changes. Figure 2.3 illustrates the structural change at the aggregate level. While the primary industry, mainly the agriculture, had more than 40% of the industrial workers in 1955, the workers in the primary industry declined sharply after that. Meanwhile, the workers in the secondary and tertiary industries increased. In this sense, the high growth was a process of resource reallocation from the primary industry to the secondary and tertiary industries. Furthermore, within the secondary industry, a structural change occurred as well. Figure 2.4 shows the number of workers in the secondary industry by subcategory. The workers in the machinery industry increased sharply, while workers in the textile and mining industries declined substantially. The textile and mining industries were the leading industries in prewar Japan. As these changes indicate, the postwar growth was characterized by a shift of the leading industries.

It is notable that these structural changes had a positive impact on productivity, because the direction of resource reallocation was basically from the industries with lower productivity and lower productivity growth to those with higher productivity and higher productivity growth. In order to see the effect of resource reallocation, I decompose the change in labor productivity of the private sector (value added at 1955 price/number of workers) into three components, namely, the effect of productivity change within each industry (within effect), the effect of reallocation of resource from the industries with lower productivity to those with higher productivity (between

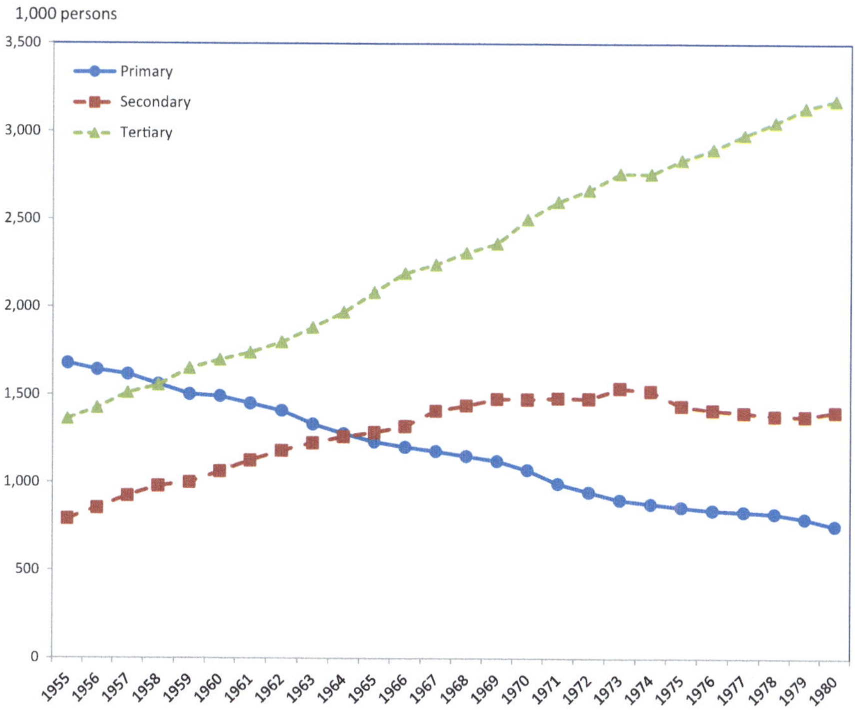

Fig. 2.3 Structural change of the Japanese economy. *Source* Economic and Social Research Institute, Cabinet Office, Government of Japan (2001)

effect), and reallocation of resource to the industries with higher productivity growth rates (covariance effect). Formally, these effects are written as:

$$\text{within effect} \sum_i \theta_{it-1} \Delta \text{LPit}$$

$$\text{between effect} \sum_i \Delta\theta_{it}(\text{LP}_{it-1}\text{LP}_{t-1})$$

$$\text{covariance effect} \sum_i \Delta\theta_{it}\Delta\text{L LPit},$$

where θ_{it} denotes the weight of industry i in terms of the number of workers in year t, and LP_{it} denotes the labor productivity of industry i in year t. We call the sum of between effect and covariance effect as reallocation effect.

First, we divide the macro-economy into the primary, secondary and tertiary sectors, and apply this decomposition formula (Table 2.1). From 1955 to 1975 labor productivity in the sense above increased from 0.213 million yen to 0.926 million yen. The increase of 0.713 million yen is decomposed into 0.508 from within effect, 0.205 from reallocation effect. It is true that most of the labor productivity increase came from within effect, but the magnitude of reallocation effect is substantial (Table 2.1).

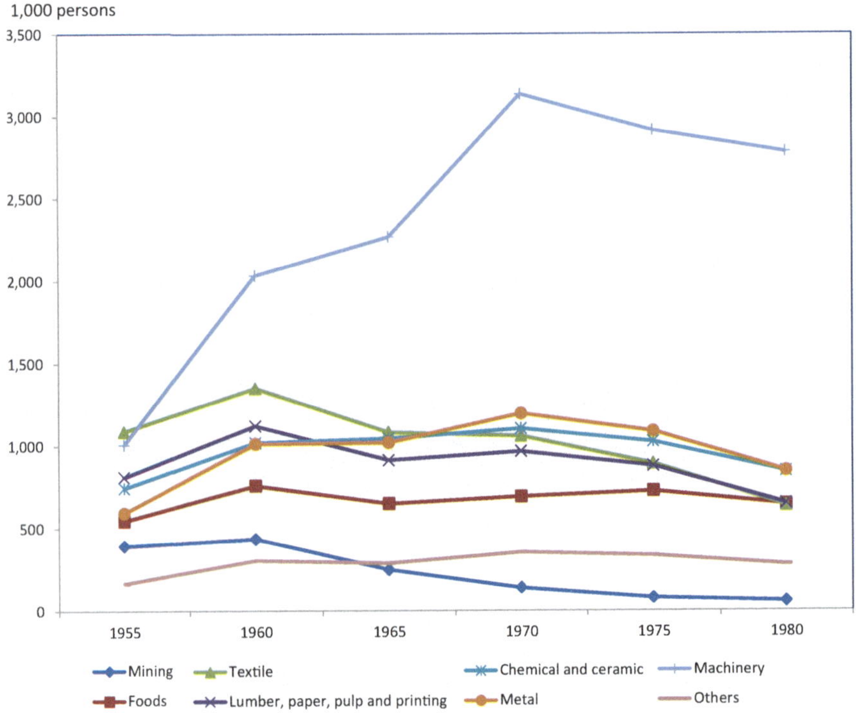

Fig. 2.4 Structural change of the mining and manufacturing industries. *Source* Economic and Social Research Institute, Cabinet Office, Government of Japan (2001)

The same decomposition can be applied to the labor productivity increase in the secondary industry, by dividing the secondary sector into 22 industries (Fig. 2.5). From 1955 to 1975, labor productivity of the secondary industry increased from 0.438 million yen to 2.710 million yen. The increase of 2.272 million yen is composed of 2.077 within effect and 0.195 reallocation effect. The contribution of within effect is much larger, but reallocation effect is not negligible here as well. Illustrating the results by industry, we find that reallocation effect is large in the machinery industries. While the machinery industries grew rapidly as we have seen in Fig. 2.3, labor productivity of those industries increased fast as well. Large reallocation effects of the machinery industries reflect the combination of their high growth and high productivity growth.

As we have just seen, the Japanese economy passed through the middle income phase in the period from the 1950s to the 1970s, and the labor productivity growth in this period was achieved by resource reallocation across industries as well as productivity increase in each industry. In the following sections, we explore how industrial policy related with these changes.

Table 2.1 Decomposition of labor productivity change [million yen/person (1955 price)]

		Total	Within	Reallocation	Between	Covariance
1955–1975	Total	0.713	0.508	0.205	0.049	0.156
	Primary	0.049	0.053	−0.004	0.029	−0.033
	Secondary	0.289	0.214	0.075	0.007	0.068
	Tertiary	0.375	0.241	0.134	0.013	0.121

Source Author's calculation from Economic and Social Research Institute, Cabinet Office, Government of Japan (2001)

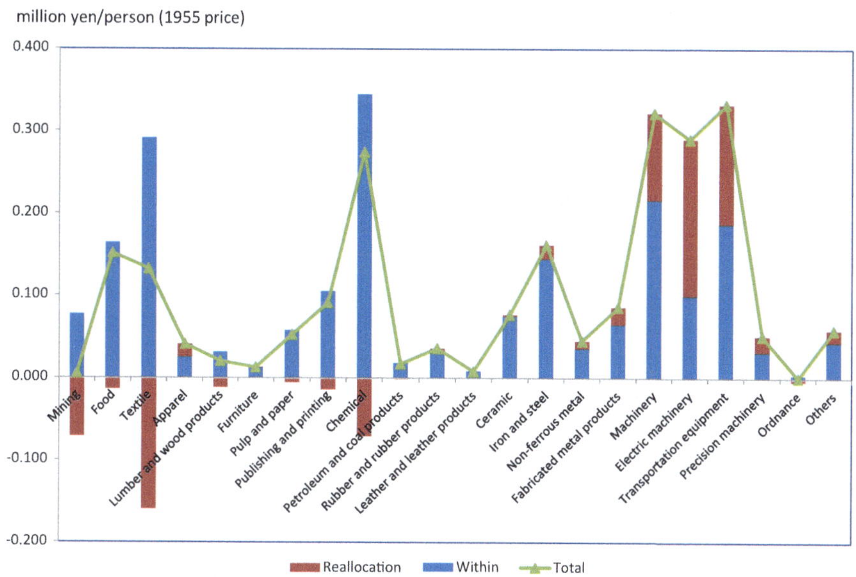

Fig. 2.5 Decomposition of labor productivity change in the mining and manufacturing industries. *Source* Author's calicuration from Economic and Social Research Institute, Cabinet Office, Government of Japan (2001)

2.3 Start of the Market-Based Industrial Policy

2.3.1 Setting the Goal: Transition to a Market Economy and the "Industrial Rationalization" Policy

The process of economic recovery can be divided into two phases, before and after the so-called "Dodge Plan". Before the Dodge Plan, the Japanese economy was under the wide-ranging government control that was taken over from the wartime. Policy measures developed for managing the war economy was used to reconstruct the economy. "Priority Production" policy (*Keisha Seisan Hoshiki*) in 1947 and 1948 was a typical case. One of the central measures for the priority production was to concentrate resource to a couple of strategic industries such as coal and steel, and for this purpose, the rationing system and the "Commodity Allocation Plan" were used. And closely tied with the rationing, prices of commodities were controlled by the government as well (Okazaki 2002).

Under the regime of planning and control, industrial production started to recover, but the government had huge deficit, and high inflation continued. In this situation, in early 1949, Joseph Dodge was dispatched by the U.S. government as the advisor of the Supreme Commander of Allied Powers. Dodge stressed balancing the government budget to stop inflation, but at the same time he instructed to abolish government controls and to unify exchange rates. By this set of policies, the Japanese economy transited from a controlled economy to a market economy in 1949.

It is notable that this transition was enforced by the occupation authorities. As the Japanese economy was under the strict government controls, private firms and their employees had been accustomed to the economy without market competition for more than ten years. Indeed, even under the occupation, harsh labor disputes tool place to resist layoffs by the firms which had hoarded excess employment (Okazaki and Okuno-Fujiwara 1999). If Japan had been an independent nation with democracy, such a drastic change in economic regimes would not be easy.

Just after the Dodge Plan, the Japanese government was seriously concerned about the international trade of Japan. The *Annual Economic Report* for 1953 focused on the fact that the international trade of Japan was still smaller than a half of that in 1937, although the international trade of major European countries recovered to the prewar level. The Report pointed out three concerns about the international trade. First, the trade with the colonies and China, which was around 40% of the prewar trade, disappeared. Second, raw silk, the major export commodity to the U.S. in the prewar period was substituted by synthetic fibers. And finally, export of cotton products to Asian counties is declining because of the industrialization of those countries. Based on this observation, the Report stressed the necessity of economic restructuring (Economic Planning Agency 1953).

This view was taken over by the Five Years Plan for Economic Independence (*Keizai Jiritsu Gokanen Keikaku*), the first official long-term economic plan in post-war Japan, decided by the Cabinet Meeting in 1955. The final goal of the Plan was "economic independence," which meant balancing the international payments without foreign aids and the Special Procurement Demand from the U.S. Army. Given this goal, the Plan argued, "Because of the development of light industries in developing countries, we need to change the main part of export from light industries products to heavy industries products. For this purpose, we should change the industrial structure, strengthening and expanding the secondary industry, especially heavy industries" (Economic Planning Agency 1955, 30–31). In particular, the iron and steel industry and the machinery industry were expected to be major export industries in this plan (ibid., 40).

The vision that Japan should upgrade the industrial and export structure with heavy industries as a leading sector, was shared in the government when Japan transited to a market economy. This vision was reflected in the organizational reform of the government. In April 1949, the Ministry of International Trade and Industry (MITI) was established, by integrating the Ministry of Commerce and Industry (Shoko Sho) and Agency of International Trade (*Boeki Cho*). The proposal of the law for establishing MITI wrote that the motivation of the law was directing the industrial policy to export promotion.[2]

From just after its establishment, MITI engaged in the policy of "industrial rationalization" as its central policy. To put it briefly, industrial rationalization referred to enhancing efficiency of the industries and reducing the prices. In a document titled "On industrial rationalization" (*Sangyo Gorika ni kansuru Ken*, September 8, 1949), MITI wrote "Industrial rationalization has become an essential requisite to the economy by balancing of the budget, unification of the exchange rate, and implementation of the sound financial policy." [3] It clearly shows that the industrial rationalization was motivated by the Dodge Plan and the transition to a market economy.

2.3.2 Preparing New Policy Tools

As the industrial rationalization policy started given the transition to a market economy, economic controls were no longer applicable for the policy, and it was necessary to prepare a new sets of policy tools. Indeed, in the early 1950s, new policy tools were introduced.

One of the major tools was public financial institutions, more specifically, Japan Development Bank (JDB). JDB was founded in 1951 to supply long-term fund for economic reconstruction and industrial development by complementing or promoting finance by private financial institutions. There was a public financial institution, the Reconversion Finance Bank (RFB) before the Dodge Plan, but the loan policy of RFB was given the economic controls, and it sometimes disregarded the soundness of the loan. On the other hand, JDB made it a principle to achieve both sound banking and policy-based finance. In this sense, JDB was designed to be a public financial institution friendly to a market economy. There were two specific backgrounds for the foundation of JDB. First, it was essential to renew industrial equipment to enhance efficiency, as we will see in detail later, and to do that a long-term fund was needed. Second, large amount of fund was absorbed by the postal saving system, because people preferred it to private financial institutions and firms, which were damaged by the war. JDB was designed to be a channel for return the postal savings fund to the private sector. The mechanism to supply the postal savings fund to the private sector was established as the Fiscal Investment and Loan Program (*Zaisei Toyushi*, FILP) in 1953, and JDB loans were incorporated into FILP. Figure 2.6 compares the new

[2]"Tsusho Sangyo Sho Secchi Hoan yoko" (Outline for the Establishment of the Ministry of International Trade and Industry), April 15, 1949 (National Archives of Japan Digital Archive, *Hei* 14 *Naikaku* (Cabinet office) 00066100).

[3]"Sangyo gorika ni kansuru ken" (On industrial rationalization, September 8, 1949 (National Archives of Japan Digital Archive, Hei 14 Naikaku (Cabinet office) 00083100).

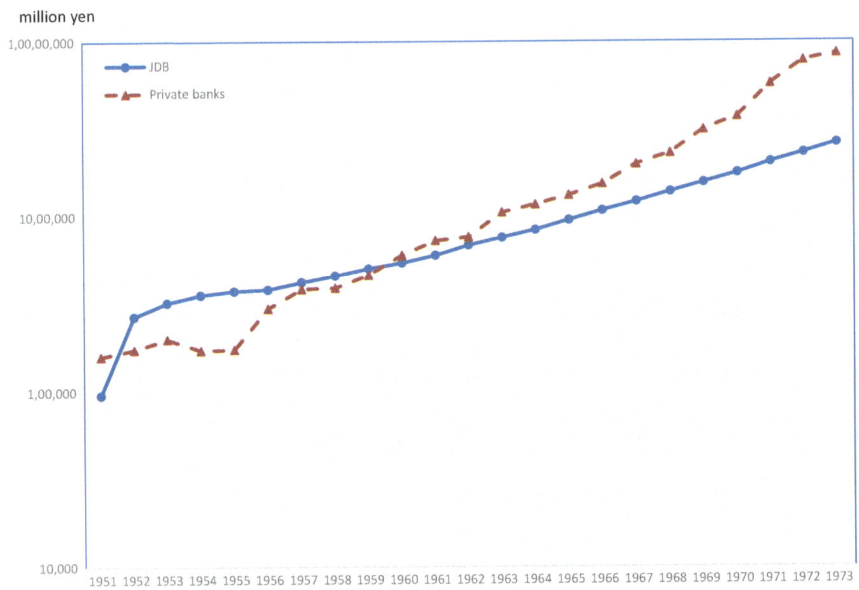

Fig. 2.6 Role of the Japan Development Bank in long-term loans. Japan Development Bank (1976), pp.52–55; Bank of Japan, Keizai Tokei Nenpo (Statistical Yearbook), various issues

loans of JDB with the new long-term loans of private banks.[4] It clearly shows how substantial role JDB loans played especially in the 1950s. There were three private long-term credit banks and other private banks supplied long-term fund, but JDB loans were larger than the total long-term loans of private banks, in the 1950s.

The second policy tool was the tax relief. In 1951, "special depreciation" was introduced by the revision of the Tax Special Treatment Law (*Sozei Tokubetsu Sochi Ho*). For the equipment recognized to contribute to the reconstruction of the Japanese economy, a firm was approved additional depreciation up to 50% of the ordinary depreciation (Ministry of International Trade and Industry 1972, pp. 194–195, pp. 210–212). In 1952, special depreciation was expanded by the Corporate Rationalization Promotion Law (*Kigyo Gorika Sokushin Ho*). By this law, for the new equipment necessary to modernization of production in the designated important industries, a firm was approved to write off a half of the book value in the year of installment (ibid., 212–213). The special depreciation enabled a firm to defer the tax payment, which had the implications of relaxing the liquidity constraint and reducing the discounted present value of tax. As the interest rate in Japan was high (around 10% per year) in this period, the latter effect was fairly large (Ogura and Yoshino 1984) (Fig. 2.7).

The third policy tool was the foreign exchange allocation system. When the direct control on the international trade was removed in 1949, a new system to regulate international trade was introduced. The legal framework was provided by the The

[4]All of the JDB loans were long-term loans.

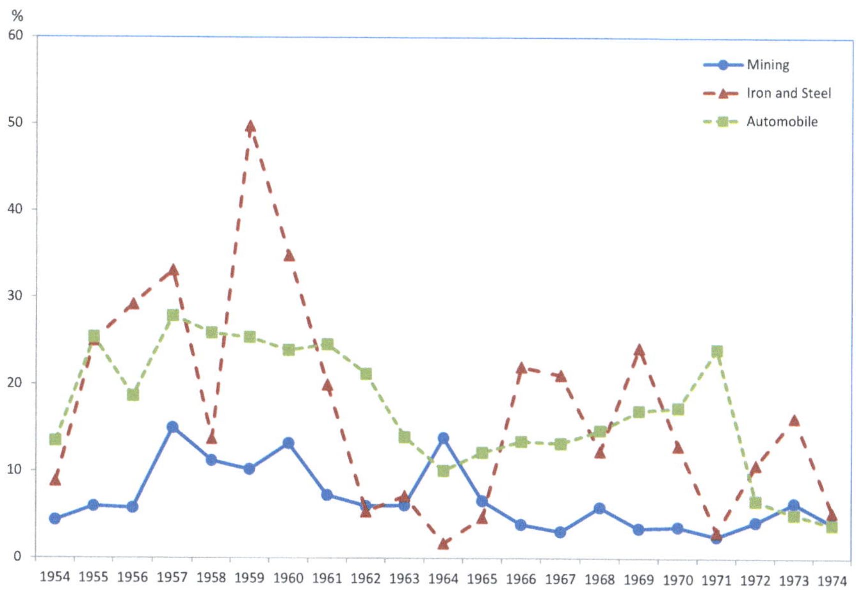

Fig. 2.7 Percentage of special depreciation in the total depreciation. *Source* Corporate Bureau of Ministry of International Trade and Industry ed., Waga Kuni Kigyo no Keiei Bunseki (Financial Analysis of Japanese Firms), various issues (1954–1959); Security Bureau of Ministry of Finance ed. (1976)

Foreign Exchange and Foreign Trade Administration Law (*Gaikoku Kawase and Gaikoku Boeki Kanri Ho*), enacted in December 1949. According to the law, all the foreign exchange was concentrated with the government, which then allocated foreign exchange based on the "foreign exchange budget". The part of the budget for commodity imports was drawn up by the MITI. The foreign exchange budget was classified into two categories, the budget for foreign exchange allocation goods (FA goods) and that for the automatic approval goods (AA goods) (Okazaki and Korenaga 1999). In the 1950s, the FA budget accounted for 70–80% of the total foreign exchange budget (Fig. 2.8).

The distinction between the FA and AA budgets was essential because, with respect to the FA goods, the budget was allocated to individual commodities. This implies that the MITI could impose de facto import quotas on FA commodities, using the foreign exchange allocation budget, given their prices. The MITI used this system to protect domestic industries. Meanwhile, in relation to industries that heavily depended upon imported raw materials, by controlling foreign exchange allocations to the raw materials, the MITI could indirectly control production in those industries. Furthermore, it is notable that the MITI allocated the foreign exchange budget for each FA good to individual firms. This implies that the MITI allocated rent to individual firms because the import of FA goods was more or less restricted.

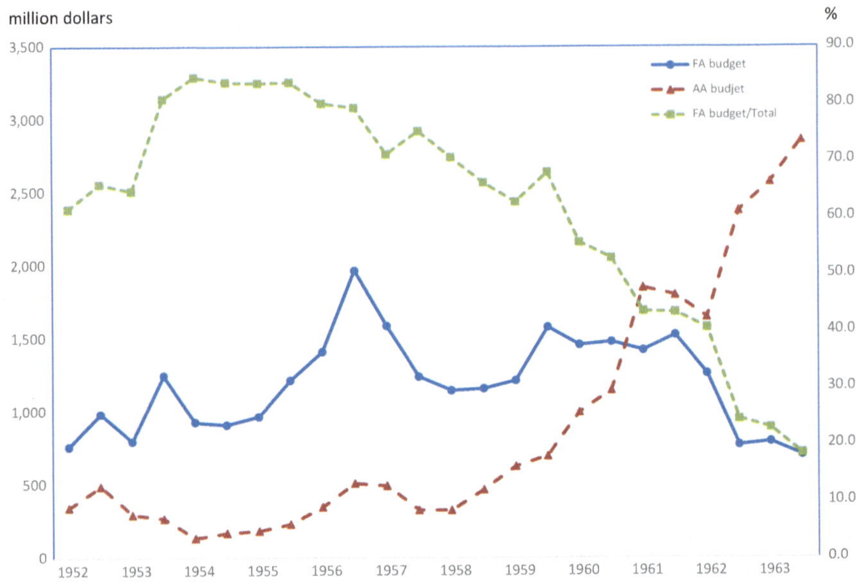

Fig. 2.8 Composition of the foreign exchange budget. *Source* Okazaki and Korenaga (1999)

Thus, the MITI promoted exports and investment of individual firms by linking the foreign exchange allocation to exports and equipment, respectively (ibid.).

2.3.3 *Updating Equipment of Basic Intermediate Goods Industries*

The main targets of the industrial rationalization policy in the early stage was basic intermediate goods industries, in particular, iron and steel industry and coal mining industry. These two industries developed in Japan in the prewar period, and were treated as the strategic industries during and after the war. However, when the Japanese economy transited to a market economy, their equipment was obsolete, and the low efficiency and high prices of coal and steel were seriously concerned.

In December 1949, MITI established the Council for Industrial Rationalization (*Sangyo Gorika Shingikai*) to examine the concrete policy measures for industrial rationalization. The first report of the Council was titled "On rationalization of the iron and steel industry and the coal mining industry" (*Tekkogyo oyobi sekitan kogyo no gorika nitsuite*, June 24, 1950), and based on this report the Cabinet Meeting decided "Outline of the policies for rationalizing the iron and steel industry and the coal mining industry" (*Tekkogyo oyobi sekitan kogyo gorika shisaku yoko*, August 18, 1950).[5]

The appendix document of the Cabinet Meeting decision explains the background of the policy that focused on these two industries .[6] It argued that the coal price was much higher than the international price, which in turn was an impediment for the competitiveness of other industries. Especially the impact of the high coal price was serious to the iron and steel industry, because the percentage of the coal cost was high in its total cost. The document pointed out that a high price of steel was a problem not only because it would impede steel export, but also because it would an obstacle to the export of machinery. In this sense, the rationalization of the iron and steel industry and the coal industry was designed to promote export of machinery.

The decision of the Cabinet Meeting committed to take some specific measures for supporting rationalization of the iron and steel industry and the coal industry. The measures included supply of low interest rate fund, priority allocation of foreign exchange to the import of equipment and technologies from foreign countries. Figure 2.9 indicates the investment in the iron and steel industry and the percentage of JDB loan in the total fund raised for investment by the iron and steel industry. Although the scale was not so large compared with the high growth period, the iron and steel industry resumed investment in the early 1950s, and in this early stage, JDB loan played a substantial role. Also, as shown in Fig. 2.7, in the 1950s, the iron and steel industry extensively utilized the program of special depreciation. It is notable that in the 1950s, the iron and steel industry introduced new equipment that embodied advanced technologies, in particular oxygen top blowing converters for steelmaking and strip mills for rolling (Figs. 2.10 and 2.11), which established the competitiveness of the Japanese iron and steel industry in the international market.

2.3.4 Promoting New Industries

As stated above, the government expected the machinery industry to be a major export industry from the early 1950s. The automobile industry, a part of the machinery industry, was included as an object of promotion from the early stage, at least by the authorities of industrial policy in the government. In October 1948, the Ministry of Commerce and Industry (MCI), the predecessor of MITI, announced "Basic plan on the automobile industry" (*Jidosha kogyo kihon taisaku*). This plan was related to the "Plan for Economic Recovery" (*Keizai Fukko Keikaku*), whose first draft was drawn up in May 1948. In the "Basic plan" MCI argued that the demand for new automobiles based on the "Plan for Economic Recovery" should be met by increase in the domestic production, and that they would promote automobile export focusing on the East Asian market. (Sakurai 2005, 124–125).

---

[5]National Archive of Japan Digital Archive, *Rui* 03511100-014.

[6]Ministry of International Trade and Industry, "Appendix to "Outline of the policy to rationalize the iron and steel industry and the coal mining industry".

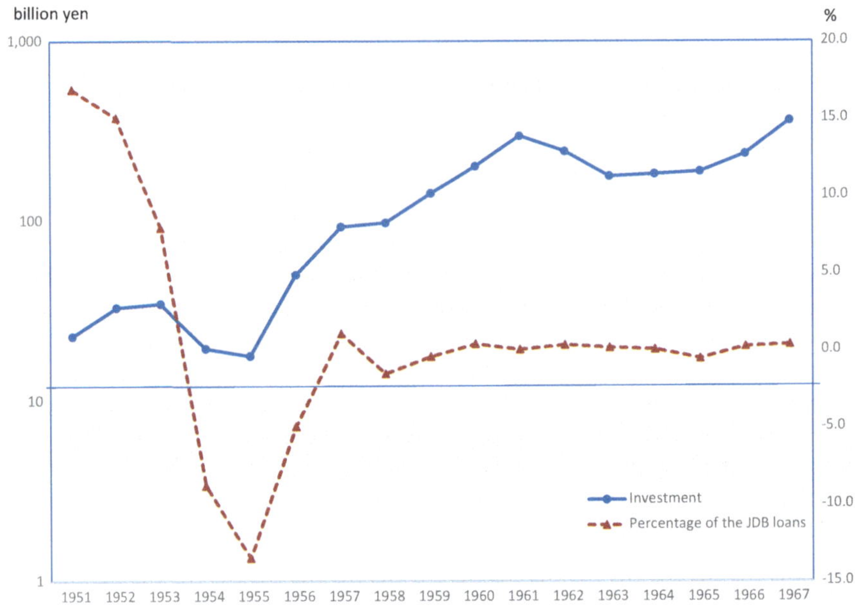

Fig. 2.9 Investment of the iron and steel industry and the role of JDB. *Source* Japan Federation of Iron and Steel (1959), pp. 480–481; Japan Federation of Iron and Steel (1969), pp. 698–699

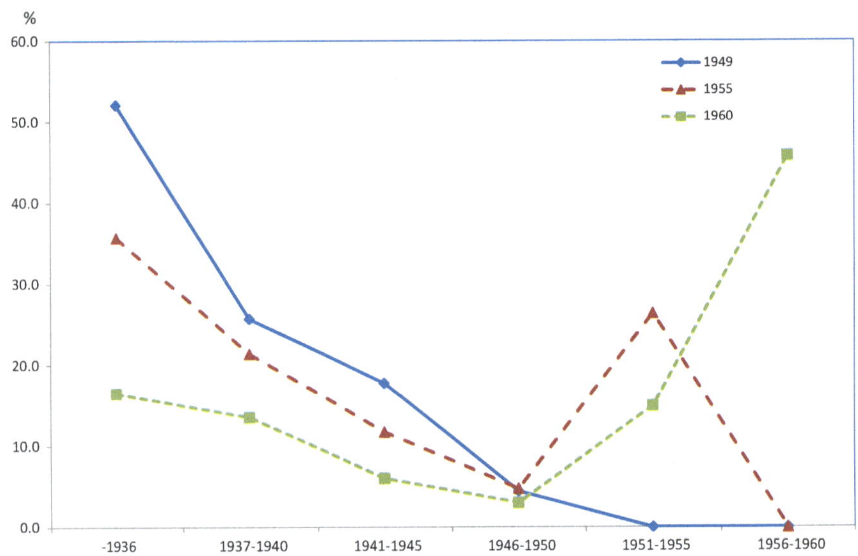

Fig. 2.10 Renewal of rolling mills. *Source* Okazaki and Korenaga (2015)

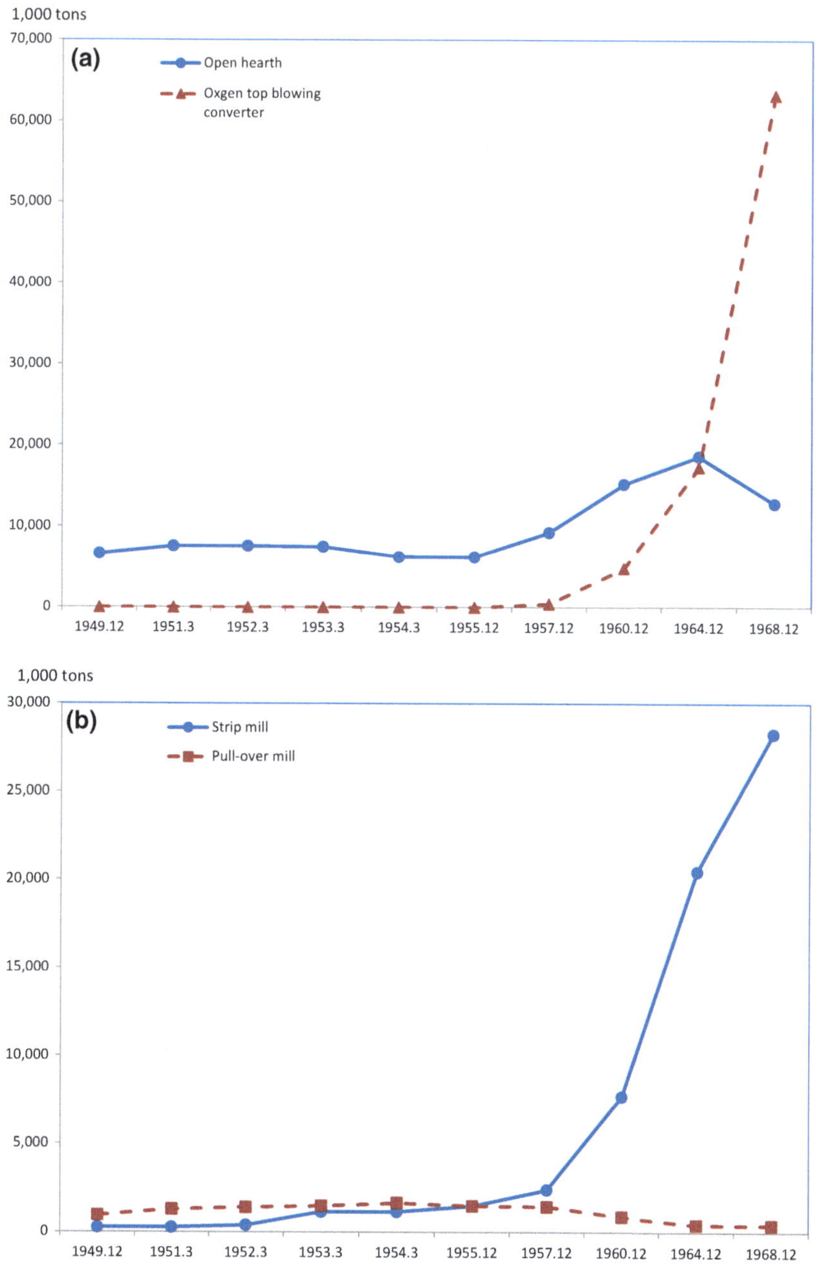

Fig. 2.11 Adoption and diffusion of advanced technologies in the iron and steel industry. **a** Steelmaking. **b** Rolling

MITI's argument that the automobile industry should be promoted, was not a consensus in the early 1950s. Indeed, the Ministry of Transportation and the transportation industry preferred imported cars, while the Bank of Japan was skeptical on the protection of the domestic automobile industry from the stand point of comparative advantage (Japan Automobile Manufacturers Association 1988, 81). Given these criticism, MITI published a pamphlet titled "For understanding of the domestic cars" (*Kokusan joyosha no rikai no tameni*) in 1952 to appeal to the mass people. In this pamphlet MITI argued, "The automobile industry is the only general assembly industry substituting the aircraft industry, and the development of the automobile industry and its related industries is essential to the development of the Japanese economy," and until the domestic automobile industry develops well, we should ensure its survival by some measures". (ibid., 83–84).

First MITI protected the automobile industry by regulating foreign direct investment. In June 1952, MITI decided "The basic policy on the capital import concerning the passenger car industry," to restrict the foreign direct investment. Meanwhile, MITI promoted domestic automobile firms to adopt foreign technologies. Following this policy, several domestic firms adopted technologies, such as Nissan from Austin (UK), Isuzu from Hillman (UK) and Hino from Renault (France) (ibid., pp. 106–107; Ministry of International Trade and Industry 1990, 552–553). Restriction of FDI increased the incentives of foreign automobile firms to license their technologies to Japanese firms.

Based on the technology adoption, the government took a measure to reduce car import strictly. That is, the government curtailed the foreign exchange budget for passenger car import in 1954 (Industry Research Meeting, Long-term Credit Bank of Japan 1975, 438). As stated above, this measure implied de facto import restriction by quota, and hence the passenger car import declined sharply in 1954 and stayed at a low level from then (Fig. 2.12). In this sense, the Japanese automobile industry developed under strict government protection from import.

A characteristic of the automobile industry promotion policy in Japan is that the government took measures on automobile parts industries as well as on the assembling industry (ibid., p. 558). This characteristic partly reflects the feature of the industrial organization of the Japanese automobile industry. That is, compared with the US counterpart, the extent of vertical integration of parts producing processes has been much smaller in the Japanese automobile industry. In other words, Japanese car assembling firms heavily depended upon outside parts suppliers (Asanuma 1989). Given this feature and that the qualities of the parts were low, MITI took the policy to upgrade the automobile parts industry.

In 1956, the Act on Temporary Measure for the Promotion of Machinery Industry (*Kikai Kogyo Shinko Rinji Sochi Ho*) was legislated. The targets of this law were "basic machinery" including machine tool and mold, "common parts" including gear and bearing, and "specific machinery" including automobile parts and watch parts. With respect to each of those machines and parts, MITI drew up a "basic plan" for cost reduction and investment. And based on the plan, firms were provided policy treatments such as low interest rate loan from JDB, tax relief by special depreciation and exemption of Antitrust Law (Odaka and Matsuhima 2013, 4–7). Figure 2.13

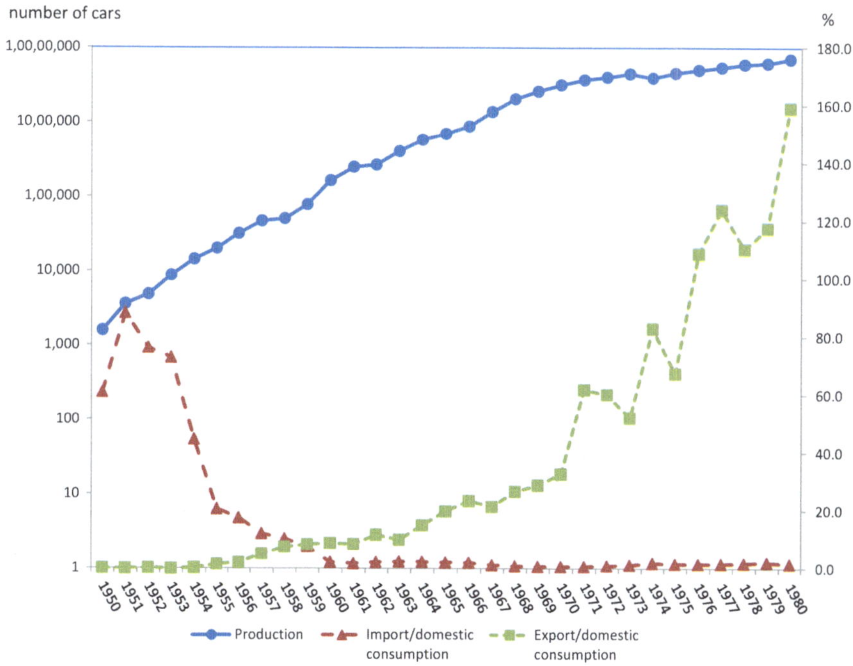

Fig. 2.12 Import substitution and development of the passenger car industry. *Source* Japan Automobile Manufacturers Association ed. (1988), p.387; Toyo Keizai Shinpo sha ed. (1991b), p.162 and p.175

indicates JDB loans by industry. Increase in the loans to the machinery industry in 1956 reflect the enactment of the Act on the Temporary Measures for the Promotion of Machinery Industry. According to Odaka (2013, 86) this law contributed to improving qualities of automobile parts and labor productivity.

2.4 Trade Liberalization: Upgrading the Trade and Industrial Structure

2.4.1 Trade Liberalization and Industrial Structure Policy

As we have just seen in the previous section, the foreign exchange allocation system was a powerful tool for industrial policy, and for that reason Japan had a pressure from foreign countries and international organizations to abolish this system. For example, the annual meeting of IMF in September 1959, adopted a statement that Japan was imposing restriction on import and utilized it for industrial policy, although the Japanese economy had already recovered (Ministry of International Trade and

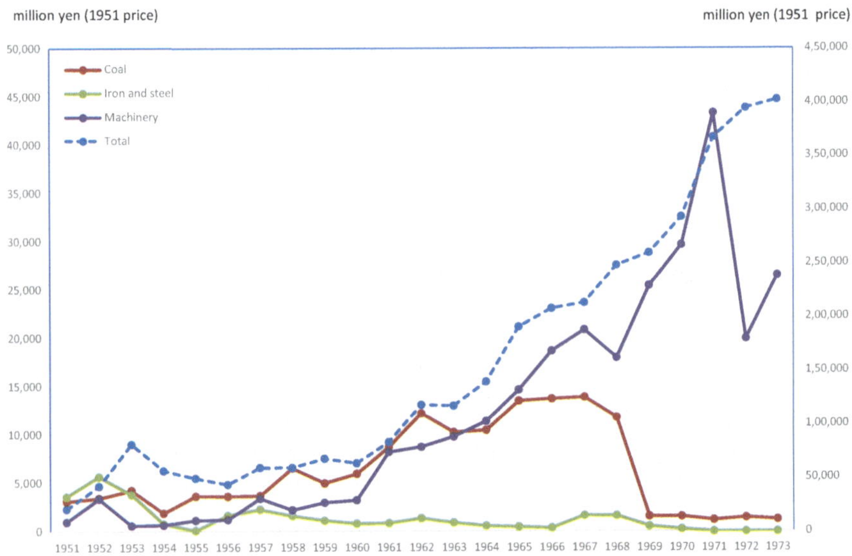

Fig. 2.13 JDB loans by industry. *Source* Japan Development Bank (1976), pp. 52–55

Industry 1990, 179–180; Asai 2015, 250). Also, at the annual meeting of GATT in October 1959, many countries criticized Japan for continuing import regulation for the reason of balance of payments (Ministry of International Trade and Industry 1990, 180–181; Asai 2015, 251–252).

Expecting the external pressure for trade liberalization, MITI started to examine the countermeasures to trade liberalization. In January 1959, MITI established the Committee on the Countermeasures to Trade Liberalization (*Boeki Jiyuka Taisaku Iinkai*), which was composed of relevant section chiefs of MITI (The Ministry of International Trade and Industry ed., vol. 6, 174). MITI thought that it was necessary to secure such measures as tariff protection, subsidies to industries and import quota for infant industries, in designing the program for trade liberalization (ibid.). Meanwhile, MITI set up another organization, Research Committee on Industrial Structure (*Sangyo Kozo Kenkyukai*) in May 1959, which was composed of MITI's stuffs and representatives of industrial society. Its mission was to explore the future prospect of the industrial structure and competitiveness of each industry.

MITI's view on the trade liberalization, based on these examinations, was systematically presented the 1960 issue of *White Paper on International Trade* (*Tsusho Hakusho*) (Ministry of International Trade and Industry 1960). On the one hand, MITI admitted the positive impact of trade liberalization:

> By trade liberalization, free and multilateral commodity exchanges become possible across countries, and thereby the price mechanism fully works and economic development is generated by international competition. Those industries accustomed to protection will be stimulated and urged through rationalization. Active interaction with the international economy will increase incentives for export.

On the other hand, however, MITI pointed out concerns about trade liberalization. First, MITI stressed that trade liberalization should not impede the policy for promoting heavy industries in progress. According to MITI, development of heavy industries was essential to the growth of national income, and also heavy industries were expected to contribute to export growth, given that developing countries were industrializing and that the share of heavy industries products was increasing in the world trade. Nevertheless, many of heavy industries in Japan did not have international competitiveness, because of shortage of capital and backwardness of technologies.

Another concern was on the natural resource-based industries, such as the agriculture, metal mining, coal mining and oil mining. With respect to the coal mining industry, MITI argued that although the coal price was substantially higher than oil price at that time, it would be possible to reduce the price for the domestic coal to compete with oil, and the drastic rationalization plan was on the process. Based on these reasons, MITI insisted that liberalization of trade of coal and oil was difficult for the time being. In this sense, MITI presented a view that trade liberalization was unavoidable and had a positive effect, but that it should be implemented sequentially, depending upon each industry's condition, more specifically present and future international competitiveness (Okazaki 2012).

Under the external pressure, the Cabinet Meeting decided "Outline for the program of liberalizing trade and foreign exchange" (*Boeki kawase jiyuka keikaku taiko*) in June 1960. It announced that "liberalization rate" would be raised to around 80% by June 1963. Liberalization rate here refers to the ratio of the import of AA goods to the total import, which was 41% in June 1961. As shown in Fig. 2.8, this goal was fully achieved. Sharp rise in the liberalization rate in this figure reflects the rapid reclassification of FA goods into AA goods. Given the progress of the trade liberalization, the foreign exchange budget was abolished in April 1964, and the for the remaining FA commodities, the import quota system was introduced (Kiyota and Okazaki 2016).

It is notable that MITI's opinion on the sequential liberalization was adopted and authorized in this decision of the Cabinet Meeting. That is, the document stressed that the government should be careful about transitory negative effects on the economy, given that there were numerous small-sized farms and firms, and that many industries were still in the infant stage. On these grounds, a sequential liberalization plan by commodity was presented. Namely, the document classified the major 104 commodities into the following four categories according to the target year of liberalization; (a) those that should be liberalized promptly, (b) those that should be liberalized in about three years, (c) those for which they should make effort to liberalize soon after three years, and (d) those that would be difficult to liberalize for several more years (Naoi and Okazaki 2013). For example, coal and oil were classified into category (d), ordinary steel was classified into category (a), and small-sized car was classified into category (c).

As we can see in the description of the 1960 issue of *White Paper on International Trade*, this sequential liberalization strategy of MITI was based on its vision of the future industrial structure. MITI's vision echoed with another important decision of the Cabinet Meeting, namely "Income Doubling Plan" decided in December 1960. The Plan stressed the importance of upgrade of industrial structure in order to achieve its goal of income doubling, and stated in particular that "Machinery industry is a strategic industry that leads jumping development of the economy and upgrade of the industrial structure" (Economic Planning Agency 1961).

Given these two decisions of the Cabinet Meeting, MITI started the policy for upgrading industrial structure. For this purpose, MITI established the Investigation Committee on Industrial Structure (*Sangyo Kozo Chosakai*) in June 1961. In 1963 it published the report. The report stressed that the process of upgrading industrial structure would be accompanied by continuous restructuring of industries. While some industries would lead upgrade, other industries should carry out drastic restructuring with scraping inefficient equipment and layoffs of workers. The report argued that this process will be executed by the market mechanism in the long-run, but to fix conflicts in the process, policy interventions are required. That is, the government should support investment for cost reduction, reduction of production capacity and shift of labor force to growing industries. It is notable that MITI recognized the importance of adjustment of declining industries, which started in the 1960s as we will see on the coal mining industry below, and became the major issue of industrial policy in the 1970s and 1980s, after the two Oil Shocks.

2.4.2 Promotion of Automobile Industry

The trend of trade liberalization had a substantial impact on the automobile industry in the early 1960s. In April 1961, the trade of bus, truck, motor bike not larger than 250 cc, and a part of automobile parts, were liberalized (Ministry of International Trade and Industry 1990, 296), while a passenger car was still under the foreign exchange allocation system. This trend urged MITI to examine the measures to upgrade the passenger car industry, so that it could survive the international competition and develop after the trade liberalization.

In May 1961, the Industrial Fund Committee of the Industrial Structure Council drew up a plan of consolidating passenger car firms into three groups, namely mass production car group, special car group and small car group. Also, in September 1962, the Special Committee for Policy on Passenger Cars (*Joyosha Seisaku Tokubetsu Shoiinnkai*) was established under the Investigation Committee on Industrial Structure (Yomiuri News Paper, September 13, 1962). The report of the Committee in December 1962, stressed the following points; Assuming that the trade of passenger cars would be liberalized by March 1965, car production should be consolidated through reduction of models, cooperation between car producers, merger, and restriction of new entries (Ministry of International Trade and Industry 1991 (vol. 8), 337).

As reflected in these plans, MITI intended to consolidate car producers into a small number of firms to improve their international competitiveness. For this purpose, MITI drew up drafts of new laws that enabled it to intervene with the process of consolidation and cooperation between private firms. The most well-known draft is the Draft Bill of the Temporary Law for Promoting Designated Industries (*Tokutei Sangyo Shinko Rinji Sochi Hoan*), which was proposed to the Diet in May 1963. The designated industries included ferroalloy, special steel, automobile, tire and petrochemical. However, this draft bill was rejected by the diet. This was because many powerful actors including Ministry of Finance, the financial business world, and Japan Socialist Party, the largest opposition party, did not support the bill (Ministry of International Trade and Industry 1990, 79–81, 296–298).

While MITI's idea of consolidating the passenger car industry by policy intervention was rejected, policies to promote the passenger car industry continued in the 1960s. In 1961, the Act on the Temporary Measures for the Promotion of Machinery Industry, which was legislated in 1956 for 5-year term limit) was renewed. As shown in Fig. 2.13, JDB loans to the machinery industry, which was according to the Act, increased sharply in the 1960s. In addition, after the renewal, Small Business Finance Corporation (*Chusho Kigyo Kin'yu Koko*) started to provide low interest rate loans to the designated industries, as most of the borrowing firms were small and medium-sized. Also, the passenger car industry continued to be protected by import quota until October 1965 (Ibid., p. 304). At the consultation on Japan's trade liberalization by IMF in June and July 1961, MITI argued that the passenger car would be under the foreign exchange allocation system after April 1963, because in order for the Japanese passenger car industry to be competitive, it was necessary to raise each firm's annual production from 4000 cars to 10,000 cars (Asai 2015, 295). It is notable that the Japanese passenger car industry was already an export industry, when the trade of passenger cars was liberalized in 1965 (Fig. 2.12). That is, MITI continued protection until the passenger car industry was well established in the international market.

2.4.3 Adjustment of Coal Mining Industry

The coal mining industry was one of the leading industries in Japan from the prewar period, and especially during and just after the war, it was promoted by the government as a strategic industry. Indeed, increasing coal production was the most important target of the so called "priority production" policy in the late 1940s. In 1953, coal was the largest source of energy in Japan and the coal mining industry employed around 322 thousand workers (Figs. 2.14 and 2.15). However, as imported oil became an alternative source of energy and the international price of oil declined, coordination between coal production and oil import was getting a serious policy issue.

In the 1950s, MITI and the government took a position of giving priority to coal production. In March 1954, MITI decided the document titled "Coordination between coal and oil," which was approved by the Cabinet Meeting. In this document, MITI stated that they should decrease coal price, while restricting consumption of heavy oil. MITI's idea was that coal was an important domestic natural resource and by

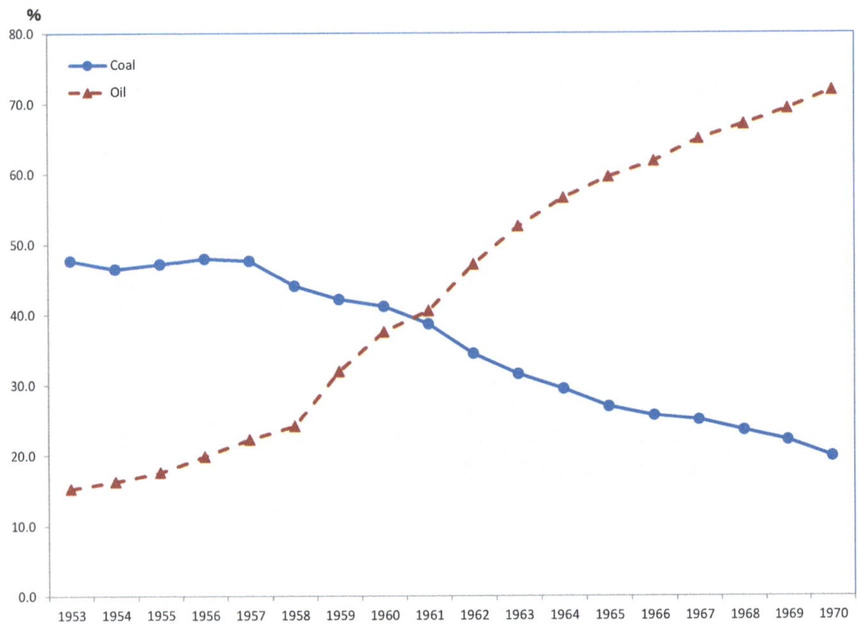

Fig. 2.14 Sources of energy in Japan. *Source* Toyo Keizai Shinposha ed. (1991a), p.458

exploiting it they could save foreign exchange. This policy was endorsed by another decision by the Cabinet Meeting in May 1955, "General Policy Measures on Energy." (Ministry of International Trade and Industry 1991, 334–335, 341–342, 348–350). Based on this decision, MITI implemented two policies in the late 1950s, that is, regulation of oil consumption and rationalization of coal production. For regulation of oil consumption, the Law for Regulation of Heavy Oil Boiler was legislated in August 1955. According to this law, new installment of a heavy oil boiler was prohibited in principle, and MITI instructed firms with heavy oil boilers to remodel them for other fuels (ibid., 363–364).

Meanwhile, the Temporary Law for Rationalization of Coal Mining Industry was legislated in August 1955. This law provided the basic legal framework of rationalization and restructuring of the coal mining industry. According to the Law, first, MITI drew up a long-term rationalization plan and annual rationalization plans, which set the targets of production and labor productivity. Second, Corporation for Restructuring of Coal Mining Industry (*Sekitan Kogyo Seibi Jigyodan*) was established. It was a public corporation whose major role was acquiring inefficient coal mines to shut down and payment of compensation to workers of closed mines. Also, MITI was given the authorities to approve the open of a new coal mine (ibid., 354–356). Under this legal framework, coal production and labor productivity increased gradually, while employment was maintained in the late 1950s (Fig. 2.15).

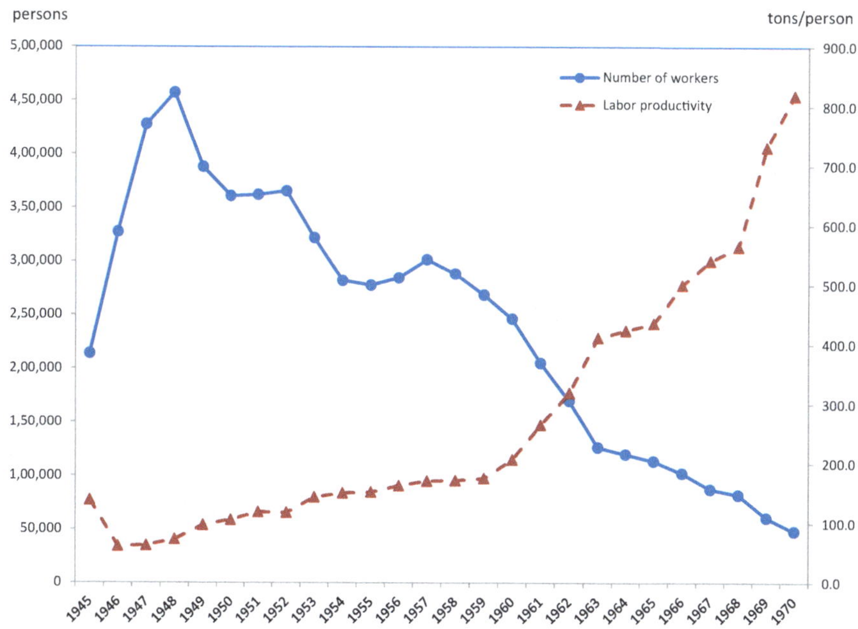

Fig. 2.15 Adjustment of the coal industry. *Source* Toyo Keizai Shinpo Sha ed. (1991a), p. 303

However, the environment of the coal mining industry changed rapidly from 1958. Figure 2.16 compares the coal price and the heavy oil price per 1000 kcal. In 1958, the heavy oil price declined sharply to be substantially lower than the coal price. In addition, by the pressure from IMF, the Japanese government decided to liberalize trade of crude oil in October 1962, in the "Plan for Accelerating Liberalization of Trade and Foreign Exchange" (September 1961) (Asai 2015, 303). Given the declining price and increasing availability of heavy oil due to trade liberalization, energy consuming industries criticized MITI's restriction of heavy oil boilers (Ministry of International Trade and Industry 1991, pp. 407–408; Kobori 2010, 189–190). In 1960, the Law for Regulation of Heavy Oil Boiler was renewed and revised substantially. That is, heavy oil boilers smaller than 50 m^2 and heavy oil boilers for power generation were exempt from the regulation. This implies that the regulation was de facto removed (Kobori 2010, 190–191).

In this situation, MITI was still stick to maintain coal production. Figure 2.17 shows the production target in the long-term plan decided in each year. Until 1966, the production target of 55 million tons was not revised (Shimanishi 2011, 200–201). Based on this plan, MITI expanded the support to rationalization of efficient coal mines and shut down of inefficient mines. For this purpose, Corporation for Restructuring Coal Mining Industry was reorganized to be Corporation for Rationalization of Coal Mining Industry in 1960, which had roles of supplying low interest loans and paying subsidies to closed mines, in addition to acquiring inefficient mines. For the

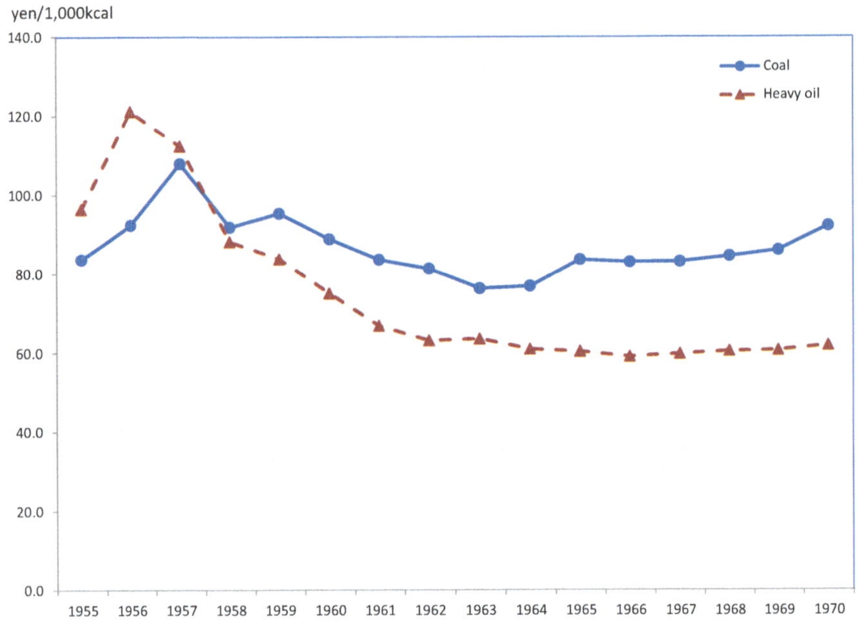

Fig. 2.16 Comparison between coal price and heavy oil price. *Source* Ministry of International Trade and Industry (1990), p.498; Utility Industry Bureau of Ministry of International Trade and Industry (1964), pp. 346–347

workers who quitted coal mines, the government supported re-employment by the Temporary Law for Job Losers from Coal Mines (*Tanko Rishokusha Rinji Sochi Ho*) in 1959 (Yada 1995, 1002; Corporation for Rationalization of Coal Mining Industry 1976, 100–103). Loans from JDB to the coal mining industry increased in the 1960 (Fig. 2.13).

Finally in 1967, MITI changed the policy to accept the gradual exit from the coal mining industry. To support the gradual exit, a new law, the Temporary Law for Restructuring Coal Mining Industry was legislated in 1967, which enabled the government to assume the debts of coal mining firms (ibid., 1003). After that, production of coal declined sharply.

The process of adjustment of the coal industry above has two implications. First, MITI's policy was not appropriate. Until the late 1960s, MITI was too optimistic about the prospect of the coal mining industry, and based on the optimistic prospect, MITI continued to invest resource to the coal mining industry, which, in turn, delayed Japan's exit from it. Second, however, this mistake was corrected finally in the late 1960s. This was because of the pressures from both inside and outside of Japan. That is, the industries consuming coals criticized MITI's policy to protect the coal mining industry excessively, while IMF and foreign countries continued to request the Japanese government to liberalize trade, in particular, the trade of crude oil.

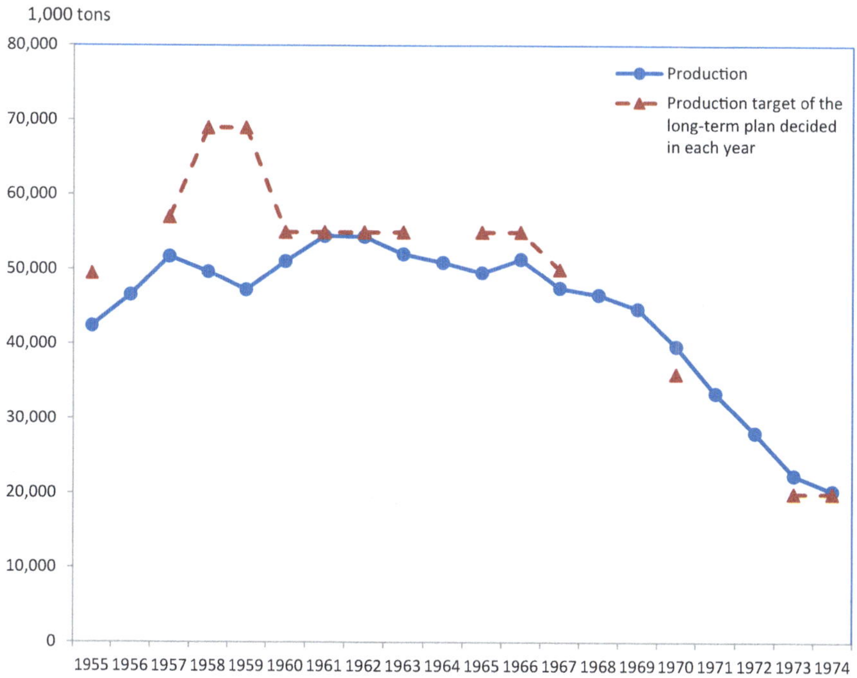

Fig. 2.17 Production targets and production of coal. *Source* Toyo Keizai Shinpo Sha (1991a), p.291; Corporation for Rationalization of Coal Mining Industry (1976), p.376

2.5 Concluding Remarks

Japan transited from a middle income country to a high income country in the period from the 1950s to the 1970s. This process was characterized by a large structural change, such as resource reallocation from the primary industry to the secondary and the tertiary industries as well as resource reallocation within the secondary industry. One of the difficulties that middle income countries face is that they should compete with low income countries in the markets of labor-intensive industries as well as with high income countries in the markets of capital and technology intensive industries (Bulman et al. 2017).

The Japanese government recognized this difficulty in the early 1950s, just after the Japanese economy transited to a market economy. Based on this recognition, the government, more specifically MITI, pursued two goals of upgrading major existing industries and promoting new leading industries at the same time. The former industries included the iron and steel industry and the coal mining industry, and the latter included the automobile industry, more specifically the passenger car industry. For these purposes and given the transition to a market economy, new policy tools were devised, namely public financial institutions, tax reliefs, subsidies and the foreign exchange allocation system. Especially, the foreign exchange allocation system was a powerful policy tool for protecting industries from international competition and for preferential treatment of imports by targeted industries. This regime of industrial policy worked through the 1950s.

However, as the Japanese economy well recovered from the war damage, international organizations and advanced countries came to be critical to the foreign exchange allocation system, and requested trade liberalization. Given the pressure of trade liberalization from the outside, MITI intended to prepare a new policy measure substituting the foreign exchange allocation system in the early 1960. At the same time, MITI aimed at restructuring the industrial organization of strategic industries including the automobile industry. Also, MITI was stick to maintaining coal production even in the middle of the 1960s. These attempts of MITI indicate that it tended to intervene with the private sector excessively, but these attempts of excess intervention were finally withdrawn by the criticism and resistance of the domestic actors.

Transition to a high income country is a challenging task for a middle income country. With respect to Japan, the industrial policy played a positive role in the transition. However, positive effects of industrial policy were achieved not only by the contribution of MITI but also by the contribution of various actors inside and outside Japan, who constrained and corrected MITI's policy.

References

Agenor PR, Canuto O (2012) Middle-income growth traps. World Bank Policy research working paper 6210

Asai Y (2015) IMF 8-jo koku iko: Boeki kawase jiyuka no seiji keizaishi (Japan's transition to an IMF article VIII country). Nihon Keizai Hyoron Sha: Political Economic History of Trade and Foreign Exchange Liberalization, Tokyo

Asanuma B (1989) Manufacturer-supplier relationships in Japan and the concept of relation-specific skill. J Jpn Int Economies 3(1):1–30

Bulman D, Eden M, Nguyen H (2017) Transition from low-income growth to high-income growth: Is there a middle-income trap? J Asian Pac Econ 22(1):5–28

Corporation for Rationalization of the Coal Mining Industry (ed) (1976) Dan shi: Seibi kindaika hen (History of the corporation: the volume on restructuring and modernization). Corporation for Rationalization of the Coal Mining Industry, Tokyo

Economic and Social Research Institute, Cabinet Office, Government of Japan (2001) Report on national accounts from 1955 to 1998. Printing Bureau of Ministry of Finance, Tokyo

Economic Planning Agency (ed) (1953) Keizai hakusho (Annual economic report), 1953 issue. Keizai Tokei Kyokai, Tokyo

Economic Planning Agency (ed) (1955) Keizai jiritsu 5 kanen keikaku (Five-year economic plan for economic autonomy, unpublished document)

Economic Planning Agency (ed) (1956) Keizai hakusho (Annual economic report), 1956 issue. Shiseido, Tokyo

Economic Planning Agency (ed) (1961) Kokumin shotoku baizo keikaku (Income doubling plan). Printing Bureau of Ministry of Finance, Tokyo

Eichengreen B, Park D, Shin K (2011) When fast growing economies slow down: International evidence and implications for China. NBER working paper 16919

Felipe J (2012) Tackling the middle-income trap: what is it, who is in it, and why? Asian Development Bank working paper 306
Gill I, Kharas H (2007) An East Asian renaissance: idea for economic growth. The World Bank, Washington DC
Im FG, Rosenblatt D (2015) Middle-income traps: a conceptual and empirical survey. J Int Commer Econ Policy 6(3):1–39
Industry Research Meeting, Long-term Credit Bank of Japan (1975) Shuyo sangyo sengo 25 nen shi (25 year history of major industries after the World War II). Sangyo to Keizai, Tokyo
Japan Automobile Manufacturers Association (ed) (1988) Nihon jidosha sangyo shi (History of the Japanese automobile industry). Japan Automobile Manufacturers Association, Tokyo
Japan Development Bank (1976) Nihon kaihatsu ginko 25 nen shi (25 year history of Japan Development Bank). Japan Development Bank, Tokyo
Japan Iron and Steel Federation (ed) (1959) Sengo tekko shi (Postwar history of the iron and steel industry). Japan Iron and Steel Federation, Tokyo
Iron Japan, Federation Steel (eds) (1969) Tekko ju-nen shi (Ten-year history of the iron and steel industry). Japan Iron and Steel Federation, Tokyo
Johnson C (1982) MITI and the Japanese miracle: the growth of industrial policy, 1925-1975. Stanford University Press, Palo Alto
Kiyota K, Okazaki T (2016) Effects of industrial policy on productivity: the case of import quota removal during postwar Japan. J Jpn Int Econ 40:31–42
Kobori S (2010) Nihon no enerugi kakumei: Shigen shokoku no kingendai (Energy revolution in Japan: contemporary history of natural resource poor country). Nagoya University Press, Nagoya
Ministry of International Trade and Industry (ed) (1960) Tsusho hakusho (White paper on international trade). Research Institute of International Trade and Industry, Tokyo
Ministry of International Trade and Industry (ed) (1972) Shoko seisaku shi (History of Commercial and Industrial Policy), vol.10. Shoko Seisakushi Kankokai, Tokyo
Ministry of International Trade and Industry (ed) (1990) Tsusho sangyo seisaku shi (History of trade and industrial policy) vol 6. Research Institute of International Trade and Industry, Tokyo
Ministry of International Trade and Industry (ed) (1991) Tsusho sangyo seisaku shi (History of trade and industrial policy) vol 7. Research Institute of International Trade and Industry, Tokyo
Naoi M, Okazaki T (2013) Political economy of trade liberalization: the case of postwar Japan. CIRJE Discussion Paper Series F-893, The University of Tokyo
North DC (2005) Understanding the process of economic change. Princeton University Press, Princeton
Odaka K (2013) Kishin ho to jidosha buhin: Kodo keizai seityoki tyokuzen ni okeru sangyoseisaku no keizaiteki koka ni tsuite. In: Odaka, K and S. Matsushima (eds) Maboroshi no sangyo seisaku kishin ho: Jissho bunseki to oraru hisutori ni yoru kaimei (Act on temporary measures for the promotion of machinery industry, a phantom industrial policy: empirical analyses and oral history). Nihon Keizai Shinbunsha, Tokyo, pp 75–105
Odaka K, Matsuhima S (2013) Maboroshi no sangyo seisaku kishin ho: Jissho bunseki to oraru histori ni yoru kaimei (The act on temporary measure for promotion of machinery industry as a legendary industrial policy: investigation by empirical analyses and oral history). Nihon Keizai Shinbun Sha, Tokyo
Ogura M, Yoshino N (1984) Zeisei to zaisei toyushi (Tax system and fiscal investment and loan program). In: Komiya R, Okuno M, Suzumura K (eds) Nihon no sangyo seisaku (Industrial policy in Japan). The University of Tokyo Press, Tokyo
Okazaki T (2002) 'Keisha seisan' to Nihon keizai no fukko ('Priority production' policy and the recovery of the Japanese economy). In: Hara A (ed) Fukkoki no Nihon keizai (Japanese economy in the recovery period). The University of Tokyo Press, Tokyo
Okazaki T (2012) Boeki jiyuka no seiji keizaigaku (Political economy of trade liberalization). In: Hara A (ed) Kodo seityo tenkaiki no Nihon keizai (The Japanese economy in the high growth period). Nihon Keizai Hyoron Sha, Tokyo

Okazaki T, Korenaga T (1999) The foreign exchange allocation policy in postwar Japan: Its institutional framework and function. In: Ito T, Kreuger A (eds) Changes in exchange rates in rapidly developing countries: Theory, practice, and policy issues. University of Chicago Press, Chicago
Okazaki T, Korenaga T (2015) 1950 nendai no Nihon niokeru setsubi kindaika to seisansei: Tekkogyo niokeru 'sangyo gorika' (Update of industrial equipment and its productivity implication in 1950s Japan: "Industrial rationalization" in the iron and steel industry). RIETI Discussion Paper Series 15-J-016
Okazaki T, Okuno-Fujiwara M (eds) (1999) Japanese economic system and its historical origins. Oxford University Press, Oxford
Sakurai K (2005) Nihon jidosha sangyo no hatten, vol 2. Hakuto Shobo, Tokyo
Security Bureau of Ministry of Finance (ed) (1976) Hojin kigyo tokei nenpo shuran (Collected volume of statistical yearbook of corporations)
Shimanishi T (2011) Nihon sekitan sangyo no sengo shi: Shijo kozo henka to kigyo kodo (Postwar history of the Japanese coal mining industry: change in the market structure and firm behavior). Keio University Press, Tokyo
Takagi Y, Kanchoochat V, Sonobe T (2018) Introduction: the nexus of developmental policy and state building. In: Takagi Y, Kanchoochat V, Sonobe T (eds) Developmental State building: The politics of emerging economies. Springer, Berlin
Toyo Keizai Shinpo Sha (ed) (1991a) Kanketsu showa kokusei soran (Statistical handbook of showa era, final version), vol 1. Toyo Keizai Shinpo Sha, Tokyo
Toyo Keizai Shinpo Sha (ed) (1991b) Kanketsu showa kokusei soran (Statistical Handbook of Showa Era, Final Version), vol 2. Toyo Keizai Shinpo Sha, Tokyo
Utility Bureau of Ministry of International Trade and Industry (ed) (1964) Denki jigyo yoran, 1964 issue, Nihon Denki Kyokai, Tokyo

Chapter 3
Tigers at Critical Junctures: How South Korea, Taiwan and Singapore Survived Growth-Led Conflicts

Veerayooth Kanchoochat

3.1 Catch-up and Conflicts

Early studies on the developmental state examined the characteristics of East Asian economies that, despite deviating from the conventional free-market model, succeeded in catching up with the developed world within a few decades after the Second World War. The general consensus is that developmental states are those that possessed: a centralized state structure; effective and autonomous bureaucracy; and a close and productive relationship between states and industries (Johnson 1982; Amsden 1989; Wade 1990; Evans 1995). Most states in the developing world do not share such characteristics and are thereby incapable of achieving economic performance of the East Asian calibre (see Evans and Rauch 1999). However, an agenda following this strand of studies is clear: enhancing state capacity is key to sustaining long-term economic growth.

Although the developmental state literature provides us with an alternative set of development model and policy choices, it understates one critical aspect of the catch-up process, that is, *conflict*. Take Thailand, Brazil and Turkey, for example. These three countries were promising economies in their respective regions and were on the verge of reaching a high-income level following East Asian tigers – if they maintained their growth momentum for another decade or so. Thailand was once the world's fastest-growing economy between 1987 and 1996, with the average annual growth rate of real GDP per capita at 9.5%. Brazil flourished during the Lula presidency (2003–10), with its praiseworthy attempts to maintain macroeconomic stability and to reduce inequality through effective social policies. Turkey was a thriving upper-middle-income country in the early 2000s when its poverty headcount ratio halved within a decade.

V. Kanchoochat (✉)
National Graduate Institute for Policy Studies (GRIPS), Tokyo, Japan
e-mail: kanchoochat@grips.ac.jp

Y. Takagi et al. (eds.), *Developmental State Building*, Emerging-Economy State and International Policy Studies, https://doi.org/10.1007/978-981-13-2904-3_3

Nonetheless, what these three countries have in common in the 2010s are a string of violent confrontations between conflictual groups in society. The state capacity of these three countries may increase with the passage of time, but their impenetrable barrier seems to lie in the realm of socio-political conflict—the issue that is overlooked in the traditional developmental state literature. Have South Korea, Taiwan and Singapore undergone economic transformations with neither social nor political conflict?

Actually, economic catch-up is, by its very nature, a contentious process laden with political and social conflicts along the way. As Kuznets (1972) pointed out, technological development that characterizes modern economic growth and a structural change process inevitably leads to dislocation of productive factors, making the process extremely conflictual. If factors of production are perfectly mobile, as in theory, this should not cause a problem. However, when the mobility of certain physical and human assets is limited, as is the case in the real world, their owners face the prospect of obsolescence and induce them to take non-market or political actions to redress the situation (e.g. petitions, strikes, bribing). Therefore, the process of structural change will be full of conflict and generate pressures for an explicitly political management of the economy by the state (Chang 1994, 302). Without the effective role of the state and institutions of conflict management, socio-political conflict not only diverts resources away from economically productive activities but also discourages such activities as a result of the uncertainty it generates (Rodrik 2008, 161).

The growth-led conflict could be even more detrimental in the developmental states, whose ruling elite tends to favor certain social forces (e.g. capitalist and bureaucratic) over others (e.g. labor and peasant). To understand successful catch-up more fully, the process of developmental state building should not simply be seen as a story about effective economic policies implemented by capable states. An equally important, but far less explored, dimension is how East Asian states "managed" the socio-political conflicts that accompanied their rapid economic transformation. This puzzle forms the key question of this chapter: *How have the East Asian states (South Korea, Taiwan and Singapore) dealt with the domestic conflicts arising from their catch-up process?*

3.1.1 The Argument

Economic development in East Asia has been neither smooth nor harmonious. Conflict has been an integral part of their growth and created dangerous tensions from time to time. This chapter seeks to underline the growth-led conflicts in the East Asian tigers and discusses the implications that are relevant to today's emerging economies.

It argues that the characteristics of growth-led conflict vary across countries. The diversity within the East Asian development models is key to understanding the multiplicity of these conflicts as well as the way in which each country reached a socio-political "settlement".[1] South Korea has undergone a series of *contentious settlements*, in which opposing forces clashed for a few decades before reaching a compromise. Taiwan has pursued a *gradual process of political opening* in which competing groups of elite reached an agreement. A distinctive trajectory of *continuous consolidation* is found in Singapore, whereby interests and ideologies among the ruling party, key government agencies and the middle class have been readjusted periodically to maintain their symbiotic relationship.

Existing analyses usually highlight the common features of the East Asian model, pointing to the export-oriented industrialization and quality human resources. This statement may not be wrong per se, but it does overlook the varieties within; and it is such varieties of catch-up strategy that shape the subsequent path to settlement. South Korea was single-minded on growth and driven by a small circle of large conglomerates. Taiwan pursued a growth-with-equity strategy from the start, with the intention of nurturing small and medium-sized enterprises (SMEs). Singapore mixed the use of state-owned enterprises (SOEs) and interventionist social policies with free trade and foreign investment. These varied strategies have led each one to different economic outcomes and have a significant bearing upon each country's pattern of socio-political settlement in the later phase of catch-up.

The following sections explore the empirical cases of South Korea, Taiwan and Singapore respectively. The conclusion summarizes the findings on the varieties of catch-up strategy and multiple paths to settlement, and discusses a broader implication that goes beyond a conventional wisdom on liberal democracy.

3.2 South Korea and Contentious Settlements

The settlement process in South Korea is characterized by confrontation and fragmentation. Its catch-up strategy, led by General Park Jung Hee, produced relatively clear-cut winners and losers. Confrontation began as early as the start of the catch-up, but became more intense in the late 1980s, in which the mass protestors forced the military to grant a direct presidential election in 1987. Yet, fragmentation within pro-democracy movements paved the way for the electoral success of the military-backed candidate. Contentious politics have continued alongside political opening until recently.

[1] A socio-political settlement has narrow and broad definitions. A narrow one is defined by the UK Department for International Development (DFID) as "the forging of a common understanding, usually between political elites, that their best interests or beliefs are served through acquiescence to a framework for administering political power" (cited in Di John and Putzel 2009: 4). This chapter follows a broader definition that considers political settlement as "social order based on political compromises between powerful groups in society that sets the context for institutional and other policies" (Khan 2010, 4).

3.2.1 Catch-up Strategy: Chaebol-Led Growth

After the Korean War, South Korea was ruled by President Syngman Rhee from 1953 to 1960, followed by a brief spell with a democratic government. The substantive catch-up project got off to a flying start under the regime of General Park Chung Hee, who was in power for almost two decades (1961–79).

Park's catch-up strategy can be characterized by a formula of "growth-first, distribution and stability later" (Jeon 1995, 72). The Park regime was founded on the coalition between the ex-military administrators and civilian technocrats on the one hand, and between the government and the large-scale conglomerates (chaebols) on the other. The catch-up strategy reflected Park's endeavors to legitimize the regime mainly through economic growth, while price stability and distributive measures were taken less seriously.

In the take-off phase from 1961 to 1973, South Korea's basic theme of state intervention was the making of an independent economy (*Jarip Gyongje*). The Economic Planning Board (EPB) controlled the budget and placed a strong emphasis on directing investment to achieve scale economies in targeted industries. Its policy-makers were primarily concerned with "excessive competition", which would result in social waste. Therefore, lead firms were instructed to build plants of efficient production scale, which in turn compelled them to engage in global markets to avoid losses due to low capacity utilization (Chang 1993, 139–40). To control resource allocation, the government nationalized the commercial banks in 1961, exercising tight control over the lending activities until the early 1980s. This led to the use of "policy loans", which accounted for 57.9% of total bank loans made approximately between 1962 and 1987 (Heo 2001, 222). The second phase of catch-up (1973–79) focused on industrial deepening through the production of heavy and chemical industries (HCI). The regime expanded low-interest loans and relied heavily on deficit-and-debt-financing and directed an excessive resource transfer from light to heavy industries.

Park's regime was increasingly authoritarian over time and ended with an assassination in 1979 amid growing political unrest. Ultimately, his growth-oriented strategy produced a sustained investment boom and resulted in rapid economic growth throughout the 1960s and 1970s. Yet, Park's single-minded quest for hyper-growth was accompanied by high inflation and an upward trend in income inequality. Overall, under the Park regime, annual per capita income was growing at 9.5%, with an average inflation rate of around 15.5% (Jeon 1995, 73). However, inequality has increased over time, with the Gini coefficient rose from around 0.35 in the 1960s to 0.40–0.45 from the 1970s to the 1990s (Solt 2009).[2]

[2]Income inequality figures are based on Frederick Solt, "The Standardized World Income Inequality Database," Version 3, http://hdl.handle.net/1902.1/11992 (accessed June 9, 2018), with a detailed description is in Solt (2009).

Table 3.1 The chaebols' total assets compared with the government's fiscal budget (billions won)

	1980	1985	1990
Sum of top four chaebols	8511	26,984	85,249
Sum of top ten chaebols	14,592	38,718	127,292
Sum of top thirty chaebols	21,800	54,914	167,655
South Korean government's fiscal budget	8648	15,000	32,537

Source Summarized from Lim (2003)

3.2.2 *Winner and Losers in Structural Transformation*

Rapid industrialization has led to a dramatic change in the socio-economic structure. Industrial production, which accounted for 9% of the gross national product (GNP) in 1962, increased to 31% in 1985, while the share of agricultural production decreased from 43 to 15% (Koo 1991, 487).

South Korean catch-up strategy has created clear-cut winners and losers. In the private sector, resources have been concentrated within a small circle of chaebols at the expense of small enterprises. To support the chaebols, the state pushed the peasantry to become wage labor. Between 1955 and 1985, industrial-wage workers (in factories, mining, construction and transportation) increased from 5.9 to 25.7% of the labor force. They constituted the core of the emerging working class in South Korea, and by the mid-1980s they represented the largest occupational grouping. The middle class also flourished, with the proportion of professional, managerial and clerical workers increasing from 6.7 to 16.6% between 1963 and 1983 (Koo 1991, 485). Meanwhile, the total assets of the top 50 chaebols *exceeded* the governments' fiscal budget by approximately three times in 1980, four times in 1985, and six times in 1990 (see Table 3.1).

Along the industrialization path, it was labor who made the greatest sacrifice. Export-oriented strategy was based on low wages, with the state-sponsored labor union used to controlling workers and their wages. Legally, South Korean workers did not have the right to collective bargaining until 1987. However, with "neither the buffer of the agricultural economy nor the prospect of becoming small entrepreneurs" in sight (Chu 1998, 190), South Korean workers were inclined to appreciate collective movement as a realistic option to better their life chances. The continued militancy of South Korean unions originated from this long period of authoritarian exclusion and the absence of political parties to represent their interests (Lee 2011, 6).

3.2.3 Ongoing Confrontations, from the 1960s to the 1980s

Popular resistance to the military regime, led by student groups and intellectuals, took place from the April Uprising in 1960 and continued to challenge Park's legitimacy throughout his regime. However, other sectors of civil society were largely dormant, due to an impressive economic performance and the regime's extensive surveillance (Kim 2000, 75). In the 1970s labor unions emerged as a major anti-government force, staging strikes for higher wages and better working conditions, in alliance with sections of civil society. Although the alliance was unable to force authoritarian departure, it generated a serious internal split within the ruling elite and ultimately led to critical junctures in the following decade (see Kim 2000, Ch. 4).

The confrontation became more intense from the late 1970s. After the assassination of Park, General Chun Doo Wan staged a military coup in December 1979 and became President from 1980 to 1988. Following the slaughter of hundreds of people in the Gwangju Uprising in May 1980, Chun carried out a series of coercive campaigns to "cleanse" the entire civil society. In June 1980 the government arrested 329 politicians, professors, pastors, journalists and students. In July 1980 the military purged thousands of public officials, employees of public corporations, employees of agricultural and fisheries cooperatives, and teachers. In August 1980 the authorities arrested 16,599 "hooligans and gangsters" and sent them to military courts or labor camps (Kim 2000, 78–79).

3.2.4 A Critical Juncture, 1984–1987

The military succeeded in not only restoring political order but also rescuing the growth rate from −3.7% in 1980 to 12.6% in 1983. With politics and the economy under control, the military moved to pursue an appeasement policy from 1983 to 1984. It permitted 1,000 college and university students to return to their schools, pardoned 300 political prisoners and lifted bans on political activities for politicians and activists. Why so suddenly? Many studies attribute Chun's appeasement to his miscalculated confidence. However, Choe and Kim (2012, 59–60) pay more attention to *timing and sequencing*, pointing out that, for Chun, the appeasement policy appeared to be an inevitable political choice if the regime intended to shine in the forthcoming events, that is: the 1985 general election; the 1987 presidential election; and hosting the 1986 Seoul Asian Games and the 1988 Seoul Olympic Games—all of which were expected to heighten the political stature of the Chun regime in the shadow of the Gwangju massacre.

Nonetheless, contrary to Chun's expectations, rather than being satisfied with the relaxed measures, the former democratic alliance, together with the New Korea Democratic Party (NKDP) established in 1985, took this opportunity to threaten the regime's political stability. They began an active struggle, proposing constitutional revision for a *direct presidential election*.[3] In the 1985 general election, the turnout reached 84.6%, the highest since the 1950s. With this agenda, the NKDP won 29.3% of the votes, slightly behind Chun's ruling Democratic Justice Party (DJP), which won 35.2%, thus reinforcing the gathering momentum of pro-democracy movements (Kim 2000, 86).

In early 1987 civil society organizations and the opposition party formed a grand coalition that saw the triple solidarity of student groups, labor unions and religious organizations formed under the National Centre for Democratic Constitution (*Gukbon*). The nationwide demonstrations were aroused by the military's ongoing oppression of political dissenters, especially the killing of student activist Park Jong-cheol in January 1987, and Chun's decision to ban any discussion on constitutional revisions later in April (Lee 2011, 64–65). In June 1987 Chun's nomination of Roh Tae Woo as the DJP's presidential candidate triggered large pro-democracy rallies in Seoul and other cities. The demonstrations were critical enough to push Roh to announce the "June 29 Declaration" that covered eight points, the most important of which were a direct presidential election, the rehabilitation of political criminals, and the guaranteeing of media freedom.

The settlement in 1987 resulted from the intensification of street protests. As shown in Fig. 3.1, the number of protests rose sharply from 1984 to reach a peak in 1987. Between July and August 1987, approximately 3,000 strikes occurred, more than 12 times the number of strikes in the entire year of 1986 and quadrupling the number of strikes in 1980. Moreover, 1,278 new labor unions were created during the same period, which amounted to one-third of the total number of unions in existence at the end of 1987 (Kim 2000, 93). Yet, it is not just about number; the *composition* of the protesters also matters. Prior to 1987 street demonstrations had been the preserve of student activists and labor unions. There were no mass-rooted nationwide pro-democracy organizations until the founding of *Gukbon*, in which the middle class, salarymen and housewives took part in the central area of main cities (Lee 2000, 197). In sum, the military's political concession in the late 1980s was brought about by a series of contentious and dramatic confrontations.

3.2.5 An Unfinished Transformation

Despite military concession in 1987, the term "settlement" reflects South Korea's political development better than democratization since post-1987 politics has seen the continuity of the military's ruling party (DJP) and the fragmentation of pro-democracy forces.

To begin with, even with a free direct presidential election in December 1987, the pro-democracy forces did not win the race because of the internal split of their

[3]Until then South Korea had an indirect presidential election, or what many called the "gymnasium elections", in which members of the "national electoral college" gathered in a huge gymnasium and, irrespective of the genuine popular will, elected a president (Kim 2000, 85).

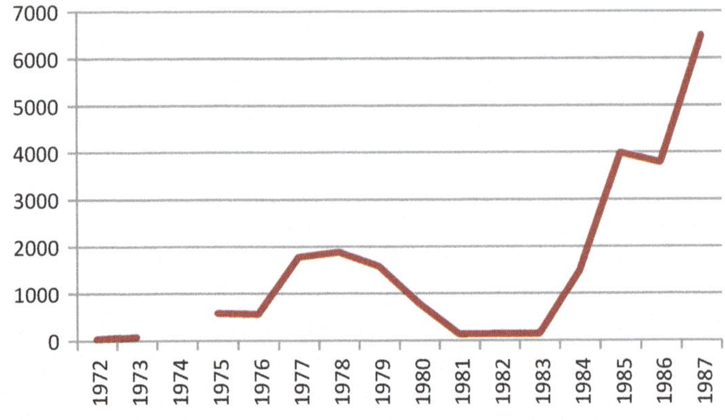

Fig. 3.1 Number of political protests from 1972 to 1987. *Source* Lee (2000: Fig. 2). No data on 1974

key leaders, known as the "two Kims" (see Kim 2000, Ch. 6). Advantaged by this fragmentation, DJP's Roh Tae Woo won the presidency with a 36.6% vote, while Kim Young Sam and Kim Dae Jung received 28 and 27% respectively. Roh's victory meant that South Korea's authoritarian elites survived and coexisted with the democratization process (Lee 2007, 111).

In addition to the political fragmentation that led to Roh's victory, the interests of social forces in South Korea seem to be divergent over time, making it difficult for more political consolidation. For much of the 1990s and the 2000s, South Korea was plagued by regional factionalism, labor–management conflict and right/left ideological cleavages (Kim 2003, 4). Of greatest concern seems to be regional divide. Im (2004) argues that, as soon as the country reached a general consensus on democratization in the late 1980s, voters lost their common agenda, Meanwhile presidential contenders tended to mobilize regional interests and sentiments for gathering votes. In the early 1990s regionalism deepened when the three parties merged to create a hegemonic regionalism designed to isolate minor regions. Some call it the "regional rivalry sentiment", while others point to urban concentration and an imbalance of regional development (see Choi 2009, 12–14), which have been the pitfalls of South Korea's successful catch-up.

The long legacy of authoritarian rule also left many people nostalgic for strong leadership, as seen in the case of Park Geun-hye, a daughter of General Park Chung Hee, who won the presidency in 2012 "thanks to older voters who remembered with fondness the regime of her father" (*The Economist*, 4 May 2017). Mass demonstrations returned in late 2016 against her alleged abuse of power. Lee Jae-yong, the son of Samsung's chairman, has also been involved in the scandal, accused of paying bribes in return for government support for corporate restructuring. However, early calls for Park Geun-hye to step down did not work until around a million protesters mobilized. Protests against Park Geun-hye are not just about disenchantment with the personnel; they also reflect a deeper frustration of the South Korean younger generation with an unlevel playing field in daily life. The US' Pew Research Center recently found that only 20% of young South Koreans were satisfied with the direction of their country, compared with four in ten of those aged fifty and over (*The Economist*, 4 May 2017). Although the presidential victory of Moon Jae-in in 2017 has brought hope of resolving the catch-up legacies, it is obvious that political settlement in South Korea takes much longer than its economic catch-up and is still very much in process.

3.3 Taiwan and Gradual Opening

In contrast to South Korea, Taiwan's catch-up strategy was driven by SMEs, while price stability and income equality were part of the initial plan. This strategy facilitated a gradual process toward political opening, largely under the control of the ruling leaders. Dominant studies in comparative politics typically portray Taiwan's political development as a top-down process under elite control. For example, Haggard and Kaufman (2016, 165) characterize it as the elite's "pre-emptive democratization". However, such a decision could not be made without a supportive context, especially the country's catch-up strategy and continuous local elections.

3.3.1 Inclusive Growth with Political Reasons

Taiwan's catch-up process was manned by the Kuomintang Party (KMT) and can be characterized as a "shared growth" model designed to achieve economic prosperity together with equitable distribution and a mild level of inflation. Its average growth was 9.7% from 1960 to 1980, while Gini coefficient remained between 0.31 and 0.35 until the 1990s (Jeon 1995, 73).

This growth model is a calculated political move. The KMT attributed its defeat to the Chinese Communist Party in the civil war (1945–9) to a vicious cycle of social inequality, rampant inflation, intra-party factionalism and corrupt state–business ties. To avoid another political downfall, upon settling in Taiwan in 1949, the KMT began developmental state-building by a substantive land reform, which not only undermined local landlords but also allowed the party to gain legitimacy among agrarian smallholders (Lauridsen 2014, 434). The KMT later sought to maintain relatively tight fiscal and monetary policies, with surplus budgeting, high real interest rates, low money supply, and stable foreign exchange rates.

Taiwan helped its firms to develop technologies and open export markets through state agencies. That the KMT was considered an *occupation force* by the local Taiwanese population unintentionally benefited the catch-up process. Due to this political distance, local business interests could not influence state-led technology acquisition to favor particular groups at the expense of national interests (Khan and Blankenburg 2009). The KMT was also reluctant to allow native conglomerates to flourish, as they could threaten the party's dominance. As a result, most large-scale firms in the Taiwanese economy have been state-owned enterprises (SOEs), or rather "party enterprises", while the private sector consisted mainly of SMEs, with a few exceptions, such as the Tatung group or Formosa Plastic (Chang 2006, 117–18).

Taiwan entered the advanced phase of catch-up in the mid-1980s. The KMT introduced a comprehensive set of technology-upgrading policies and institutions. Favorable fiscal and financial incentives were granted to special public science and technology projects, as well as initiatives for private-sector technological development. Wong (1999) attributed Taiwan's success to its public research institute innovation network, involving the promotion of indigenous SMEs coupled with the large-scale development of public research institutes to facilitate technology assimilation/transfer and cooperative R&D promotion. Yet again, such industrial upgrading policies and dense public–private ties reflected the KMT's changing political strategy. As detailed in Lauridsen (2014, 438), the strong focus on high-tech industries was driven by the termination of the 1954 Mutual Defense Treaty, urging the KMT to move toward a more self-sustaining defense sector.

3.3.2 Capital and Labor in Structural Transformation

Successful catch-up in Taiwan led to rapid structural transformation. From 1956 to 1988, the proportion of small farmers went down from 45 to 10%, while manual workers rose from 20 to 45%, and the middle class (professional, managerial and clerical workers) from 11% to more than 20% [collected from Burris (1992) and Koo (1991)].

However, compared to South Korea, Taiwan's catch-up strategy led to a different impact on the organization of social forces. In 1981 SMEs made up 55% of non-agricultural production and employed 70% of the entire population in Taiwan (Lim 2003, 130). This structure facilitated the KMT's political domination. Until the 1980s several surveys found that 70–80% of industrial and commercial associations supported the KMT, believing that the KMT not only provided the best guarantee of the social order required for business but also supported the broader interests of the private sector in economic development (Mcbeath 1998, 317).

Although Taiwan has a higher rate of unionization (22.3% in 1986) than South Korea (7% in 1986), labor unions in Taiwan had been largely under state control. No autonomous union existed before 1986, as local branches of the KMT were active in intervening in union activities or maintaining security offices inside large-sized factories (see Chu 1998). Moreover, the government's incentives did not favor large enterprises as in South Korea, but rather encouraged them to subcontract parts of their production to small firms. Thus, until the late 1980s many Taiwanese workers would regard factory jobs as an apprenticeship toward starting their own entrepreneurial careers. As a consequence, the political role of labor in Taiwan was less active and contentious than its South Korean counterpart. Although the number of labor disputes increased markedly during the 1980s, there were rare large-scale industrial demonstrations. It was after the rescinding of martial law in 1987 that workers began to get organized (Chu 1998, 192).

3.3.3 Continuity of Local Elections

Despite maintaining a tight grip on the national polity and economy, elections have been held continuously at local districts, laying a firm foundation for competing forces to negotiate on political opening at the national level.

To strengthen its legitimacy as much as its control across regions, the KMT continued to expand the scope of local elections from the 1950s. The KMT also used local elections to identify authentic local leaders and co-opted them into the party. From 1951 the Taiwanese could cast their votes for the Provincial Assembly, along with elections for village executives and councils, on a regular basis and without significant interruption. Independent candidates were permitted to run in the competition, but KMT candidates tended to win, with the help of the single non-transferable vote and multi-member district electoral system (SNTV–MM system) that undermined the chances of independent candidates (Wong 2001, 343).

Despite the KMT's manipulation, a close study by Rigger (1999) found that grassroots elections were a powerful process for political socialization in Taiwan. By the early 1980s, opposition and independent candidates had already played the electoral game for nearly 30 years. The experience of voting in competitive local elections encouraged the Taiwanese to express their preferences and focus on party identification. Meanwhile, the opposition forces could use local elections to develop their skills of political mobilization. Accordingly, the continuity of local-level elections provided an effective institutional infrastructure for full-blown democratization in the later period, as it "created and reinforced party identification, which made retreating from reform doubly difficult" (Rigger 1999, 181).

3.3.4 Elite Bargains in the 1980s

The contexts of shared-growth catch-up and continuous local elections paved the way for elite bargaining in the process of gradual political opening. The three major power blocs that facilitated organized negotiations in the late 1980s were the KMT moderates, the opposition moderates and student protesters, with the hardliners in each bloc being marginalized (Fell 2012, 37).

As detailed in Huang et al. (1998), in the wake of the 1980 elections, one faction of the opposition, led by Kang Ning-hsiang, approached a group of reform-minded members of the KMT and initiated a consultative meeting with opposition leaders. And from 1981 KMT soft-liners and leaders of the *Tangwai* (meaning "outside the party") started arranging informal meetings, in which opposition leaders gave the impression that they were willing to work with the KMT in facilitating democratic transition. Political persecution did continue in the 1980s but less severely than before. An important milestone came in September 1986 when the *Tangwai* formally founded the Democratic Progressive Party (DPP) to contest the year-end supplementary elections. Although technically illegal, the KMT allowed the DPP to run its first election campaign in December 1986 and won 12 legislative and 11 National Assembly seats—which could be counted as Taiwan's first multi-party election at the national level (Fell 2012, 33).

Whether Chiang Ching-kuo—KMT leader from 1978 to 1988—was a true democratic reformer remains a debatable issue. However, note that Chiang Ching-kuo and the KMT allowed competitive national elections to take place only when they were confident that the party itself possessed sufficient organizational and political capabilities to prevail in a more competitive political setting (Haggard and Kaufman 2016, 165).

The martial law was lifted in July 1987, having been in operation for almost four decades. Moreover, in 1988 the KMT decided to choose Lee Teng-hui to be party chairman and ultimately president. This was an *unconventional* choice. The KMT had been led by mainlanders for almost four decades: Chiang Kai-shek (1950–75), Yen Chia-kan (1975–8) and Chiang Ching-kuo (1978–88). Lee was a native Taiwanese, US-educated technocrat who was the appointed Taipei City mayor from 1978 to 1981. This selection suggested that reformist leaders in the KMT were beginning to realize that the party's reputation as a "mainlander redoubt" was a political liability, indicated by the overwhelming success of Taiwanese candidates in elections and the increasing popularity of the opposition party throughout the 1980s (Rigger 1999, 122).

A series of gradual political openings arose under the presidency of Lee Teng-hui (1988–2000). In March 1990 President Lee announced his intention to host the National Affairs Conference (NAC), bringing together elites from both the ruling and opposition camps to negotiate, bargain and forge compromises on the country's key issues. The NAC marked the first time that politicians from both parties formally met to hammer out extremely sensitive political projects (Wong 2001, 350). Again, it is worth noting that the NAC did not merely result from the elite's decision. Rather, it came from the demands of students and intellectuals, who arranged the so-called Wild Lily student movement, an unprecedented 22,000-strong demonstration in Taipei, from 16 March until Lee's presidential inauguration on 21 March 1990 (Chao and Myers 1998, 192).

3.3.5 Gradual Political Opening from the 1990s

The NAC marked a critical juncture in Taiwan's political development. It brought formerly exiled or jailed dissidents face-to-face with the KMT leaders who had exiled or jailed them. More importantly, it set an agenda for political reform, which would be followed even though the NAC had no statutory force (Huang et al. 1998, 153).

Most of the reforms discussed at the NAC were enacted. National Assembly elections in 1991 and legislative elections in 1992 featured full-scale electoral and free-party competition. March 1996 saw the direct presidential election, which was sufficiently freely contested for the Freedom House to rank Taiwan as a "politically free" country for the first time (Huang et al. 1998, 148).

A next step in the political development of Taiwan was the creation of the National Development Conference (NDC), an extra-constitutional forum, in December 1996. The NDC consisted of 170 representatives from all of the important sectors of society. At the end of the NDC, Lee Teng-hui reached a new position, from which he could lead the KMT beyond its founders and previous legacy, while the DPP's leaders learned to play the game of electoral and legislative politics successfully and to contain their party's ingrained factional struggles (Huang et al. 1998, 159–60). With the NDC's key resolutions becoming part of the revised Constitution, Taiwan entered 1997 with considerable consensus over the country's key issues of relations with China and the rules of the political game (Jacobs 1997, 155).

The DPP eventually won a presidential election in 2000 thanks to its social welfare policies and a split within the KMT. However, President Chen Shui-bian (2000–8) and the DPP had lost its popularity over time due to various reasons. As detailed in Lauridsen (2014, 441), the facts that economic bureaucracy was still KMT-dominated while the DPP itself could not win the majority in the Parliament caused several cases of policy paralysis under Chen's tenure. Meanwhile, the lack of a direct mode of financing (such as KMT's party enterprises) incentivized the DPP to distribute giveaway subsidies to favored firms, leading to corruption and embezzlement, on which Chen and his wife were convicted in 2009.

Despite the fall of the DPP in 2008, Taiwan's contemporary political economy is generally open and inclusive. From 1996 until 2016, the Freedom House rated Taiwan as a "free" country, with high scores on both political rights and civil liberties, generally a step higher than South Korea.[4] There is an increasing tendency toward a healthy two-party system in which, after the introduction of a direct presidential election in 1996, the government has alternated between the KMT (in office 1996–2000 and 2008–16) and the DPP (2000–8 and 2016–present).

3.4 Singapore and Continuous Consolidation

Although South Korea and Taiwan have taken varying paths to socio-political settlement, both have ended up with a generally democratic procedure. In this respect, Singapore's path has been fundamentally different. Until the mid-1990s, Levitsky and Way (2010: 34) considered Singapore to be a "fully authoritarian" regime because "restrictions on speech and association made it nearly impossible for opposition groups to operate publicly and because legal controls and other institutional obstacles prevented opposition parties from contesting most seats in parliament". Even in

[4]https://freedomhouse.org/report/freedom-world/freedom-world-2017.

2017, when the country has a per capita income of USD 52,889, making it the world's tenth richest country, the Freedom House still counts Singapore as being "party free".[5] A general election may be fully contested, but television and the traditional media are "mostly aligned with the ruling People's Action Party",[6] facilitating the party to capture 93% of the seats and 70% of the popular vote in 2015. Put together, this chapter characterizes Singapore's path to settlement as *continuous consolidation*.

3.4.1 Stable Growth with Peculiar Compositions

Singapore's catch-up strategy can be categorized as a "stable growth" model, in which the emphasis was placed on economic growth together with political and macroeconomic stability, but relatively less on income distribution. Singapore grew at an average rate of 10.2% between 1965 and 1979, with its Gini coefficient reducing from 0.50 (1965) to 0.43 (1980) and 0.41 (1990) (Jeon 1995, 75 and Solt 2009).

Singapore adopted a free-trade regime and strongly supported foreign direct investment (FDI), making its industrial policies distinct from other East Asian countries. Even so, Singapore did not pursue a laissez-faire approach, as usually assumed. Although adopting a pro-FDI approach, the Singaporean government has worked hard to attract FDI into strategic areas by investing in particular types of manpower and infrastructure, as well as providing custom-designed financial incentives (Chang 2006, 118). More importantly, the government set up SOEs, known as government-linked corporations (GLCs) across key industrial sectors, including Singapore Airlines, telecommunications, financial services, energy and natural resources, transport, shipping, semiconductors, health care and engineering. As a result, the public sector share of gross fixed capital formation in Singapore was 35.6% in the 1960s, 26.7% in the 1970s and 30.3% in the 1980s, much higher than in Taiwan and South Korea (see Shin 2005). Singapore often used these GLCs to pump-prime the economy whenever there was any sign of economic downturn, while profits from GLCs were used to subsidize deficits in government priority areas such as housing (Chowdhury 2008).

In sum, Singapore's successful catch-up was driven by a "peculiar" policy mix of free trade, pro-FDI with custom-designed incentives, and heavy use of SOEs. This resulted in an annual growth rate of 10.2% and an inflation rate of 4.3% between 1965 and 1979 (Jeon 1995, 73).

3.4.2 Tying the PAP–Bureaucracy Nexus

The above catch-up strategy had been crafted and carried out by the People's Action Party (PAP), which has ruled Singapore since its independence in 1959. The PAP

---

[5] http://freedomhouse.org/report/freedom-world/2017/singapore (accessed 17 May 2017).

[6] http://freedomhouse.org/report/freedom-world/2016/singapore (accessed 17 May 2017).

has been led by three prime ministers: Lee Kuan Yew (1959–90); Goh Chok Tong (1990–2004); and Lee Hsien Loong (2004–present).

The PAP had a landslide victory in the 1959 elections. Initially, social tensions surrounding the issue about a merger with the Federation of Malaysia in the early 1960s encouraged PAP leaders to intimidate its opponents, particularly trade unions, journalists and student leaders. For example, in the particular swoop in 1963, 111 people were arrested under the Internal Security Act (ISA), legislation inherited by the British and giving the authorities the power of detention without trial. However, over time, the PAP has developed a more nuanced approach to social organization. As detailed in Rodan (2006), it began by strengthening ties between the party and public bureaucracies. Policy formation was completely removed from wider party organization and became a matter that was discussed only between the PAP executive, led by Lee Kuan Yew, and senior civil servants. New civil service appointments then extended PAP control over the state apparatus and, subsequently, the upper echelons of the civil service became the standard route to political leadership (Rodan and Jayasuriya 2009, 29).

Since then the state machinery has been part and parcel of the PAP's social organization. On the one hand, grass-roots para-political state institutions (e.g. People's Associations, Community Centres and Citizens' Consultative Committees) were initiated under the Prime Minister's Office. These organizations became avenues to foster support for the PAP's candidates and ideology. The most important achievement was the National Trades Union Congress (NTUC), through which the PAP fostered a political allegiance with selected elements of the working class (Rodan 2006, 7). On the other hand, the state set up strategic social schemes to reach more citizens, ranging from investments in education to public housing. The latter policy resulted in three-quarters of the Singaporean population living in apartments on 99-year leases from the government (Rodan and Jayasuriya 2009, 29). These schemes enabled the PAP to harness estate development and resettlement programmes during the 1960s and 1970s in an effort to dilute the electoral impact of political opposition (Rodan 2006, 8).

Another key mechanism used to tie the party–state nexus is manipulation of the electoral system. The institutionalization of authoritarian rule during the early 1960s has had a number of long-lasting impacts. In the context of elections, the most debilitating tools included: the detention of opposition leaders; the denial of permits to hold campaign rallies; the shutting down of hostile printing facilities; increasing the candidate registration fee; limiting the campaign period to nine days; and placing the Elections Department within the Prime Minister's Office to facilitate the incumbent (Morgenbesser 2017, 8).

3.4.3 New Industrial Revolution and Political Participation

Since the mid-1980s, the government's successful attempt at the "new industrial revolution" has led to a surge of the middle class. The Singaporean middle class (defined as professionals, technicians and those employed in administrative and managerial work) increased from 10.3% (1970) to 13.6% (1980), 25.0% (1989) and then 40.3% (1999) (Tamura 2003). A steep rise after the 1980s was caused by government policies designed to train a large number of skilled workers required for industrial upgrading.

Accordingly, the PAP initiated new forms of political participation in response to the emerging middle class (Rodan 2006, 11–18). First, legal and administrative tools have become the PAP's essential mechanism to control opposing groups and the mass media. By design, the ruling party holds authority over appointments and renewal of the Supreme Court, as well as the transfers of lower court judges between judicial and government service. Regarding the media, amendments to the Newspaper and Printing Presses Act in 1986 have been instrumental in restricting the circulation of foreign publications.

Meanwhile, political participation has been encouraged through state-controlled channels. In the mid-1980s, the PAP established a group of extra-parliamentary units such as the Feedback Unit, under the Ministry of Community Development, to collate the public's response to policy issues. The Government Parliamentary Committee and the Institute of Policy Studies were also founded to incorporate professionals with specific policy expertise. Another significant step was taken in 1990, with constitutional revisions to create a new category of parliamentarians—*Nominated MPs* (NMPs)—to mediate the widening interests of Singaporean citizens, including domestic business, labor, women and ethnic organizations. Yet, the number and authority of the NMPs were decided by the PAP. For example, the NMPs were initially allocated with six positions with limited voting rights and gradually increased with the following elections.

Finally, economic dependence is also important. Much of the middle class was either employed by government departments and GLCs or received state services through the provision of professional legal, commercial or other assistance (Rodan and Jayasuriya 2009, 30). For example, from the 1980s to the 1990s more than 80% of Singapore's population lived in public housing built by the government's Housing Development Board (Tamura 2003, 191; Barr 2014, 33).

3.4.4 Governance Ideology

Approaching the 1980s, "technocracy" has become a new approach to legitimizing the PAP's domination, replacing the old paradigm of "pragmatism" that was powerful in the 1960s and 1970s. Technocratic governance was heralded by the introduction of professional, non-elected town councils helmed by local MPs to manage the delivery of services in the government's estates, in which the majority of Singaporeans lived. Under the concept of technocratic governance as a grand ideological theme, the PAP is adaptable to changes in broader contexts (Rodan 2006, 16–18). For example, when Asian economies were at their height in the 1990s, the government was keen to promote "Asian values". The implications of Asian values were that liberalism would create conflicts and would not be compatible with the Asian tradition of the consensual style of management. Yet, when the Asian financial crisis in the late 1990s delegitimized this discourse, the PAP was sufficiently responsive to shift toward a new idea of the "Singapore 21" vision, developed to forge a "partnership" between the government, the private sector and the people toward the common national interest.

A more practical application of technocratic professionalism is found in electoral regulations. That electoral laws have been manipulated to favor the PAP is well documented (see Tan 2013). However, the PAP never ceases to find a new "creative" way to undermine the opposition, as recently seen in the presidency, which since the 1990s has been an elected office vested with the power to veto any senior appointment in the civil service and Cabinet, including that of prime minister (Barr 2014). In January 2016 Prime Minister Lee Hsien Loong pushed forward a constitutional amendment to create stricter qualifying criteria for the presidency. It is now required that, to be president, one must have held, for no less than three years, one of several high offices—such as cabinet minister, Chief Justice, Speaker of Parliament, Attorney-General or Permanent Secretary. Alternatively, a person is qualified only if he or she has held the position of chief executive officer of a company with a paid-up capital of at least $100 million (Lee 2016, 3). In effect, in almost every election, all alternatives to the PAP nominee have been ruled ineligible under these rules (Barr 2014, 34). This is because the PAP holds authority over appointments of almost all those positions through the government and the GLCs.

3.4.5 *A Prototype for High-Income Authoritarianism?*

The current Prime Minister Lee Hsien Loong, a son of Lee Kuan Yew, clearly stated that "a democratic system is inherently adversarial, and there are risks to it".[7] Does this mean that Singapore is set to be a prototype for high-income authoritarianism?

The most recent election in 2015 saw the PAP's landslide victory, winning 69.9% of the popular vote and 83 out of 89 parliamentary seats. It is possible that the PAP will retain its hold on power for the foreseeable future, underpinned by its political adaptability, as well as the existing institutional infrastructure. Meanwhile, research finds that opposition membership grew significantly in the 2000s, with a surge in young and well-qualified opposition candidates in their 20s and early 30s in the 2011 and 2015 general elections (Singh 2012). In fact, the PAP was more responsive after the opposition's strong showing in 2011, leading Lee Hsien Loong to apologize for the ruling party's mistakes and to promise improvements. The PAP has since strengthened its community involvement and introduced more social programs to deal with citizen complaints. It also granted some political "opening", such as the relaxed measures that allow protests without police permits in a designated area, and political parties to use online media and videos during electoral campaigns (Ng 2016, 439).

[7]"Not Everything Debatable in Public", *Channel News Asia*, 13 April 2011 (cited in Barr 2014).

As Morgenbesser (2017) puts it, the PAP's source of stability lies in the art of balancing *legitimation* and *repression*—it always "encourages laws to be bent, not broken; media outlets to be regulated, not censored; public gatherings to be controlled, not outlawed; civil society organizations to be circumscribed, not eliminated; and elections to be managed, not blatantly stolen" (Morgenbesser 2017, 13).

3.5 Concluding Remarks

This chapter has pointed out that socio-political conflict is an integral part of catch-up and is worthy of more analytical consideration. It has also stressed the multiplicity of paths to settlement and how each path hinges heavily on the country's catch-up strategy. This concluding section recaps the main findings and discusses some broader implications.

3.5.1 Catch-up, Conflicts and Multiple Paths to Settlement

In South Korea, the catch-up strategy led by General Park focused single-mindedly on industrial growth and created clear winners and losers. Resources were relocated to support the large-scale production of the chaebols in target industries. To force the ruling military into political concession, labor movements needed to ally with moderate civil society and middle classes to stage a series of contentious demonstrations. However, the rift within the pro-democracy forces extended the military's grip in the first direct presidential election in 1987. Subsequent politics in South Korea have continued to be shaped by confrontation and fragmentation.

The KMT learned from its political mistakes in mainland China and crafted Taiwan's catch-up in the direction of an inclusive growth model. On the surface, the KMT and the opposing forces seemed to reach a consensus to liberalize the political economy gradually from the late 1980s. However, such elite bargaining was made possible by an equitable development outcome, as well as the continuity of local elections in the background since 1950. Moreover, political opening through elite bargaining has also allowed the preservation of some authoritarian legacies, such as the KMT's control over state assets and the limited implementation of transitional justice (Fell 2012, 38).

In contrast to South Korea and Taiwan, where democracy has been the "only game in town" since the 1990s and witnessed an alternation of the ruling party, the PAP has managed to rule Singapore for almost sixty years since its independence. Right from the start the PAP has tied the party–bureaucracy nexus and undertaken social policies to render the emerging middle class heavily dependent upon it. The PAP has regularly adapted channels of political participation, as well as governance ideology, to suit the changing contexts. Table 3.2 summarizes these three paths to settlement in East Asia.

Table 3.2 Comparing varieties of catch-up and settlement path in East Asia

	Catch-up strategy	Development outcomes	Path to settlement
South Korea	Chaebol-led growth	• Clear winners (chaebols, middle class) and losers (labor, SMEs) • Increasing inequality	Contentious settlements
Taiwan	Inclusive growth	• SME-based economy • Relatively equitable society • Strictly controlled labor	Gradual political opening
Singapore	Free trade + strategic FDI and SOEs	• Close ties between PAP–state–middle class • Tight control over party politics and participation	Continuous consolidation

3.5.2 Broader Implications

The findings herein differ from the conventional suggestion that a developing country needs a set of institutional prerequisites—especially a level playing field for new businesses and democracy—in order to sustain economic growth toward a high income level (Acemoglu and Robinson 2012; North et al. 2009). South Korea, Taiwan and Singapore have escaped the so-called "middle-income trap" despite their institutions being highly deficient in both the political and economic arenas. Even when South Korea and Taiwan democratized, they did so in an uneven and non-linear fashion. More interesting is the case of Singapore, which has hardly democratized at all by most standards. Settlement is therefore a better word than democratization to describe the way in which each society tries to manage the socio-political conflict arising from the rapid industrialization that changes the composition of class structures, as well as resource allocations.

The findings from this chapter may have different implications for the elite and non-elite in developing countries. The former may best look to Taiwan, while the latter could learn more from South Korea and Singapore.

The ruling elite typically considers Singapore to be the dream authoritarian, high-income destination, exemplified by the Chinese Communist Party's eagerness to follow the Singapore model (see Ortmann 2012). However, size does matter, while the absence of an agricultural sector makes it less difficult for the PAP to steer the economy in the way it has done. A relatively large country with a significant amount of agriculture needs a substantive land reform to reduce tensions at an early stage of industrialization. The ruling elite and policy-makers in today's developing countries should learn from Taiwan regarding the timing and preparation required for political concession and opening. A catch-up strategy that creates clear-cut winners and losers with no pre-emptive compensation, like that of South Korea, will heighten tensions over the course of development. A good growth strategy is one that comes with complementary policies to maintain price stability and income parity. In short, it is an inclusive development model that lays a solid foundation for the elite themselves in the bargaining process, as well as their survival in the post-authoritarian era. Unequal growth is inclined to arouse confrontation, which, in turn, impedes further economic restructuring at the later phase of catch-up—the Gordian Knot currently faced by countries like Thailand, Brazil and Turkey.

While the elite should learn from Taiwan, civil society and the citizens of developing countries may learn practical lessons from South Korea and Singapore. Political opening in South Korea has been driven mainly by labor unions—but they cannot achieve this without forming an alliance with civil society, students, religious organizations and parts of the middle class. After all, it is a *cross-class coalition* that makes the movement powerful. Moreover, Singapore also shows us that political opening could take place in various ways, even if such an opening were under state control. Civil society and social movements in other countries can make a pre-emptive move to demand Singaporean-style representation and participation, such as nominated MPs and the partnership consultation, before developing them into a more substantive channel such as Taiwan's National Conferences.

References

Acemoglu D, Robinson J (2012) Why nations fail: the origins of power, prosperity, and poverty. Profile, London

Amsden AH (1989) Asia's next giant: South Korea and late industrialization. University Press, Oxford

Barr MD (2014) The bonsai under the banyan tree: democracy and democratisation in Singapore. Democratization 21(1):29–48

Bellin E (2000) Contingent democrats: industrialists, labor, and democratization in late-developing countries. World Polit 52(2):175–205

Burris Val (1992) Late industrialization and class formation in East Asia. Research in Political Economy 13:245–283

Chang HJ (2006) Industrial policy in East Asia: lessons for Europe. EIB Papers 11(2):106–132

Chang HJ (1994) State, institutions and structural change. Structural Change and Economic Dynamics 5(2):293–313

Chang HJ (1993) The political economy of industrial policy in Korea. Camb J Econ 17(2):131–157

Chao L, Myers RH (1998) The first Chinese democracy: political life in the Republic of China on Taiwan. Johns Hopkins University Press, Baltimore, Md

Choe H, Kim J (2012) South Korea's democratization movements, 1980–1987: political structure, political opportunity, and framing. Inter-Asia Cultural Studies 13(1):55–68

Choi S (2009) Labor welfare in South Korea. J Workplace Behav Health 24(1–2):265–273

Chowdhury A (2008) Growth-oriented macroeconomic policies for small islands economies: lessons from Singapore. Research Paper No. 2008/47, UNUWIDER, Helsinki

Chu YW (1998) Labor and democratization in South Korea and Taiwan. Journal of Contemporary Asia 28(2):185–202

Di John J, Putzel J (2009) Political settlements. Discussion Paper, University of Birmingham

Evans P (1995) Embedded autonomy: States and industrial transformation. Princeton University Press, Princeton

Evans P, Rauch JE (1999) Bureaucracy and growth: a cross-national analysis of the effects of Weberian state structures on economic growth. Am Sociol Rev, 748–765

Fell D (2012) Government and politics in Taiwan. Routledge
Fleckenstein T, Lee SC (2017) Democratization, post-industrialization, and East Asian welfare capitalism: the politics of welfare state reform in Japan, South Korea, and Taiwan. J Int Comp Soc Policy 33(1):36–54
Haggard S, Kaufman R (2016) Dictators and democrats: masses, elites, and regime change. Princeton University Press, Princeton
Heo Yoon (2001) Development strategy in Korea reexamined: an interventionist perspective. Soc Sci J 38(2):217–231
Huang TI, Tse-min L, Higley J (1998) Elite settlements in Taiwan. J Democracy 9(2):148–163
Im HB (2004) Faltering democratic consolidation in South Korea: democracy at the end of the 'three Kims' era. Democratization 11(5):179–198
Jacobs JB (1997) Democratisation in Taiwan revisited. Asian Stud Rev 21(2–3):149–157
Jeon JG (1995) Exploring the three varieties of East Asia's state-guided development model: Korea, Singapore, and Taiwan. Stud Comp Int Dev 30(3):70–88
Johnson C (1982) MITI and the Japanese miracle: the growth of industrial policy: 1925-1975. Stanford University Press, Stanford
Khan M, Blankenburg S (2009) The political economy of industrial policy in Asia and Latin America. In: Cimoli M, Dosi G, Stiglitz JE (eds) Industrial policy and development: the political economy of capabilities accumulation. Oxford University Press, Oxford
Khan M (2010) Political settlements and the governance of growth-enhancing institutions. SOAS Working Paper
Kim SS (2003) Korea's democratization. Cambridge University Press, Cambridge
Kim S (2000) The politics of democratization in Korea: the role of civil society. University of Pittsburgh Press, Pittsburgh
Koo H (1991) Middle classes, democratization, and class formation. Theor Soc 20(4):485–509
Kuznets S (1972) Innovations and adjustments in economic growth. Swed J Econ 74(4):431–451
Lauridsen L (2014) Governance and economic transformation in Taiwan: the role of politics. Dev Policy Rev 32(4):427–448
Lee JTT (2016) Singapore's elected president: an office that is still evolving. Paper presented at 16th international symposium on wearable computers, Newcastle, United Kingdom, 18–22 June 2012
Lee J (2000) Political protest and democratization in South Korea. Democratization 7(3):181–202
Lee S (2007) Democratic transition and the consolidation of democracy in South Korea. Taiwan J Democracy 3(1):99–125
Lee Y (2011) Militants or partisans: labor unions and democratic politics in Korea and Taiwan. Stanford University Press, Stanford, California
Levitsky S, Way LA (2010) Competitive authoritarianism: hybrid regimes after the cold war. Cambridge University Press, Cambridge
Lim S (2003) Chaebols and small and medium-sized capitalists: the forgotten players in Korean and Taiwanese democratization. Pac Focus 18(1):123–149
McBeath GA (1998) The changing role of business associations in democratizing Taiwan. J Contemp China 7(18):303–320
Morgenbesser L (2017) The autocratic mandate: elections, legitimacy and regime stability in Singapore. Pac Rev 30(2):205–231
Ng HY (2016) What drives young people into opposition parties under hybrid regimes? A comparison of Hong Kong and Singapore. Asian Politics Policy 8(3):436–455
North DC, Wallis JJ, Weingast BR (2009) Violence and social orders: a conceptual framework for interpreting recorded human history. Cambridge University Press, Cambridge
Ortmann S (2012) The 'Beijing consensus' and the 'Singapore model': Unmasking the myth of an alternative authoritarian state-capitalist model. J Chin Econ Bus Stud 10(4):337–359
Pak S (1998) Two forces of democratisation in Korea. J Contemp Asia 28(1):45–73
Rigger S (1999) Politics in Taiwan: voting for democracy. Routledge, London

Rodan G (2006) Singapore exceptionalism: authoritarian rule and state transformation. Murdoch University, Asia Research Centre, Working Paper No. 131
Rodan G, Jayasuriya K (2009) Capitalist development, regime transitions and new forms of authoritarianism in Asia. Pac Rev 22(1):23–47
Rodrik D (2008) One economics, many recipes: globalization, institutions, and economic growth. Princeton University Press, Princeton
Shin JS (2005) Globalization and challenges to the developmental state: a comparison between South Korea and Singapore. Global Econ Rev 34(4):379–395
Singh B (2012) Politics and governance in Singapore: an introduction. McGraw-Hill Education, Singapore
Solt F (2009) Standardizing the world income inequality database. Soc Sci Q 90(2):231–242
Tamura KT (2003) The emergence and political consciousness of the middle class in Singapore. Dev Econ 41(2):184–200
Tan N (2013) Manipulating electoral laws in Singapore. Electoral Stud 32(4):632–643
Wade R (1990) Governing the market: economic theory and the role of government in East Asian industrialization. Princeton University Press, Princeton
Wong J (2001) Dynamic democratization in Taiwan. J Contemp China 10(27):339–362
Wong PK (1999) National innovation systems for rapid technological catch-up. Paper at the DRUID Summer Conference on National Innovation Systems, Denmark, 9–12 June 1999

Chapter 4
Reemerging Developmental State in Democratized Indonesia

Yuri Sato

4.1 Introduction

This chapter discusses challenges facing emerging states that promote development under democratization and globalization. It compares two types of developmental state; that is, 'authoritarian developmental state' and 'democratic developmental state'. Indonesia experienced both types of developmental states during the last five decades. The chapter looks at similarities and differences between the two types from the viewpoint of institutions, policies, and policymakers under the respective given external conditions. By doing so, it explores the key characteristics inherent in 'democratic developmental state' in the context of the twenty-first century.

As Chap. 1 emphasizes, this volume reexamines the concept of developmental state beyond the so-called 'East Asian bias' prevalent in the existing literature. This chapter provides a reexamination from the Southeast Asian perspective. Southeast Asia has been considered as a region where one can hardly find developmental states in the sense in which Japan, Korea, and Taiwan were viewed as developmental states. As Chap. 1 reviews, the term 'developmental state' was coined by Johnson (1982) on the model of Japan, where the Ministry of International Trade and Industry (MITI) materialized 'plan rationality' in the bureaucratic system and in the collaborative relationship between state and business in promoting development. Johnson's focus on capacity of the developmental state was enriched with broader evidences from Korea (Amsden 1989; Haggard 1990; Haggard et al.1992) and Taiwan (Wade 1990; Hattori and Sato 1996). Setting this model of developmental states as a benchmark, Southeast Asian states are rated as having lower capacity than a developmental state. Doner et al. (2005), defining developmental states as 'organizational complexes in which expert and coherent bureaucratic agencies collaborated with organized private

Y. Sato (✉)
Institute of Developing Economies (IDE), Japan External Trade Organization (JETRO), 3-2-2 Wakaba, Mihama-ku, 261-8545 Chiba, Japan
e-mail: yuri_sato@ide.go.jp

Y. Takagi et al. (eds.), *Developmental State Building*, Emerging-Economy State and International Policy Studies, https://doi.org/10.1007/978-981-13-2904-3_4

sectors to spur national economic transformation', deem Southeast Asian states not to fulfill the definition, as these states are featured by uneven bureaucratic coherence, clientelism in public-private linkages, and private-sector factionalism.

Southeast Asian studies, however, set eyes on the features common to some states that have been pushing development as intermediate states (see Chap. 1 of this volume). As Iwasaki (1994) argued, Thailand, the Philippines, Indonesia, Singapore, and Malaysia have had 'a development-oriented organic unity of political and economic institutions'. He called it a 'developmental regime', featured by four elements; (i) developmentalism to place 'development' as a source of legitimacy of the state, (ii) a centralized administrative system of bureaucrats-technocrats with state intervention, (iii) authoritarianism, and (iv) pro forma parliamentary democracy led by the military or a dominant political party. Suehiro (1998, 2002) saw the developmental regime fit in wider area including Korea, Taiwan, the above-stated five original ASEAN member states, and Vietnam, and extracted a concept of 'developmentalism' as the most essential element. He defined developmentalism in the context of East and Southeast Asia as 'a state ideology for intensively mobilizing physical and human resources to catch up with advanced countries by achieving economic growth through industrialization'.

According to Chap. 1, this volume sets the concept of developmental state free from a specific historical (e.g. the Cold War era) and geographical (e.g. Japan, Korea, and Taiwan) milieu by broadening the scope of observation in terms of time (twentieth and twenty first centuries) and space (Asia and Africa). As an essential element of a developmental state, it underlines the 'shared commitments of leaders and policymakers to development', rather than a specific set of policy instruments.

Similarly, this chapter is based on the following understanding. In Southeast Asia in the latter half of the twentieth century, there emerged some developmental states entailing the 'shared commitments of leaders and policymakers to development', though the degree of coherence in the state system and the quality of state-business relationship may have been lower than those of the advanced model of Japan. One of the common features of the Southeast Asian developmental states in those days was that they took the authoritarian regime. However, as the Cold War that had tolerated the authoritarian regime ended in 1989, the world turned into the era of globalization and democratization. At the beginning of the twenty first century, Southeast Asia saw reemergence of developmental states in the sense of increasing shared commitments of leaders and policymakers to promoting development. It occurred under globalization and democratization, the circumstances greatly changed from the latter half of the previous century.

Indonesia is a typical example in Southeast Asia experiencing developmental state building under authoritarianism in the era of the Cold War and reemergence of developmental state under democracy in the globalization era. I call them 'authoritarian developmental state' and 'democratic developmental state' respectively. Section 4.2 below overviews these two types of developmental state observed in Indonesia and provides an analytical framework this chapter adopts. Sections 4.3 and 4.4 examine the process of policy making under the respective types of developmental state. The main questions are who the key policy makers are; who involves in the policy making;

how the relationship among stakeholders is; and how external and internal conditions influence the policy making process. Economic development policy and social welfare policy are taken up in the third and fourth sections respectively. Section 4.5 summarizes the analysis and elicits challenges facing developmental states in the twenty first century.

4.2 Authoritarian Versus Democratic Developmental States

It is widely accepted that the rule of Indonesia's second president Soeharto was authoritarian and that it set *pembangunan* or 'development' as a state ideology (Thee 2002, Robison 1988, Yasunaka and Mihira (eds) 1995, Shiraishi 1997). Soeharto, after seizing power in 1966, succeeded the authoritarian rule that concentrated power in the president on the basis of the 1945 Constitution from the first president Soekarno, while making a historic turnaround from closed socialism to open capitalism in managing the national economy under the banner of *pembangunan*. The nature of development-oriented authoritarianism remained unchanged throughout his administration until 1998 when democratization movement amid the Asian financial crisis forced Soeharto to step down. I designate Indonesia under the Soeharto's rule (1966–1998) as an 'authoritarian developmental state'. The Soeharto-led authoritarian developmental state is positioned on the left (II and III quadrants) in Fig. 4.1, an area with a high degree of power concentration, while its position in terms of state intervention into the economy changed over time as discussed in Sect. 4.3.

With the fall of Soeharto, the pendulum of Indonesia's state governance swung sharply from power concentration to de-concentration, from centralization to decentralization, and from active state intervention to least state intervention. The position of state governance moved to the extreme of libertarianism, the upper right corner of Fig. 4.1. In 2004, the first direct presidential election in the Indonesian history was carried out peacefully, which led to the recognition that Indonesia established a foundation of democracy through vigorous institutional transformation in the period of 1998–2004.

In the post-Soeharto transition period, policymakers, business agents, and the general public shared sentiment to reject state intervention, perceiving it as an evil practice of authoritarianism, and espoused laissez-faireism. After a decade of laissez-faireism, however, the government changed gear toward more active state intervention, having realized the necessity of shared commitments that would drive the state towards the common goals of development even under a decentralized democracy. I designate Indonesia recognizing the importance of shared commitments for development under democracy as being a 'democratic developmental state'. The democratic developmental state is positioned in the center right (asride I and IV quadrants) in Fig. 4.1, a position with a low degree of power concentration and some degree of state intervention in managing the economy.

A consensus has not reached about the concept of Indonesia being a 'democratic developmental state' and when it started. This chapter suggests it started in 2009,

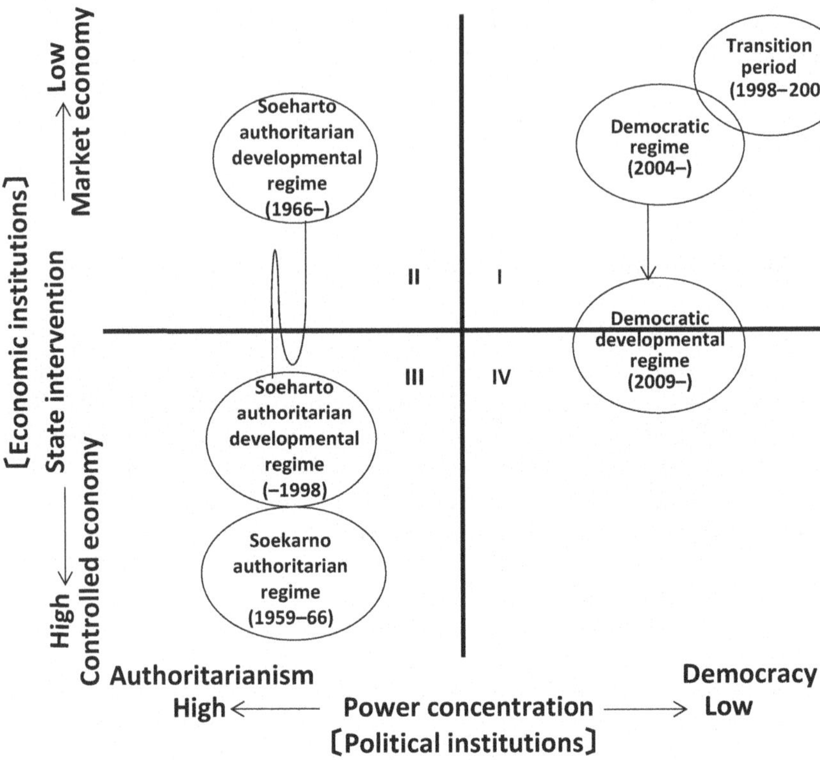

Fig. 4.1 State governance in terms of political and economic institutions: positioning of Indonesian regimes. *Source* Created by the author

when the second-term administration of Susilo Bambang Yudhoyono (2009–2014) began.

Some signs of a gear change can be observed during the Yudhoyono's second-term. The first sign was the National Medium-Term Development Plan 2010–2014 formulated in early 2010. Every Indonesian administration should provide a comprehensive 5-year plan of policies as the National Development Plan or Program at the beginning of its term, but the post-Soeharto administrations avoided setting numerical targets that were perceived as a top-down custom of the Soeharto's authoritarianism. However, the Plan of the second-term Yudhoyono administration set detailed numerical targets not only in the macro indicators, but also in the attached 'policy matrices' of micro policy items (Sato 2010, 164–5). This style was followed by the Plan of the Joko Widodo administration for its 2015–2019 term. The second signpost was the "Masterplan for the Acceleration and Expansion of Indonesian Economic Development 2011–2025" announced in May 2011. While some criticized this Masterplan as a mere rhetoric, its significance lies in the official recognition of greater state commitment to national development. In the launching speech, President Yudhoyono stated that 'for an efficient economy, the invisible hand is important, but the visible hand is also necessary for a fairer and more balanced economy' (Presidential Secretariat 2011). In the Masterplan, the government, for the first time, proclaimed the explicit state developmental target that Indonesia would 'transform into a developed nation in the 21st century' and 'place itself in the top ten advanced economies in the world by 2025 and the top six by 2050' (Republic of Indonesia 2011, 8–9).

Table 4.1 compares 'authoritarian developmental state' (1966–1998) and 'democratic developmental state' (2009–present) in Indonesia in terms of socio-economic performance, external conditions, institutions, and policies.

Three major changes had an impact on policy making in the democratic developmental state, compared to the authoritarian developmental state in Indonesia. The first is the change in external conditions, that is, globalization after the end of the Cold War. Accountability, transparency, and good governance came to be global-standard principles, which policymakers could not ignore. Also, economic liberalization became a global standard policy. Together with the impact of information technology revolution, it promoted cross-border economic activities and value chain development.

The second and third major changes are those in internal conditions. One is the appearance of the constituency. After Indonesia introduced a system of direct presidential election in 2004, the approval of the constituency became the most crucial indicator of the administration's legitimacy. The political leaders became conscious of the voices of the constituency. They came to appeal to the people for Indonesian self-identity and their commitment to the national interests.

The other internal major change occurred in the power structure, that is, deconcentration and decentralization. As a consequence, the number of stakeholders involved in the policy making process have increased greatly. While the president, ministers, technocrats and bureaucrats in the executive branch are central policymakers, veto players such as politicians in the legislature and the constitutional court in the judiciary have emerged. Local governments and non-state players, such as economic organizations, workers unions, religious and social organizations, civil society watchdogs, mass media, and the public through opinion polls as well as social network services (SNS), have increased their voice. With these internal major changes, the democratic developmental state is characterized by a less state-centric policy framework, with more players involved in the policy making, and an interactive relationship between state and non-state domains.

To accommodate the major change in the external conditions explicitly in the analytical framework, I add the third axis to Fig. 4.1. Figure 4.1 shows political institutions in terms of power concentration with the extremes of authoritarianism and democracy as the abscissa axis, and economic institutions in terms of state intervention with the extremes of controlled economy and market economy as the ordinate axis. The third applicate axis represents external relations in terms of conformity with globalization between the extremes of global standard and national interests. Policies can be categorized into eight spaces divided by the three axes as seen in

Table 4.1 Comparison between authoritarian developmental state and democratic developmental state in Indonesia

	Authoritarian developmental state	Democratic developmental state
Administration (Period)	Soeharto (1966–1998)	2nd Yudhoyono and Joko Widodo (2009–present)
Socio-economic performance		
GDP per capita (current US$)	57→1154 (1967→1996)	2400→3570 (2009→2017)
Average GDP growth (%)	7.4 (1968–1997)	5.4 (2009–2017)
Poverty ratio (%)	60.0→11.3 (1970→1996)	14.2→10.1 (2009→2017)
GINI index	0.35→0.36 (1970→1996)	0.37→0.39 (2009→2017)
External conditions	the Cold War	Globalization, economic liberalization, regional integration, global value chains[a]
Institutions		
Political institutions		
Source of legitimacy	Developmentalism (*Pembangunan*)	Public support of the constituency[b]
Power structure	Concentration and centralization	De-concentration and decentralization[c]
Variety of stakeholders	Low	High
Economic institutions		
Institutions for development	Created and established	Revived and developing
State intervention	Active	
Development strategy	Exists	
Aims of the strategy	Economic and social development + distribution of the outcomes of development	
Key element of the strategy	Industrialization	Infrastructure, resource-based industry, digitalization
Policies		
Legal and policy framework	State centric	Accountability, transparency, governance[a]
		Liberalization as global standard[a]
		Nation-state self-identification[b]
		Participation of various stakeholders[c]
Players in policymaking	President, technocrats, foreign organizations, techonologues	President, politicians, technocrats, business/workers organizations, local governments, civil society

(continued)

Table 4.1 (continued)

	Authoritarian developmental state	Democratic developmental state
State = non-state relationship	Vertical, with the least interaction	Horizontal, with various forms of interaction
Policy elements		
Economic development	Boom: state-led investment	Infrastructure investment, deregulation
	Bust: deregulation and rationalization	
Social development	Village development (school, health center)	Universal social security system

[a]External major change
[b]Internal major change
[c]Internal major change
Source Created by the author. Figures are calculated from BPS Indonesia and *World Development Indicators*

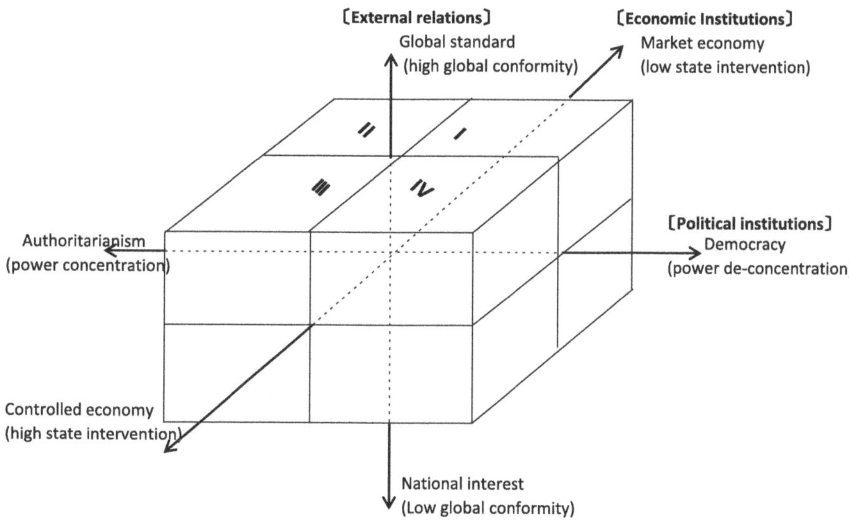

Fig. 4.2 Policy area in three dimensions. *Source* Created by the author

Fig. 4.2. In this framework, it is assumed that policies in the authoritarian developmental state are observed in the four spaces on the left rear side, and those in the democratic developmental state are seen in the four spaces on the front right side, both of which contains the polarities between controlled economy (regulation) and market economy (deregulation), and between the global standard and national interests.

4.3 Development Policies in the Soeharto-Led Authoritarian Developmental State

In the authoritarian developmental state, development policies were formulated and implemented under the concentrated power structure with President Soeharto at the apex. Soeharto, as an ultimate decision maker, used two camps of policy makers —technocrats and technologues—, depending on whether the economy was in a boom or bust cycle.

4.3.1 Technocrats and American Organizations—Deregulator and Market Guardian

The first camp was technocrats. Technocrats, which usually mean bureaucrats with expertise in technology and engineering, here refer to bureaucrats with expertise in economy and finance. Soeharto placed his full trust in technocrats to rescue the economy from difficulties and to manage stability. Technocrats, who started as economic advisers of Soeharto, played the role of architects of institutional foundation when the state converted to the capitalist economy. They also performed as diplomats in negotiating with the donor community and worked as therapists to mitigate every economic crisis. The original key figures were five scholars with Ph.D. in economics who were organized in an 'advisory team' for Soeharto in September 1966: Widjojo Nitisastro (the head of Bappenas in 1968–83, Coordinating Minister of Economy, Finance and Industry in 1973–83), Ali Wardhana (Minister of Finance in 1968–83, Coordinating Minister of Economy, Finance and Industry in 1983–88), Emil Salim, Subroto, and Mohammad Sadli.[1] The former three, having graduated from University of Indonesia, completed the doctoral course at the University of California, Berkeley in 1961, 1962, and 1964, respectively, with support of the Ford Foundation. The Ford Foundation started in 1956 to provide scholarships for master's and doctoral candidates to some universities in USA, and Widjojo became the first Indonesian who gained the Ph.D. from the Berkeley (Bresnan 2006). Subroto and Sadli obtained master's degrees from McGill University in Canada and MIT in USA respectively, before receiving a doctorate in economics from the University of Indonesia. They were very few scholars who studied neoclassical economics that underscored the effectiveness of a market mechanism at the time of the Soekarno reins approaching to the Communist bloc.

We can see the policy area led by technocrats in Table 4.2. The table organizes development policies into three broad categories; an action to build a new institution, a policy to intervene in the economy (regulation), and a policy to reduce intervention in the economy (deregulation). The second and the third categories run in the

[1] Interview with Widjojo Nitisastro conducted by the author on May 25 2007 at Jakarta. Widjojo told that "In September 1966, we five were asked by Pak Harto to be an advisory team. An official team".

opposite direction along the axis of economic institutions with higher to lower state intervention. The table lists intervention policies for two purposes; promoting industrial development and promoting equity (redistribution). The policies shown in bold type in the table represent those in conformity with the global standard, which here means the international standard among the capitalist bloc under the Cold War.

The first policy area in which technocrats' competence works best is deregulation that makes the market function better. Most of the policies in the column of intervention reduction (deregulation) and market establishment in the column of institution building in Table 4.2 are categorized in this policy area. The central position of the technocrat camp was in the upper II space in Fig. 4.2, a space of market orientation in conformity with the global standard under authoritarianism. In 1966–1970, they took a key part in transforming the closed controlled socialistic economy to the open liberal capitalist economy: Sadli drafted the Foreign Investment Law (Law No. 1/1967) that provided an open-door policy for foreign investment[2]; Ali Wardhana took the initiative in liberalizing foreign exchange control in 1970, a bold decision in the early stage of economic development. The next phase where the technocrats demonstrated their expertise as a deregulator was in 1983–88, the period of post-oil-boom recession, when a series of reforms were needed to adjust the oil-dependent economy, to activate manufactured exports and investments, and to mobilize domestic savings through fiscal and banking channels. Ali Wardhana as the Coordinating Minister of Economy announced a series of policy packages for deregulation. Soeharto, calling for the national solidarity under difficulties, stood behind the technocrats' reform.

The second policy area the technocrats managed well is macro-economic stability in terms of inflation, fiscal and current account balances, the level of debts, and foreign exchange rates. These policies are categorized in the upper III space in Fig. 4.2, a space with a certain level of intervention, as the policies need to enforce discipline in accordance with the internationally accepted standard. While the technocrats were routinely engaged in this task at such offices as Bappenas, the central bank, and the Ministry of Finance, they took a pivotal part in building some fundamental institutions as seen in Table 4.2. The principle of balanced budget was introduced in 1966, given that the biggest culprit of hyper-inflation in the mid-1960s had been fiscal deficit and central bank lending to make it up by issuing money. The Central Bank Law (Law No. 13/1968) stipulated check functions over the central bank lending to the national treasury (Mihira 1995: 204–5). Another example was an introduction of single foreign exchange rate in 1970. In concurrence with the above-stated full liberalization of foreign currency possession by abolishing the Foreign Exchange Bureau that had handled the multiple rates, technocrats were required full operation to avoid capital flight by raising interest rates and to create a new system of the single rate in the newly-established foreign exchange market. Ali Wardhana had analyzed on the balanced budget as a theme of Ph.D. dissertation at the UC Berkeley, and

[2]Mohammad Sadli told about the drafting of the Foreign Investment Law that "I worked in consultation with Soeharto regarding a rough outline" in an interview with the author conducted on 17 May 2007 at Jakarta.

Table 4.2 Development policies under the authoritarian developmental regime in Indonesia

Year	Institution building	State intervention/regulation		Intervention reduction/deregulation
		For industrial development	For equity/redistribution	
1966	**Balanced budget principle**			**Deregulation of state control on economy**
1967	**Establishment of IGGI (donors' association)**	Recognition of Chinese capital as domestic capital		**Open-door policy for foreign investment**
	Establishment of foreign exchange market			**Open-door policy for foreign bank branches**
	Mandate of Bappenas to design and budget for development plan			
1968	**Control on central bank loan to state treasury**	Promotion of domestic investment		
1969	Start of Five-Year National Development Plan	Automobile import substitution policy		
1970	**Single foreign exchange rate**	Investment incentives to priority sectors		**Liberalization of foreign exchange control**
1971		Establishment of state-owned steel company		
1973			Elementary school development in villages	
1974		Restriction on foreign ownership and employment	*Pribumi* priority policy as FDI partner	
		Establishment of 2 LNG companies under Pertamina	Subsidized loan to *pribumi* business	

(continued)

Table 4.2 (continued)

Year	Institution building	State intervention/regulation		Intervention reduction/deregulation
		For industrial development	For equity/redistribution	
			Public health center development in districts	
1975		Refund system of import duties on materials used for export products		**Pertamina debt crisis: curtailing Pertamina's investments**
1976	**Reopening of capital market**	Automobile component localization policy		
		Establishment of state-Japan-joint aluminium company		
		Establishment of state-owned aircraft company		
1979		Export substitution policy from log to plywood	*Pribumi* priority policy in government procurement	
1982	**Environmental Law**	Export finance with low interest rates		
	Copyright Law			
1983				Suspension of SOEs' 48 capital-goods investments
				1st banking reform: Liberalize interest rates
1984	**Tax reform to increase non-oil revenue (ex. VAT)**	Declaration of rice self-sufficiency	6-year compulsory education system	
1985		Ban on log exports		**Entrust custom clearance to foreign surveyor (SGS)**

(continued)

Table 4.2 (continued)

Year	Institution building	State intervention/regulation		Intervention reduction/deregulation
		For industrial development	For equity/redistribution	
1986	**Establishment of commodity exchange market**	Bonded zone for export production		**Import liberalization for exporters/tariff reduction/deregulation of foreign investment**
1987				**Conversion of non-tariff barriers (NTB) to tariffs/simplification of investment procedures**
				Privatization of expressways construction (Soeharto's first daughter)
1988				**2nd banking reform: Freer new entry**
				Deregulation of capital market and financial services
				Privatization of TV broadcasting (Soeharto's second son)
1989	**Patent Law**	Establishment of Agency for Managing Strategic Industries (BPIS)		
1990			President request to 31 business group owners to transfer shares to cooperatives	
				Privatization of oil exploration (Soeharto's third son)
1992	**Trade Mark Law**			
1993			Poverty reduction for underdeveloped villages	**Lift of automobile import ban, component tariff reduction**

(continued)

Table 4.2 (continued)

Year	Institution building	State intervention/regulation		Intervention reduction/deregulation
		For industrial development	For equity/redistribution	
1994			9-year compulsory education system	**Deregulation for FDI to enable 100% ownership**
1995	**Company Law**			
	Capital Market Law			
1996		National Car Program (Soeharto's third son)		
1997	**IMF crisis lending with conditionality for reform**			

Source Compiled by the author
Bold: action in conformity with global standard (of the capitalist bloc under the Cold War)

he as the Minister of Finance was the key person to execute the unification of the exchange rates by lifting the foreign exchange control.[3]

The third policy area of the technocrats is social development. While the above two policy areas, economic liberalization and macro-economic management, are well known as technocrats' specialty, they were also highly conscious of the importance of social development, especially those working at Bappenas, the headquarters of overall development throughout the country. Tilaar (2007) calls Widjojo Nitisastro, the then head of Bappenas, as a 'pioneer of social development', because Widjojo took the leadership to create the program of 'one elementary school in each village' by *Inpres* (Presidential Instruction) in 1973, and the program of 'one *puskesmas* (public health center) in each district' by *Inpres* in 1974. These two programs came to be symbolistic social services distributed uniformly all over the country by the authoritarian developmental regime. Widjojo himself recalled as follows: "Primary education and public health were under the jurisdiction of local governments, but they had no money, while the central government liked big projects for universities and hospitals; when the oil boom came in 1973, I came up with the idea of flowing part of the money directly to villages, not through the ministries".[4] These social development policies are a sort of intervention for the sake of equity and redistribution (Table 4.2), and are put in the lower III space in Fig. 4.2, a space of state intervention in the context of national interests.

Of the three policy areas the technocrats specialized in, deregulation and macro-economic management conformed with international standards. In these area, foreign organizations from the Western bloc, especially those from USA, were heavily involved in the technocrats' policy making. Key organizations were the IMF, the World Bank, the Ford Foundation, and the Harvard Institute for International Development (HIID). Just after Soeharto came to power on 11 March 1966, these organizations reacted swiftly. In April 1966, the Ford Foundation sent its representative back to Jakarta after a nine-month office closure, and in 1968 it started to finance policy advisers from the Development Advisory Service (DAS: renamed HIID in 1974) of Harvard University working for the five scholars' advisory team (Bresnan 2006). IMF sent a study team in June 1966, and then stationed an adviser before Indonesia officially rejoined the IMF in February 1967 (Mihira 1995). Starting September 1966, the World Bank closely cooperated with technocrats in debt rescheduling and new loan negotiations, and opened an office in 1968 for routinizing advisory services. In the 1983–88 period of post-oil-boom reforms, in concert with the World Bank's structural adjustment programs in general, dozens of the HIID project experts were

[3]Interview with Ali Wardhana conducted by the author on May 23 2007 at Jakarta. Regarding the liberalization of foreign exchange control, he told as follows; when he consulted his idea of this radical policy, Soeharto said to submit it to the cabinet meeting; the ministers criticized the proposal as horrible, and after all the criticisms were out in the open, Soeharto said 'I've listened. But there is some good', and concluded to accept the proposal; he was astonished to hear that and became sleepless; IMF and the World Bank said 'don't', 'see the failure of Latin America', 'stabilization first, and then liberalization'; and he thought he must think how to solve the issue by using the law of economy.

[4]Interview with Widjojo Nitisastro (see Footnote 1).

committed the process. Malcolm Gillis, a HIID Fellow, led a 28-member expatriate team to design and undertake the tax reform during 1981–84 (Gillis 1985). David Cole from the Harvard University was engaged in the HIID project of banking and financial reforms in the Ministry of Finance in the 1980s (Cole and Slade 1996).

4.3.2 Technologue—Locomotive of Industrial Development

The second camp was technologue, which refers to bureaucrats with expertise in technology and engineering, mainly working at the Ministry of Industry, the State Ministry of Research and Technology, and state-owned enterprises (SOEs). Soeharto used technologues as the locomotive to push forward with industrial development. They were particularly active when the economy turned favorable and was able to afford state-led, large-scale, capital-intensive investments. Some leading figures were Ibnu Sutowo (the president of Pertamina in 1968–76), A. R. Soehoed (the Minister of Industry in 1978–83), and B. J. Habibie (the State Minister of Research and Technology in 1978–98).[5]

Technologues' policy area is simply categorized as state intervention for industrial development in Table 4.2 and in the lower III space in Fig. 4.2, a space with state intervention on the basis of national interests. Some policies started earlier than the oil boom began. The typical case was the automobile industry, for which the Soeharto government pressed ahead with import substitution policy. The starting point was 1969, when the government banned the import of complete-built-up (CBU) commercial cars to Java and Sumatra, only allowing the import of complete-knock-down (CKD) kits, which required local assembly putting all parts together. In 1976, the import substitution proceeded to component production with introducing a 'deletion program', in which components designated to be procured domestically were deleted from the CKD import kits according to the designated schedule. The key person in designing and implementing a series of this mandatory localization policy was Suhartojo, an engineer bureaucrat and the then Director General for the Metal and Machinery Industry of the Ministry of Industry (Suhartojo 1991). The policy was backed by ministerial collective actions in the form of decrees of ministers of industry, trade, and finance, indicating that there was a political will from Soeharto in favor of the policy.

Ibnu Sutowo, an ex-army doctor who had been managing oil and gas businesses since 1957, assumed the first president of a merged oil and gas SOE, Pertamina, in 1968. Pertamina developed Batam island as an oil logistic base and resumed the suspended plan of the country's first steel company, Krakatau Steel, in 1971. Sutowo influenced the government's decision that Pertamina financed investment in Krakatau Steel, and that this steel SOE adopted natural-gas-based direct reduction furnace, rather than a coke-based blast furnace. The first oil boom starting in 1973

[5] B. J. Habibie replaced Soeharto as the 3rd President in May 1998, after he served as the Vice President for two months from March 1998.

fueled Ibnu Sutowo's expansionism: Pertamina, not only expanded its oil and gas production, but also invested in oil refineries, LNG plants, urea fertilizer plants, gas pipelines, oil tankers and so on. These diversified investments using short-term finance caused the 'Pertamina crisis' in 1975. Sutowo lost his position, but most of the projects were saved and survived.

Sutowo's role was succeeded by Soehoed. In the 1970s, Soehoed, an ex-airforce engineering officer, assumed charge of the Indonesia Asahan Aluminium project, which consisted of the first aluminum smelter and hydropower plants, jointly invested by the Indonesian government and Japanese private companies. After being appointed as the Minister of Industry, he used the second oil boom in 1979 to accelerate his plan of capital-intensive SOE projects, including oil refineries, petrochemical plants, and an alumina (raw materials of aluminum, processed from domestic bauxite) plant. In 1983 when the oil boom was over, 48 of the 52 projects were suspended.

Habibie, who completed a doctoral degree in aeronautical engineering in RWTH Aachen, West Germany, and served as a vice president of Messerschmitt-Bolkow-Blohm, a German aircraft manufacturer, was persuaded by Soeharto to return to serve the nation. Earning Soeharto's full trust, Habibie had been consistently devoted to the state-led development of technology-intensive 'strategic industries': He set up BPPT, the Agency for Assessment and Application of Technology, in 1974, established the first aircraft SOE in 1976, took a post of the State Minister of Research and Technology in 1978, and in 1989 set up and became a head of BPIS, the Agency for Managing Strategic Industry, responsible for 10 SOEs including aircraft, shipbuilding, railway vehicle, diesel engine, steel, telephone exchanges, weapons, and explosives.

4.3.3 Two Camps, the Balancer, and Degeneration

There was persistent tension between the technologue camp and the technocrat camp. Technologues were interventionists who believed that state intervention was indispensable for the catching-up of infant industries with their counterparts in advanced countries. Technocrats criticized this argument, since they believed the state intervention as the chief culprit for market distortion, lack of competition, and welfare loss. Technologues asserted that priority resource allocation into capital and technology intensive industries would lead to 'leapfrogging' or what Habibie called 'jump system' helping developing countries jump to the competence in cutting-edge technology, rather than tracing the sequential trajectory of technological development. Technocrats criticized this view, stressing the importance of 'comparative advantage' that Indonesia should first focus on labor and natural resource intensive industries making use of the nation's comparatively advantageous resources. This controversy constitutes a conventional 'state versus market' argument, or 'Habibienomics versus Widjojonomics' in the Indonesian jargon, or confrontation between the lower III space versus the upper II space (Fig. 4.2), which would never intersect with each other.

It was Soeharto that functioned as a balancer, swinging between the two camps in response to the economic situations. As shown in Table 4.2, Soeharto relied on the technocrats for setting up open capitalist institutions in the depths of hyper stagflation (1966–early 1970s), encouraged the technologues to accelerate national industrial development particularly during the oil boom with utilizing state oil revenues (early 1970s–early 1980s), and relegated transformation from the oil-dependent inward-looking economy to the manufactured-export-driven outward-looking economy to the technocrats (1983–88).

In the last phase of the Soeharto era (late 1980s–1997), the economy boomed as a result of reforms. Unlike the previous phases, the last one showed no clear tendency to turn into state intervention for industrial development (Table 4.2). There were some reasons. First, there was less room for state-led investment, since the government had no longer had financial power that it used to have under the oil boom. Private capital led investments as the five-year development plan stipulated. Second, the trend for deregulation continued, as required by the external conditions of the post-Cold-War globalization. Third, a form of deregulation associated with preferential treatment increased, favoring Soeharto's inner circle, particularly his eldest daughter, second son, and third son. Their companies were allowed to enter SOE-managed sectors as the first private players along with the global trend of privatization; the sectors included expressways, television broadcasting, oil and gas exploration, transportation of LNG, airports, water supply, and so on. This phenomenon was an evidence of degeneration of Soeharto's authoritarian developmental state, which later sparked the democratization movement against *KKN* (corruption, collusion, and nepotism) after the outbreak of the Asian Financial Crisis. The policies in this degeneration phase are positioned in the lower II space in Fig. 4.2, a space with orientation to the market economy (privatization) but based on narrow interests of the authoritarian power.

4.4 Development Policies in the Democratic Developmental State

4.4.1 Driving Forces Toward Libertarianism

Before the appearance of democratic developmental state, there was a sharp swing to libertarianism after the fall of Soeharto, driven by two forces. The first force was external, with the IMF as a major driver, with which the technocrats acted harmoniously. The force enhanced marketization conforming with the global standard, a change captured by an upward shift in Fig. 4.1, and as a shift going from the lower III space to the upper I space in Fig. 4.2. As its loan conditionality, the IMF pressed a wide range of reforms in line with global-standard concepts, such as accountability, transparency, and good governance. The reforms included ensuring independence of the central bank, reforming nontransparent monopolistic government organs (e.g. Bulog, Pertamina, etc.), enacting the Anti-Monopoly Law and so on.

The second force was internal democratization movement called *reformasi*, which strongly criticized *KKN* and power concentration in Soeharto. Its direction was power de-concentration, captured by a rightward move in Fig. 4.1, and from the lower II and III spaces to the lower I space in Fig. 4.2. Politico-bureaucrats under the Soeharto regime took concerted actions with *reformasi* movement leaders. Their enthusiasm empowered the legislative body, local governments, labor unions, and civil society watchdogs, which in turn restructured Soeharto's power centers (Bappenas, Bulog, Pertamina, Golkar, the military, etc.), annulling *KKN*-related contracts with SOEs, and legalizing private sector engagement in the SOE-monopolized public works sectors. The *reformasi* efforts came to fruition in the four-time amendments to the 1945 Constitution and the enactment of many new laws. These external and internal forces operated synergistically to drive Indonesia towards libertarianism.

4.4.2 Technocrats—Dual Functions of Regulator and Deregulator

In the democratic developmental state, the structure of policymakers became not as simple as that of the authoritarian developmental regime, which consisted of liberal technocrats, interventionistic technologues, and Soeharto as a balancer. Now the number of stakeholders increased, and the division of roles became complicated. Technocrats widened their scope to assume the roles both deregulator and regulator for growth and equity. While technologues were failing in general, multiple successors entered the policy making arena for industrial development. In addition, veto players, governmental and non-governmental watchdogs, and other players appeared. Table 4.3, which organizes development policies in the democratic developmental state in the same format as Table 4.2, shows neither alternation between deregulation and regulation by phase, nor balanced distribution of policies in conformity with global standard, like Table 4.2.

Regarding the technocrats' part, their typical product is policy packages. Under the 2nd Yudhoyono administration, policy packages started to be announced in 2013 after the 2000s commodity export boom was over. While it may have appeared to be a revival of the policy packages in the 1983–88 post-oil-boom period, the direction is opposite. In the mid-1980s, the state controls were deregulated to transform the economy heavily relying on state oil revenues into an industrialized economy. In the 2010s, the policy packages were intended to divert a laissez-faire commodity-dependent economy into an economy specializing in higher value-added sectors. A key person in reviving the policy packages was Chatib Basri, a third generation technocrat who, like Widjojo Nitisastro, taught in the Faculty of Economics, the University of Indonesia (FEUI). He took a post of the Minister of Finance in April 2013, and announced the policy packages in August and December 2013. The aim was

Table 4.3 Development policies under the democratic developmental regime in Indonesia

Year	Institution building	State intervention/regulation		Intervention reduction/deregulation
		For industrial development	For equity/redistribution	
2009	Establishment of state-owned infrastructure finance company (SMI)	Obligation of domestic processing of minerals and domestic use of coals		**Single window service for investment**
	Establishment of state-owned infrastructure insurance company (PII)	Obligation to use domestically-made products in government procurement		
	Law on National Flag, Language, Emblem, and Anthem			
2010				**ASEAN–China FTA: Tariff lift with China**
2011	**Establishment of Financial Service Authority (OJK)**	Announcement of Development Master Plan 2011–2025	Establishment of Social Security Agency (BPJS)	
	Currency Law	Progressive export tax exemption for processed palm-oil products		
		Fiscal incentives for large-scale investment in pioneer industries		
2012	Land Acquisition Law	Import restriction on agricultural products	Limitation on outsourced jobs	
			Raise in minimum wages	
2013		Low-cost eco car program		
		P1: Tax reduction for export/labor-intensive industries		

(continued)

Table 4.3 (continued)

Year	Institution building	State intervention/regulation		Intervention reduction/deregulation
		For industrial development	For equity/redistribution	
		P2: Tax exemption for imports of export industries		
		Nationalization of state-Japan-joint aluminium company		
2014	Industrial Law		Start of national health insurance	
	Commercial Law		Start of national employment insurance	
2015		Obligation to use domestically-made products in LTE telecommunication equipment		
		P1: Promotion of industrial estates	P1: Promotion of village fund utilization	**P1: Simplification of visa procedures**
		P2: Tax reduction for interests on exporters' obligatory deposits		**P2: Speed up of procedures for industrial estates, environmental licenses, tax allowance**
		P3: Reduction in electricity tariffs	P3: Reduction in MSME finance interest rates	
		P4: Introduction of minimum wage formula to improve predictability	P4: Expansion of coverage of SME finance/low-interest finance for SME exporters	
				P5: Abolition of double taxation to promote Real Estate Investment Trust

(continued)

Table 4.3 (continued)

Year	Institution building	State intervention/regulation		Intervention reduction/deregulation
		For industrial development	For equity/redistribution	
		P6: Promotion of Special Economic Zone (KEK) by tax reduction and foreign ownership		**P6: Simplification of KEK procedures/Speed up of import of pharmaceutical materials**
		P7: Tax reduction for labor-intensive export companies	P7: Easing of issuing land certificates to promote land redistribution	
		P8: Investment incentives for oil refinery/aircraft component industries		
2016		P9: Promotion of electric power infrastructure		**P9: On-line port services to deregulate logistics**
			P10: Expansion of sectors reserved for MSMEs	**P10: Deregulation for foreign investment**
		P11: Incentives for pharmaceutical material/medical equipment industries	P11: Export financing for MSMEs	
				P12: Speed up of doing business procedures and MSME start-up
			P13: Simplification of construction procedures of low-income housing	
		P14: Roadmap of development of e-commerce and digital economy		
2017		P15: Promotion of shipping and transportation insurance		**P15: Cost reduction in logistics industry**
				P16: Integrated online licensing system

Source Compiled by the author
Bold: action in conformity with global standard
P refers to a policy package consisting of several regulations, and the attached number is a serial number of the package announced by the same administration

conventional—to ensure macro-economic stability with reducing current account deficits that was supposed to depreciate the rupiah. However, the packages placed more emphasis on industrial promotion than deregulation; tax reduction for labor-intensive industries, resource-processing industries, and those with more than 30% exports; investment promotion for oil refining industries to reduce processed oil imports; and tax exemption, instead of restitution, on the imported materials of export industries.

The Joko Widodo administration inherited the practice of policy packages. A central figure is Darmin Nasution, a senior technocrat from FEUI, the first Indonesian Ph.D. from the University of Sorbonne in France. It was after Darmin took office as the Coordinating Minister of Economy in the first reshuffle of Joko Widodo cabinet in August 2015 that policy packages began to come out continuously. As seen in Table 4.2, policy packages under the Joko administration are a mix of regulation and deregulation. The former includes policies for industrial development and for redistribution to micro-, small-, and medium-sized enterprises (MSMEs). The latter are policies directed toward improving business environment, often assessed by international comparative rankings. All the policy packages were announced by Darmin and the cabinet secretary, Pramono Anung, along with some ministers related to the issues.

Like the technocrats in the authoritarian developmental state, the technocrats in the democratic developmental state deregulate the economy and manage the macro-economic stability (the upper I and IV space in Fig. 4.2). However, they are required to be more multi-talented compared to their predecessors in the authoritarian era. First, in the globalization era, their efforts for deregulation are more severely evaluated in international rankings, and their ability to manage the macro economy is inevitably rated by global credit rating agencies. Second, they receive a greater number and scope of requests for policy intervention in accordance with national interest (the lower IV space), because in the democratization era even technocrats have no choice but to be more responsive to the public's dual desire for growth and equity. Third, technocrats require greater cordination costs if they want their policy proposals accepted, given that there is an increasing number of stakeholders including party politicians.[6]

4.4.3 Business Politicians and Business Organizations—Promoters of Industrial Development

While the technocrat camp has reproduced the next generation beyond the change of regime, the technologue camp has not yet produced outstanding leaders after Habibie.

[6]In an interview with the author on 10 August 2011 at Jakarta, Chatib Basri, the then expert staff of the Minister of Finance, said, 'Bapak Widjojo never understand why our policy making is so slow. He said, at his days, what he should do was only to meet the cabinet secretary to secure the approval of Pak Harto'.

Instead, other types of players have entered the political arena and take part in policy making on the basis of national interest (the lower IV space in Fig. 4.2), succeeding the technologues' role of advocating for industrial development.

The first type of new players is business-politicians, or business leaders turned politicians. Such a career path was rarely observed in the Soeharto era, because there was a small pool of business elites, and because they were not seen as political elites equivalent to military or bureaucratic high officers or as academic professionals. After democratization, however, business elites flowed into the political arena as the political power was deconcentrated and politics came to require a war chest. Jusuf Kalla, Indonesia's first directly-elected vice president, and Abrizal Bakrie, Coordinating Minister of Economy who received his first Cabinet post in 2004 on Kalla's recommendation, made a symbolic debut of business-politicans as the top national elite. These two figures are commonly second-generation owners of leading *pribumi* (native Malay Indonesians) business groups, and became a head of the Golkar party in 2004 and 2009 respectively. The business-politicians function as a bridge between the business community and policymakers, and as a guide to get Indonesia back to developmentalism. MS Hidayat, the then President of the Indonesian Chamber of Commerce and Industry (KADIN) and a senior member of the Golkar party, was appointed the Minister of Industry at the start of the 2nd Yudhoyono administration in 2009. He implemented a low-cost green car program—an incentive policy for manufacturers to produce affordable fuel-efficient small passenger vehicles—that the association of automobile industry had lobbied for; led the full nationalization of the Asahan project; realized strategic investments through direct negotiation with targeted foreign manufacturers; got involved in making the first and second policy packages in 2013; and prepared a draft of the new Industrial Law (Law No.3/2014) that stipulated the national interests and the role of the government in Indonesia's industrial development.

The second type of new players is business organizations. In the authoritarian era, leading businessmen lobbied Soeharto directly or through his proxies. After democratization, such system did not work any longer, because the decision-making mechanism was multi-polarized, while business organizations developed a formal channel of lobbying as the representatives of the business circle. There are two cross-sectoral national business organizations in Indonesia: KADIN and the Indonesian Association of Employers (APINDO). KADIN co-organized a national summit with the government to deliver policy recommendations from its member associations at the start of the 2nd Yudhoyono administration in 2009. When the first policy package was released in 2013, the presidents of KADIN and APINDO appeared side-by-side with ministers at the media conference, demonstrating their involvement in making the policy package and their commitment to its implementation.

The third type of new players is parliamentary speakers. The People's Representative Council (DPR), which was previously viewed as a rubber stamp organization for the holder of power in the authoritarian era, has become empowered by democratization. DPR speakers appeal to public sentiment and emphasize the national interests in the process of law making. Laws enacted under their influence after 2009 that affect economic activities include the Mineral Resources and Coal Law (Law No.

4/2009) that stipulates oblization of domestic processing of minerals and domestic use of coals; the National Flag, Language, Emblem, and Anthem Law (Law No. 24/2009) that makes using Indonesian language in all domestic contracts and product labels obligatory; the Currency Law (Law No. 7/2011) that requires Indonesian rupiah to be used in every payment of domestic transactions; and the Industrial Law (Law No. 3/2014) that emphasizes the importance of domestic value-added creation of resource-based industries.

4.5 Conclusion

This chapter discussed development policy making in the authoritarian developmental state and the democratic developmental state as experienced by Indonesia. They have some common attributes, and these attributes suggests what makes a state developmental. There are also some differences between the two, and from these differences, the challenges democratic developmental states face under the era of globalization can be ascertained.

The basic common attribute between authoritarian and democratic developmental states is that the formulation and implementation of policies for growth and equity are central. The position of this policy area is the lower III and the lower IV in Fig. 4.2 respectively in the authoritarian and democratic developmental states, the space with state intervention on the basis of national interest. Regardless of authoritarianism or democracy, core elements that make a state developmental are: (i) a series of development policies accompanying state intervention backed by the national interest, (ii) the political will of the political leader as the ultimate decision maker, (iii) one or more groups of policymakers as designers and implementers of development policies, and (iv) the commitment shared among (ii) and (iii) to have the same goals for development in the medium to long run. In the case of Indonesia, (iii) was technologues in the authoritarian developmental state, and business-politicians and some other players in the democratic developmental state.

Another common attribute between the two types of developmental states is persistent presence of technocrats. Technocrats are mainly in charge of market-oriented policies that conform to global standards (the upper II and I space in Fig. 4.2), but concurrently cover policies to intervene for the sake of securing stability in line with the global standard requirements (the upper III and IV space), and to make a commitment to development policies on the basis of national interest (the lower III and IV space). The commitment to development policies extended from policies just for equity to policies both for growth and equity. While the relationship of technologues and technocrats in the authoritarian developmental state was confrontational, that of business-politicians and technocrats in the democratic developmental state seems more interrelated and cooperative though sometimes still opposing.

A fundamental difference of the democratic developmental state from the authoritarian developmental state is the more complex structure of policy making involving more stakeholders. The challenge from such a structure is higher coordination costs and a longer time to reach a consensus, while the constituency has a louder voice to demand quick decisions and visible outcomes. One of the strategies to enable quick visible actions in the deconcentrated power structure is the centrality of the executive branch, in particular, a compact and cohesive group of ministers in the cabinet, as observed in a series of policy packages led by some technocrat ministers.

The second difference is the emerging business-politicians as key players in the democratic developmental state. Unlike technologues, business-politicians wear two hats in public office and in private business, even though they must leave their business positions during their term of public service. Their increased influence in policy making brings risk that decisions are affected by private business interests. Collusion between politics and business is not a new problem, but the same person having dual functions makes the problem more serious. To control the risk of business-politician bias, check functions of the media and civil society watchdogs are necessary. In addition, the presence of politically-neutral technocrats is significant. Hired managers in the private sector and SOE professionals who do not own individual businesses would be other alternative resources to reduce the risk of business-politician bias.

The third significant difference of the democratic developmental state is increasing orientation toward national interest, as a lower proportion of policies conform to the global standard as shown in Table 4.3 compared with Table 4.2. While globalization has promoted democratization around the world, democracy seems to have activated the constituency's consciousness of national interests, which often are at odds with global conformity. In the authoritarian developmental state, the ultimate power can manage internal conflict between global orientation and national interest. In the democratic developmental state in the globalization era, the major challenge for the political leaders is to prioritize to earn satisfaction from the constituency while facing the increased requirements from globalization. As the policy area of national interest (the lower IV in Fig. 4.2) increases in relative importance, conflicts with the policy area that requires the global conformity (the upper I) become acute. A possible way to prevent the acute conflicts would be to strategically target a set of policies that concurrently fulfill the national interest and the global conformity, such as enhancing business efficiency to attract investment by improving infrastructure, simplifying procedures, promoting e-governance, and controlling corruptive practices. To achieve visible outcomes in these targeted policies, strong political will coupled with the shared commitment of the main groups of policymakers needs to be sustained for a certain period of time.

References

Amsden A (1989) Asia's next giant: South Korea and late industrialization. Oxford University Press, New York

Bresnan J (2006) At home abroad: a memoir of the ford foundation in Indonesia 1953–1973. Equinox Publishing (Asia) Pte Ltd., Jakarta

Cole CD, Slade BF (1996) Building a modern financial system: the Indonesian experience. Cambridge University Press, Cambridge

Doner RF, Ritchie BK, Slater D (2005) Systemic vulnerability and the origins of developmental states: Northeast and Southeast Asia in comparative perspective. Int Org 59(2):327–361

Gillis M (1985) Micro and macroeconomics of tax reform: Indonesia. J Dev Econ 19(3):221–254

Haggard S (1990) Pathways from the periphery: the politics of growth in the newly industrializing countries. Cornell University Press, Ithaca

Haggard S, Moon C, Kim BK (1992) The transition to export-led growth in South Korea: 1954–1966. J Asian Studies 50(4):850–873

Hattori T, Sato Y (eds) (1996) Kankoku taiwan no hatten mekanizumu (Development mechanism of Korea and Taiwan). Institute of Developing Economies, Tokyo

Iwasaki I (1994) ASEAN shokoku no kaihatsu taisei ron (On the developmental regime of the ASEAN states). In: Iwasaki I (ed) Kaihatsu to seiji: ASEAN shokoku no kaihatsu taisei (Development and politics: the developmental regime of the ASEAN states). Institute of Developing Economies, Tokyo, pp 3–48

Johnson C (1982) MITI and the Japanese miracle: the growth of industrial policy, 1925–1975. Stanford University Press, Stanford

MacIntyre A (ed) (1994) Business and government in industrializing Asia. Allen & Unwin, Sydney

Mihira N (1995) Makuro keizai no seika (Performance of macroeconomy). In: Yasunaka A, Mihira N (eds) Gendai Indonesia no seiji to keizai: Soeharto seiken no sanju nen (Politics and economy in contemporary Indonesia: three decades of Soeharto government). Institute of Developing Economies, Tokyo, pp 193–272

Presidential Secretariat, Republic of Indonesia (2011) Pidato presiden: Sambutan pada acara peluncuran masterplan percepatan perluasan pembangunan ekonomi Indonesia (MP3EI) 2011–2025 (Presidential speech: greeting in the launching event of the masterplan for the acceleration and expansion of Indonesian economic development 2011–2025). http://www.setneg.go.id/index.php?option=com_content&task=view&id=8190. Accessed 12 June 2011

Republic of Indonesia (2011) Masterplan: acceleration and expansion of Indonesia economic development 2011–2025. Republic of Indonesia, Jakarta

Robison R (1988) Authoritarian states, capital-owing classes, and the politics of newly industrializing countries: the case of Indonesia. World Polit 41(1):52–74

Sato Y (2010) Dai ni ki Yudoyono seiken no keizai seisaku to kadai (Economic policies and challenges of the second-term Yudhoyono government). In: Honna J, Kawamura K (eds) 2009 nen Indonesia no senkyo (Indonesia's election in 2009). Institute of Developing Economies (IDE-JETRO), Chiba, pp p149–171

Sato Y (2015) Joko Widodo seiken no kihon seisaku (Basic policy of the Joko Widodo government). In: Kawamura Koichi (ed) Shinko minshushugi taikoku Indonesia (Indonesia: a newly emerging democratic power). IDE-JETRO, Chiba, pp p129–158

Sato Y (2017) State, industry, and business in Indonesia's transformation. In: Tsunekawa K, Khoo BT, Kawano K (eds) Southeast Asia beyond crises and traps. Palgrave Macmillan, Cham, pp 71–99

Shiraishi T (1997) Sukaruno to Suharuto (Soekarno and Soeharto). Iwanami Shoten, Tokyo

Shiraishi T (2010) Indonesia ni oite keizai seicho no seiji ha ikanishite hukkatsu shitaka (How did the politics for growth revive in Indonesia?). In: Otsuka K, Shiraishi T (eds) The state and economic development. Toyo Keizai Shinposha, Tokyo, pp 9–29

Shiraishi T (2014) Indonesian technocracy in transition: a preliminary analysis. Southeast Asian Studies 3(2):255–281

Suehiro A (1998) Hatten tojokoku no kaihatsu shugi (Developmentalism in developing countries). In: Institute of Social Science, University of Tokyo (Ed) 20 seiki shisutemu 4: kaihatsu shugi. (The 20th century global system 4: developmentalism). Tokyo University Press, Tokyo

Suehiro A (ed) (2002) Tonan aziashi 9 'kaihatsu' no jidai to 'mosaku' no jidai (History of Southeast Asia 9 the age of 'development' and the age of 'groping'). Iwanami Shoten, Tokyo

Suhartojo (1991) Industri mobil di Indonesia (Automobile industry in Indonesia). Kompas, 1–2 Mar 1991

Thee KW (2002) The Soeharto era and after: stability, development and crisis, 1966–2000. In: Dick HW, Houben VJH, Lindblad JT, Thee KW (eds) The emergence of a national economy: an economic history of Indonesia, 1800–2000. Allen & Unwin, Sydney, University of Hawai'i Press, Honolulu, pp 194–243

Tilaar HAR (2007) Pelopor pembangunan social (Pioneer of social development). In: Anwar MA, Ananta A, Kuncoro A (eds) Kesan para sahabat tentang Widjojo Nitisastro (Impression of friends on Widjojo Nitisastro). Kompas, Jakarta, pp p197–201

Wade R (1990) Governing the market: economic theory and the role of government in East Asian industrialization. Princeton University Press, Princeton

Yasunaka A, Mihira N (eds) (1995) Gendai Indonesia no seiji to keizai: Soeharto seiken no sanju nen (Politics and economy in contemporary Indonesia: three decades of Soeharto government). Institute of Developing Economies, Tokyo

Chapter 5
Boundaries of Nationalism Under Globalization: Reviewing Developmental State Building in Malaysia and Ethiopia

Yusuke Takagi and Boo Teik Khoo

5.1 Introduction

The 'East Asian developmental state' has been for some time a source of interest and inspiration to different regimes and leaders in different parts of the developing world. In Malaysia, for example, former Prime Minister Mahathir Mohamad (1981–2003)[1] constructed a variant of the so-called 'East Asian developmental state' to drive an ambitious program of economic transformation. In Ethiopia, too, former Prime Minister Meles Zenawi (1991–2012) attempted to implement economic policies along a similar state-guided trajectory of development.[2]

The determination of Mahathir and Meles to promote state-led paths of development was most clearly expressed in a time of crisis and was coincidentally recorded by the same author, Joseph Stiglitz, then the chief economist of the World Bank (Stiglitz 2002). The crucial moment for Malaysia was the East Asian financial crisis of 1997 when Mahathir, alone of the leaders of affected countries, declined to seek the assistance of the International Monetary Fund and chose instead to confront the global financial markets. There is comparatively little on Meles's policies of development that put Ethiopia at odds with the IMF when the former rejected the latter's prescriptions, accidentally just before the onset of the East Asian crisis.

[1] After Malaysia's fourteenth general election of May 9, 2018, Mahathir became Prime Minister again.

[2] Meles Zenawi was the acting President of the transition government from 1991 to 1995 and the prime minister from 1995 to 2012 when he died at his office.

Y. Takagi (✉) · B. T. Khoo
National Graduate Institute for Policy Studies (GRIPS), Tokyo, Japan
e-mail: y-takagi@grips.ac.jp

Y. Takagi et al. (eds.), *Developmental State Building*, Emerging-Economy State and International Policy Studies, https://doi.org/10.1007/978-981-13-2904-3_5

Their 'uncooperative' stances under crisis and the outcomes they wrought can raise important questions for any review of the developmental state, because both leaders were open to foreign investment, transfer of technology, and interfacing with private multinational corporations and international financial institutions. And yet, they were not blind followers of the so-called Washington Consensus. How should we understand the nature of their leadership? Must such 'uncooperative' responses as those demonstrated by Mahathir and Meles be evidence of parochialism, if not xenophobia? How far can economic nationalism go when domestic markets have become integrated with international ones? What are the boundaries for independent state initiatives vis-à-vis global markets and international financial institutions?

Malaysia under Mahathir and Ethiopia under Meles were far apart in space, history and political economy. Yet the leaders shouldered similar basic responsibility to achieve economic development in multi ethnic society. They were in power for more than two decades as the leaders of political coalitions. Their economies experienced rapid growth under their leadership and they did not hesitate to articulate their national aspirations. Mahathir enunciated his Wawasan 2020 (Vision 2020) while Meles prepared a series of developmental plans some of the core ideas of which had evidently been explored in his draft master thesis on economic development. Mahathir's Malaysia and Meles's Ethiopia sought to remake their economic structures in the mold of developmental states. Neither of them was a clone of the East Asian developmental state and they both sought international partners to develop their economies. But they also differed from their Northeast Asian predecessors in timing and historical conditions when they held to the feasibility of occupying the commanding heights of the economy via state intervention in an era of globalization.

This chapter offers some insights into developmental state building by comparing Malaysia and Ethiopia's trajectories of development, and the specific tasks undertaken by Mahathir and Meles, not least when their stances differed from those of the IFIs or the global markets. Our principal objective is to explore comparatively the capacities of the political leadership of new developmental states to control their paths of economic transformation in an age of globalization. While their concerns with national economic development bore basic similarities, Mahathir and Meles had to approach developmental state differently because of the contrasting political contexts in which they pursued their visions of the future. There may be an unanticipated convergence here: the 'Look East' policy that Mahathir enunciated for Malaysia in the early 1980s resonates in 21st century Africa although the gaze may not fall on Japan or South Korea this time but China.

This chapter begins with a review of academic literature and theoretical debates on the developmental state, with a focus on understanding how the vision of a strong leader can shape the character of such a state. Subsequent sections will separately focus on the development records of Mahathir's Malaysia and Meles's Ethiopia up to 1997 and beyond the East Asian financial crisis. Here, the discussion turns to the different financial crises they faced that led Mahathir and Meles to adopt policy stances that risked confrontation with the IMF and the global financial markets. Subsequent analysis concentrates on various points of commonality between the Malaysian and Ethiopian experiences. These included nationalism which found powerful but different socio-political manifestations owing to variations in the class and ethnic divides of their respective societies, the frameworks of government-business relations, and extents of cooperation with international players.

5.2 Developmental State Building: Regional Contexts and Leadership

Developmental state is a dynamic concept to appreciate multiple paths to development as well as the roles of visionary leadership to go beyond the status quo.

At first, the concept of developmental state was invented to understand deviant model of political economy. Before Chalmers Johnson introduced the developmental state as a concept to explain a heterodox model of political economy, observers of the Japanese economy were divided between regarding it as a market economy or a command economy (Johnson 1982). Johnson argued that Japan had a 'plan-rational' economy that could be distinguished from the USA's 'market-rational' economy and the Soviet 'plan-irrational' economy. In a plan-rational economy, policymakers could maximize backward advantages in the process of catching up, because they could learn from the experience of the leading developed economy. In Johnson's classic study, the bureaucrats of Japan's Ministry of Trade and Industry (MITI) were the symbols of learning for policy-making. Johnson's insights and Japan's impressive economic achievements stimulated academic debates over the role of the state in economic development. In the World Bank's study of the so-called 'East Asian Miracle', those who supported a strong role for the state, were said to form a 'revisionist school' (Amsden 1992; Wade 1990; World Bank1993).

Scholars appreciate the concept of developmental state because it allows them to capture the specific nature of Japanese economy which deviated from both capitalist and socialist models. As Johnson (1982) traces, the MITI learned from the failed experiences of the laissez-faire economy before the war and the command economy during the war and tried to find a third way by combining market economy with coordination mechanism such as administrative guidance and deliberation councils.

Those who study economic development in Southeast Asia also discuss institutional changes that boosted their economies (Suehiro 1998). While the Japanese MITI promoted local businesses through various policy tools, the counterparts in Southeast Asia promoted economic reform to invite foreign direct investment. In Thailand, for instance, Field Marshal Sarit Thanarat toppled down Luang Phibunsongkram with a coup in 1957 and established a series of economic institutions to industrialize its economy in cooperation with technocrats who had studied abroad and were conscious about macroeconomic management. Compared with the other capitalist economies in the region, Malaysia joined the club of developmental regime relatively late. Prime Minister Mahathir, who had declared the Look East policy in 1981 when he came to power, announced the Vision 2020 ten year after to accelerate economic transformation of the country as he envisioned (Khoo 1995, 2005).

In African studies, not a few developmental economists including Joseph Stiglitz begin to show their interests in the concept of developmental state (Noman et al. 2012). While they criticize a one-size-fits-all strategy such as a policy package imposing good governance everywhere, they argue for the learning, industrial and technology (LIT) policy which they developed based on the industrial policy in East Asia. Besides, it is worth mentioning that they differentiate the developmentalist state from the developmental state to highlight the efforts by Indonesia, Malaysia and Thailand which are part of the high performing Asian economies but are often neglected in the literature of traditional developmental state. In the developmentalist states, political leaders strive for economic growth through various types of LIT policy. There are indeed several pioneering efforts by African political leaders to learn from East Asian experience. Some labor union leaders in South Africa invited Alice Amsden, who had established her fame by her seminal work on the economic rise of South Korea (Amsden 1992), when they prepared for the manifest of the African National Congress in their preparation for the elections in 1994, although they failed to convince other leaders within in the ANC (Mine 1996). Botswana is an interesting case to see actual developmental state making in Africa (Taylor 2005). The country succeeded in avoiding the resource course and achieving miraculous growth based on its diamond production thanks to determination of leadership and constructive relationship between the ruling party and bureaucracy.

The concept of developmentalist states resonates with the discussion about ideational dimension of developmental regimes in Southeast Asian studies. In developmental regimes in Southeast Asia, we can observe shared belief for development, or so-called growth-ideology, with which political leaders rearrange the institutions for socio-economic policy making (Suehiro 1998). In the context of the Cold War, they avoid policy package that might resonate with class struggle. They therefore did not explicitly highlight social policy but promote economic development in general, though they actually promoted social policy to mitigate the class struggle. They worked for transformation of national economy so that they can mitigate class divide within the country.

We cannot, however, take it for granted that every political leader seeks for economic growth. They may be busy for exploit resources at the sacrifice of national development, which may result into a predatory state (Evans 1995). Not as worse as the predatory state, some political leaders may be trapped in specific interest such as his or her own ethnic group. In search for the growth-ideology in the government, we should find political leaders who consider national agenda which might go beyond economic dimension of governance. Moreover, the growth-ideology is one of national agenda, which can cover broader issues to govern the nation. Under which condition, the political leader commit himself or herself with the growth ideology?

In the following sections, we will trace the development of the political leadership of Prime Ministers Mahathir of Malaysia and Meles of Ethiopia. They were the heroes in a series of politico economic drama foreign pundits observed in 1997. Mahathir managed the politico-economic turmoil caused by the Asian Financial Crisis defying the policy prescription made by the International Monetary Fund, while Meles was in the midst of a series of tough negotiation with the IMF over the conditionality designed by the latter (Stiglitz 2002). They appeared to be devout nationalists facing the pressure from the powerful international financial institutions. It is not necessarily the case that nationalist politicians know the best about his/her countries and could lead them properly. They must be labelled as headstrong politicians who did not listen to smart technocrats, if they had failed to manage their economy well. What made them nationalist statesmen instead of outdated parochial politicians that might be found in some other countries? We should therefore carefully examine the policy process of the two economies. What did they actually do? Why did they choose particular options? Why could they implement the policy options despite the opposition from the international financial institutions? What are the politico-economic legacies of it?

In addition to the dramatic clash with the IMF, these two countries serve as good cases to study the politics of developmental state building in multiethnic society. Malaysian society is composed of Malay, Chinese, Indian and some other ethnic groups, while Ethiopian society witness more diverse ethnic groups. Why could they avoid being a political leader taking care of the interest of their own ethnic group?

In comparing the two countries, the following part of this chapter examine four issues in each country; social composition, government-business relations, international relations and political leadership. First, since the players of the politics of economic growth aim at mitigating social tensions through economic growth, we should examine the nature of social tensions in each country. The sections on each country examine ethnic issues as a potential source of social tension. Second, we study government-business relations, because the developmental state is by definition active in economic activity. The government cannot create its policy from a clean slate, but have to face existing economic structure. Third, the developmental state from the late 20th Century maximized opportunity shaped by the foreign direct investment as well as loans from international organizations. Fourth, each section scrutinizes the particular political will that the leader exerted in dealing with the above-mentioned three issues.

By examining these issues, this chapter aims at revealing a nature of leadership in developmental state building. The players in the politics of economic growth should be in dynamic political process which we cannot understand with a dichotomous perspective of the developmental state facing international pressure. The arena of the politics of economic growth is not limited within the national boundary but has been shaped throughout the context of politico-economic development of particular countries. The following section reveals the nature of leadership and context shaping it in two countries.

5.3 The Politics of Developmental State Building in Malaysia

To speak of a 'developmental state' in Malaysia is to grapple with the four issues discussed above. Linking them up provides a view of the process by which the state transformed itself at specific moments between, say, 1969, when ethnic violence broke out in what might be called Malaysia's crisis of decolonization, and 1997–98, when a crisis of globalization brought financial mayhem. The issue of leadership can be analyzed through the ideological force of nationalism—in particular, the nationalism of Mahathir Mohamad, Prime Minister from 1981 to 2003—that had peculiar expressions in Malaysian society and infused much of post-1969 state-led economic development. A guide to the complex interplay between society, political system, incumbent administrations, development strategies, economic transformation, and institutional changes—that led to a multiplicity of policy regimes—is provided by Tables 5.1 and 5.2.

5.3.1 Managing Interethnic and Class Relations

The first set of tensions lay in the internal patterns of interethnic and class relations that were reshaped by state intervention under the uninterrupted tenure of the ruling coalition. Here, the original underlying problem was a colonially constructed plural society that bore a rigid ethnic division of labor. Wheelwright (1965, 110) succinctly called the division a 'part of a class structure [that had] crystallized along ethnic lines'. The 'Outline Perspective Plan 1971–1990' of the Mid-Term Review of the Second Malaysia Plan 1971–1975, the principal document of the New Economic Policy (NEP), defined it as 'the identification of race with occupational function'. Both characterizations pointed to what were crudely called vertical and horizontal inequalities that threatened the stability of peculiar post-colonial configuration of interethnic power-sharing. After the electoral crisis and ethnic violence of 1969, the state's development strategy pursued (economic) growth with (social) distribution in parallel with the (political) management of the endemic tensions.

The strategy reserved a critical role for coherent development planning under political leadership that had the imagination, resolve, and power to make stability a prerequisite for economic growth and equitably distributed growth a determinant of stability. In good times, the strategy served an ambitious juggling of class interests and ethnic expectations although the rent-seeking conduct of competing coalitions of class interests and political power violated 'good governance'. In lean times, painful short-term choices were made 'between growth and distribution' that were amenable to the political manipulation of inter-ethnic rivalry (Khoo and Khoo 2012, 3–4).

In practice, the strategy found several institutional expressions. With the NEP, the state broke with the liberal capitalist regime of the Alliance coalition government (1957–69). The 'NEP state' projected new, active, and diversified roles for

Table 5.1 Malaysia: Administrations, Policies and Regimes 1957–90

Period	Ruling coalition/administration	Core political concerns	Regime		
			Economic policies	Social policies	Institutions and agents
1957–1969	Alliance	Decolonization, nation-building, counter-insurgency	*Laissez faire*, competitive commodity production, diversification, ISI, agricultural and infrastructural improvements	Ameliorative welfarist measures, education; revision of civil service terms and pay, credit for housing, expanded EPF coverage	Market, central bank prudence, state agencies and development authorities
1970–1980	National Operations Council, Barisan Nasional (BN)	Re-shaping political system: co-optation, more efficient administration, imposing social engineering	Promoting MNC-led EOI, state investment, employment creation, land resettlement and rural development, urbanization	poverty eradication, employment and training, restructuring wealth and ethnic division of labor, human capital formation, home ownership	Bureaucracy, SEDCs, SOEs, Malay trust agencies, state-owned banks, Petronas
1981–1985	BN: early Mahathirism	Constructing economic nationalism: new state-capital alliance, reform of administration, reorientation of mass expectations	Corporate takeovers, heavy industrialization, financial liberalization, beginning privatization, counter-cyclical spending	Bureaucratic reform, BCIC, Islamization; lowered tax rates, income bands adjusted upwards, expanded child relief	SOEs, HICOM, UMNO's fleet, domestic conglomerates, stock market
1986–1990	BN: NEP in abeyance	Surviving recession, curbing dissent, political repression	Counter-recessionary measures, austerity, debt servicing, liberalizing FDI rules, privatization, industrial deepening	Stimulating growth, creating employment, re-training unemployed graduates	FDI, privatized entities, major conglomerates, HICOM, EPU (IMP)

Source Khoo (2012, 31, Table 2.1)

Table 5.2 Malaysia: Administrations, Policies and Regimes 1991–2003

Period	Ruling coalition/administration	Core political concerns	Regime		
			Economic policies	Social policies	Institutions and agents
1991–(June) 1997	BN: triumphant late Mahathirism	Settling political succession, consolidation of oligarchy, regional triumphalism	Industrial deepening, intensifying privatization, diversifying corporatization, services (finance and tourism), new global-domestic interfaces: MSC, outward investment, foreign labor, economic regionalism	Social-market instruments for restructuring, ASN, ASB, expansion and liberalization of higher education; National Development Plan; reform of education; lowered income tax rates	Major conglomerates, FDI, Malaysian Business Council, MSC authority, IPPs
(July) 1997–1999	BN: Mahathirism in crisis	Crisis management, resistance to reform, repression of dissidence; surviving general election	Retreat from liberalization, semi-autarky: capital controls, currency peg, rescue, reflation, recapitalization; consolidation of banks	Tax cuts, reducing number of students sent abroad, no tax on 1999 personal income	State crisis agencies: Bank Negara, Danaharta, Danamodal, CDRC; IMF, foreign funds; local banks, conglomerates; Petronas, EPF
2000–(October) 2003	BN: Mahathir's last administration	Containing Malay recalcitrance; preparing succession in UMNO	Re-nationalization of ailing projects and companies; reducing capital controls; state-market rapprochement	Privatization of health care, lower tax rates, higher personal relief	Bureaucracy, conglomerates
(November) 2003 and after	BN: Old state, new administration	Recovery of legitimacy, placating core constituents, reconstituting power, Islamization	Partial return to liberalization, GLCs and governance, trimming fiscal deficit, fuel subsidy reductions, new major infrastructure; removal of currency peg, FTA negotiations	Palliative and populist measures, rural improvements, civil service pay rises, return to emphasis on NEP restructuring	Khazanah, GLCs, GLICs; new technocracy, new segments of BCIC

Source Khoo (2012, 32, Table 2.2)

state agencies that let them embark on a path of rapid economic transformation. Under Mahathir's premiership, the interventionist state grew into a 'developmental state' whose nationalist-capitalist mission required, among others, a systematic use of industrial policy, a framework of 'governing the market', and a regime of 'getting prices wrong'. That mission shaped internal politics to the extent that an authoritarian administration protected its legitimacy and kept its popularity by maintaining the mutually reinforcing conditions of political stability and economic progress. At the same time, the state undertook a number of regionalist diplomatic initiatives to safeguard national priorities vis-à-vis other states and especially more powerful regions in changing global conditions.

5.3.2 *Configuring Internal State-Capital Balance of Power*

The second set involved shifts in the balance of power between the state and the market within national borders. The NEP brought the first shift by enlarging the scope and degree of state power vis-à-vis domestic and foreign capital. The state assumed a multiplicity of roles: a provider of opportunities (principally to the Malays), a regulator of business, enforcing legal and bureaucratic compliance with the NEP, a major investor who acquired many kinds of assets, and the trustee of Malay economic interests whose state agencies and enterprises held corporate equity 'in trust' for the *Bumiputera* (the sons of the land), or the ethnic Malays. These multiple roles of the state deployed vast public financial resources for economic, social, and welfare development, expanded technocratic capability, and tightened bureaucratic control. Born of political crisis and inseparable thereafter from public controversy, the NEP state, in stark contrast to its relatively laissez faire Alliance predecessor, 'governed the market' as never before, but at the cost of a partial rupture between state and capital.

A second shift in the state-market balance of power emerged at the start of the NEP's second decade. Mahathir's early policies of bureaucratic reform, 'Malaysia Inc.', privatization, and even 'the assimilation of Islamic values' formed part of his scheme to refashion the interventionist NEP state into a variant of the East Asian developmental state.

His strong personal nationalist-capitalist impulses went beyond the ethnic fixations of many NEP advocates. Malaysia Inc. promised cooperation between the state and national capital with the latter being no longer synonymous with domestic Chinese capital. Privatization was used to reduce the fiscal burden of operating unprofitable SOEs, improve the performance of existing state monopolies, transfer state-owned corporate assets to mostly Malay capitalists, and recast a state-supported private sector as the vanguard of development investment and growth. Malaysia Inc. and privatization stood for power alignments, a corporate structure, and a governance framework within which the state 'picked winners' from politically connected Malay, non-Malay, or interethnic conglomerates.

At its most triumphant in mid-1997, the state pushed new development initiatives in alliance with national capital, and, where feasible, foreign capital. Consultative councils and meetings, such as the Malaysian Business Council, Malaysian Industry-Government Group for High Technology, and the International Expert Panel for the Multimedia Super Corridor, became the more influential the more they were tasked with passing ideas and initiatives between state and capital. In all this, Mahathir did not hasten to replace the NEP but he displaced it from the center of the nationalist-capitalist project. Twice he showed that the NEP could be realized through other developmental goals—first in September 1986 when he suspended the NEP's restructuring requirements during a recession, and, second, in 1990, when he introduced a National Development Plan that formally eschewed the restructuring language of the NEP (Khoo and Khoo 2012, 3–4).

5.3.3 Encountering the World

The third set was bound up with positioning and safeguarding the state's interests in the world. Malaysia's development proceeded under many changing conditions framed by global events and phenomena that buffeted small and non-influential states—the post-World War II struggles for decolonization; the geopolitics of the Cold War and its end; the emergence of a 'new international division of labor'; the trading and financial accords of developed states; and the reshaping of global markets under neoliberal auspices and the impositions of supranational agencies. Moreover, Malaysia's small, export-dependent, and open economy was vulnerable to fluctuations in global growth, changes in demand for commodities and manufactured goods, and shifts in the terms of trade for exports and imports, and shocks to the world economy. Its leaders and planners never threatened post-colonial nationalization but remained receptive to trade, investment flows, the transfer of technology, and ideas for development. A few developments, however, caused Mahathir to rail at foreign interests—soybean exporters who campaigned against palm oil imports (into USA), the London Metal Exchange whose abrupt change of trading and delivery rules ruined a Malaysian scheme, UK-originated criticisms of Malaysian takeovers of several plantation and mining companies on the London Stock Exchange, and the 1985 Plaza Accord that bloated Malaysian's yen-denominated loans. Mahathir's advocacy of closer East Asian economic regionalism as a bulwark against European and North American trading blocs was blocked, primarily by USA. Still, nothing had threatened the stability of the economy like the 1997 East Asian financial crisis.

Nothing that the state and the central bank, Bank Negara (BNM) attempted seemed capable of reversing 'the depreciation of the ringgit and the decline in share prices [that] reinforced each other' (BNM AR 1998, 34). Very soon, an embattled state confronted a global money market. The former's crisis management was marred by irrational statements, confrontational stances, and defensive changes of investment rules. The latter, supported by the International Monetary Fund (IMF) and economic orthodoxy, raised its demands for 'pro-market' reforms. The impasse brought damaging capital flight at the end of 1997 that turned into a foreign capital strike by mid-1998. Policy options were limited. Inviting long-term FDI for productive activity would not rescue the financial system from catastrophe. Hopes for an 'Asian solution' managed by a Japan-led 'Asian Monetary Fund' were dashed by the opposition of the USA, the IMF and even China. In addition to the IMF's standard package of structural adjustment, neoliberal prescriptions for the crisis demanded market liberalization, (domestic) financial sector reform, and 'good governance'. Such remedies, stringently applied, would have been fatal to Malaysia Inc.: a 'free market' would govern a non-interventionist state.

5.3.4 The Imperatives of Nationalism

At that juncture, the state under Mahathir bestirred itself and imposed a semi-autarkic 'shield' of currency and capital controls. The capital controls presaged a policy regime of rescuing local business, recapitalizing the financial sector, and reflating the economy. This gamble was so controversial when it was played that it attracted a lively debate over its efficacy as an instrument of crisis management and its implications for the global financial market. Rarely, however, has it been said that it was an underlying economic nationalism, long and powerfully articulated by Mahathir, that breathed life into his 'developmental state' at the very moment when it faced extinction!

Although Mahathir held and expressed many strong views on a range of subjects and was a man of different personae (Khoo 1995), Mahathir was most widely regarded to be a staunch nationalist whether or not perceptions of him as such were favorable or otherwise. He was variously involved in politics between his student days in the immediate post-World War II era and his retirement as prime minister at the beginning of the 21st century. He participated in the Malay mobilization against the Malayan Union proposal of 1946 and joined UMNO when it was founded as the organizational vehicle of Malay nationalism in the same year. His full career included an initial five-year term as a Member of Parliament (1964–69), nearly a decade of ministerial-level appointment (1972–81), and a 22-year tenure as prime minister (1981–2003).

Nationalism meant many things to Mahathir but it had an economic heart, so to speak, around which coalesced other constituent parts. His economic nationalism was a complex matter as he conceived, articulated, practiced, modified, advanced, and defended it in the course of 60 years of politics. It was not unchanging, though, just as he, Malaysia and the world did not ever stand still during that time. It would be preferable to approach Mahathir's economic nationalism in its entirety rather than reduce its complexity to a few elements or aspects. Nonetheless, for conceptual clarity, a short essay might begin by decomposing his ideas, commitments, policies, and initiatives according to some selected categories of analysis.

The core of Mahathir's economic nationalism was 'development', or *pembangunan* in the Malay language. The idea of development was cultivated in the official mind and imprinted on the public imagination as a national ideal for an independent nation, and indeed a historical imperative for an 'underdeveloped', 'developing', or 'emerging' country as such. Development as a process was expected to generate high growth, catalyze structural transformation, establish strategic sectors, promote key industries, and secure competitiveness. To achieve those ends, the state would plan and manage the process, define its goals, set targets, and launch projects. Sound and sustained development, undertaken as a major responsibility of the state, allowed economic nationalism to bear firm social objectives as well. The New Economic Policy (NEP) promulgated in 1970 placed the highest priority on two social objectives for the period from 1970 to 1990: to 'eradicate poverty irrespective of race', and to 'restructure society to abolish the identification of race with occupational function'. In fact, 'poverty eradication' and 'restructuring' were the policy demands of an ethno-nationalism whose central 'Malay dilemma' was ideologically formulated by Mahathir in 1970. But he had first raised it in 1950 (Khoo 1995, 85). The two NEP objectives supplied the justifications for the state to launch innumerable development programs and projects to provide a broad range of social services, raise an educated and skilled labor force, nurture technocratic, professional, and managerial strata, and foster a capitalist vanguard.

After 1990, Mahathir's Vision 2020 shifted the focus of the NEP objectives to the attainment of developed-country status, and the consolidation of an 'economically just society' grounded in 'a fair and equitable distribution of the wealth of the nation' (Khoo 1995, 328). Vision 2020 expressly taught that Malaysia had to avoid becoming 'an economically defenceless nation and an economically powerless state' by acquiring 'the ability to marshal influence and create coalitions in the international economic arena' (Khoo 1995, 330). And, perhaps most deeply of all, an ideological-psychological matrix of impulses—constituted of ethnic anxieties, class aspirations, state interests, and a leader's vision—motivated Mahathir's nationalism. The ultimate prize of development would be a 'secure and developed Malaysian society … justifiably proud of what it is, of what it has accomplished … psychologically subservient to none, and respected by the peoples of other nations' (Khoo 1995, 331).

5.3.5 The Political Character of Development

Whether the capital controls of September 1998 were necessary, or how effectively they aided economic recovery, stimulated a controversy that has not found a settled resolution in theory and analysis. However, the capital controls were not an economistic solution. In economic terms, the semi-autarkic regime of capital controls, recapitalization, rescue, and reflation prevented the financial collapse and IMF intervention (as happened in Thailand, Indonesia and South Korea). Politically, the semi-autarkic regime allowed the state to regain 'a greater degree of monetary independence' from the market, provide 'an environment of stability', 'restructure the financial and corporate sector' (BNMAR 1998, 36)—and salvage its nationalist-capitalist project. In a way, the crisis and the response brought things full circle.

Malaysian society has always had an intuitive appreciation of the profoundly political character of economic development. This was partly due to the NEP's overarching influence over the economy, society and political system. But it was also because mass expectations were invested in development as 'a nationalist project driven by capitalist impulses or a capitalist project imbued with nationalist aspirations' (Khoo 2003, 5). The leaders at different times had sought to suffuse development with strong ideological tones. In 1971, the principal architect of the NEP, Prime Minister Tun Abdul Razak, who spoke of combining 'rapid economic transformation' and 'social equality', called the NEP as 'nationalistic socialism' that encompassed 'state participation' and the 'doctrine of welfarism' (Khoo and Khoo 2012, 5). Two decades later, Mahathir, who launched a program of heavy industrialization and privatization, proclaimed the nation's impending arrival in the club of developed countries by dint of its continued economic growth. Between the one and the other were embedded many initiatives of a development state driven by political objectives of nation-building and national unity, and hopes of inter-ethnic equity at home, inclusion in an East Asian regionalist triumph, and an eventual parity with the advanced economies abroad.

5.4 The Politics of Development State Building in Ethiopia

The Ethiopian attempt to make a developmental state is worth studying because of its impressive growth record in the 2000s. The country enjoyed rapid economic growth without huge resource extraction or commodity exports, which are common in other emerging African economy. Besides, the country is a landlocked country surrounded by not well managed states at the Horn of Africa.

In their study on rapid growing African economy entitled, *Emerging Africa*, Radelet (2010) counts Ethiopia as one of the 17 emerging African countries which achieved more than 2% annual per capita income growth from 1996 to 2008, declined the share of the people living below the poverty line by 10% in the same time period, achieved increasing school enrollment, literacy rate and education levels for girls, and so forth (Radelet 2010, 13). These emerging Africa, according to Radelet, departed from anti-growth syndrome characterized with control-oriented economic policy, nepotism among decision makers, heavy borrowing, and failed state apparatus, and adopted more sensible economic policy, became relatively free from IMF, staffed their governments with highly educated policymakers, and were run by the new generation of political leaders.

Besides, Prime Minister Meles publicly stated that the Ethiopian government would seek for making a democratic developmental state (Clapham 2018). In the above-mentioned volume edited by Stiglitz and others, Ethiopia is indeed a model country of possible developmental state in Africa (Noman et al. 2012). Meles himself contributes a chapter, "States and Markets: Neoliberal Limitations and the Case for a Developmental State" (Meles 2012b, 170). It is true that the Ethiopian government advocated the concept of the democratic developmental state together with agricultural-led industrialization (Ohno 2013, Ch. 9).

It would be puzzling if we assume that the country enjoyed impressive economic growth with articulated program to make a democratic developmental state from the beginning of the current administration. Alex de Waal, who closely discussed with Meles on various issues, mentioned that Meles consolidated his power within the ruling coalition and carried out developmental agenda after the war with Eritrea and a successive restructuring of the party leadership in 2001 (de Waal 2012, Fana 2014). In the following sections, we will trace the process where Meles and his colleagues worked for state reconstruction after dismantling the Derg regime or the authoritarian regime led by President Mengistu Haile Mariam from 1974 to 1991.

5.4.1 Reconfiguration of the State Structure Through the Politics of Ethnicity

Before assuming the presidency, Meles was a leader of the Tigrayan People's Liberation Front (TPLF) which was a core of the governing coalition of the Ethiopian People's Revolutionary Democratic Front, EPRDF (Young 1997). The EPRDF is not only a coalition of the former guerrilla forces but rather a coalition of political groups realigned under the dominant leadership of the TPLF which was confident of its own style of governance. The TPLF leaders changed the direction of governance in following two ways. First, it came from Tigray region where most of the residents are peasants and cities were not developed or administered by the repressive rulers of the Derg regime. The TPLF provided public goods such as schools and justice system in Tigray region where the Derg systematically destroyed social system after 1974 (Young 1997, Ch. 7). Generally speaking, the TPLF leaders did not trust intellectuals and middle class in city and were concerned about rural peasants, though most of them were educated intellectuals (Markakis 2011, 247–251). Assuming that the majority of its population is in rural area, Meles even stated, "Addis Ababa [capital city] is not Ethiopia" just after he came to power in 1991 (cited from Markakis 2011, 249). There were valid political reason for the EPRDF to promote the agricultural development-led industrialization considering its leadership and its power base (Ohno 2013, 319).

Second, the TPLF emphasized the role of ethnicity as a source of legitimacy. The EPRDF government carried out a series of reform to realize the state based on the idea of ethnic federalism. The government attempted to realign the local leadership through the Peace and Development Committees from June 1991 (Markakis 2011, 234). The EPRDF recruited teachers for a month long seminar, provided political education, and search for appropriate candidates in local elections in each area. In addition, the administration declared the Proclamation to Provide for the Establishment of National/Regional Self Government in 1992 (Markakis 2011, 234). Under the proclamation, the Boundaries Commission set up by the Transitional Council of Representatives, whose members had no expertise on the issue, prepared a plan to divide the country into fourteen regions in November 1992 (Markakis 2011, 235). Because of internal migration and inter-ethnic marriage, however, the Commission could barely provide a clear cut rule to divide the country. Markakis even stated

Table 5.3 Distribution of Population by Regional State, 2007

Region	Number	Percent
Tigray	4,314,456	6
Afar	1,411,092	2
Amhara	17,214,056	23
Oromia	27,158,471	37
Somali	4,439,147	6
Beni Shangul Gumuz	670,847	1
SNNP	15,042,531	20
Gambella	306,916	0
Harar	183,344	0
Addis Ababa	2,738,248	4
Dire Dawa	342,827	1
Special enumeration	96,570	0
Country total	73,918,505	100

Source Markakis (2011, 235)

in his intensive study on Ethiopian state building, "as a result [of complex nature of ethnicity] no official *kilil* (regional) map has been issued to this day" (Markakis 2011, 236). The ethnicity created by the EPRDF's ethnic federalism was in essence political.

It is misleading to assume the politicization of ethnicity as the hegemony of the ethnic majority over minority. As Table 5.3 reveals, the Tigray people who promote ethnic federalism are minority in the country.

It is obvious that the Tigray region, where the TPLF comes from, occupied only the fifth largest population in the country. Under this situation, the TPLF would be located as an automatic minority group with general elections. Why did they do this?

In order to understand the politicization of ethnicity by the TPLF leadership, we should contextualize the regime change in the history of Ethiopia. The TPLF aimed at dismantling the traditional Amhara hegemony in Ethiopia. It accused the Derg regime of imposing Ethiopian nationalism on ethnic minority such as Tigray. The Derg indeed imposed the usage of Amharinga in school and public offices. As a result, 67% of city dwellers said that they spoke Amharinga at home while only 29% of the population claimed that they were Amhara in 1984 (Markakis 2011, 185–186). Against this background, the TPLF established schools throughout Tigray region to mobilize the peasants by advocating Tigrayan nationalism (Young 1997, 172–174). Once coming to power, the EPRDF kept pushing for political realignment based on the ethnic federalism. A symbolic example of the realignment is a transformation of the Amhara People's Democratic Movement (ANDM) from the Ethiopian People's Democratic Movement, EPDM in 1994 (Markakis 2011, 243). The ANDM supposedly represents the voice of Amhara people, while the EPDM was assumed a pan-Ethiopian movement and did not limit its membership to Amhara people. The

Table 5.4 Number of privatized enterprises, 1994–2001

1994	12
1995	122
1996	27
1997	15
1998	13
1999	22
2000	10
2001	2

Source Ethiopian Privatization Agency cited from Getachew (2003, 35)

EPRDF finally made a new constitution stipulating ethnic federalism in August 1995. The TPLF leaders succeeded in transforming the political system of Ethiopia as they desired.

5.4.2 Liberalization: Transition from Socialist Economy

The TPLF did not seem to have a clear vision for economic development except its emphasis on the benefits of the peasants' population. In the midst of constitution making for a new government, President Meles established the Ethiopian Privatization Agency in 1994, which was a part of the Public Enterprises Reform Program supported by the World Bank and IMF. In implementing the privatization, the agency received financial and technical assistance from Germen Technical Assistance (GTZ), African Development Bank, and the World Bank (Getachew 2003, 58).

As Table 5.4 shows, the EPRDF boldly carried out a series of liberalization facing sporadic opposition in civil society, it for instance even cracked down the Confederation of Ethiopian Trade Unions when the latter publicly condemned the structural adjustment program by the World Bank in 1994 (Markakis 2011, 251–252). Despite the opposition in civil society, the EPRDF left an impressive economic performance through various deregulatory measures, removal of price controls, export taxes and exchange controls (Markakis 2011, 262).

5.4.3 Encountering the World

The policymakers in fact accepted a policy package prepared by the international financial institutions until the late 1990s. The board of the IMF approved Enhanced Structural Adjustment Facility (ESAF) program in 1996 (Wade 2001, 70). The Ethiopian government defied against the IMF when the former supported the Ethiopian Airlines or the national flag career of Ethiopia despite the opposition of the

IMF's advice late in the same year. While the Ethiopian government approached the World Bank led by its chief economist, Joseph Stiglitz, the IMF decided to stop the ESAF program in Ethiopia. After several negotiation supported by the World Bank, the Ethiopian government accepted a new program with the IMF only in April 1998 (Wade 2001, 73).

Stiglitz revealed his first encounter with Prime Minister Meles in his provocative book, *Globalization and its Discontents* (Stiglitz 2002, 25–33). When he visited the country in March 1997, Prime Minister Meles was in the midst of heated debate with the IMF over the ESAF program providing $127 million loan with highly subsidized rates (Stiglitz 2002, 27). Stiglitz praised the macroeconomic management as well as the budget allocation reducing the military budget and increasing the budget for rural development of the country, while he criticized the IMF of its obsessive concern about Ethiopian budget's dependence on foreign aid (Stiglitz 2002, 28). He further pointed out that the Ethiopian government was wise enough so that it did not follow the IMF's advice to open its financial market, which resulted into the decision by the IMF to suspend the ESAF program (Stiglitz 2002, 32). Stiglitz eventually mobilized his network in the World Bank and the Clinton administration to lift the suspension of the program by the IMF (Stiglitz 2002, 32).

Meles and his aides were nationalist policymakers who were different from isolationists or rent seekers. They did not hesitate to contact with the World Bank, but rather sought for the help from the Bank. Moreover, they succeeded in convincing the chief economist who could have been critical at economic policy management if the Ethiopian policymakers were irresponsible for their countries' macroeconomic condition.

Meles and the policymakers might have shifted their economic policy management much earlier, if they haven't had faced an untimely war with Eritrea in 1998 as we will see below.

5.4.4 Developmental State Building in a Series of Political Turmoil

It took three more years for the Ethiopian government to prepare a new development plan not because of the clash with the international financial institutions but rather because of military clash with its neighbor, Eritrea. In May 1998, Tigray regional administration published a map to figure out the national boundary between the two countries. After a small skirmish led by Eritrean Army, the Ethiopian Army fought back with its full force, which resulted into a classic type of trench warfare between the two countries. They remained at war until the time Organization of African Union brokered and arranged the Cessation of Hostilities Agreement in May 2000. In December same year, the U.S. pushed two countries to sign the Technical Agreement with which two countries submit their differences in international arbitration

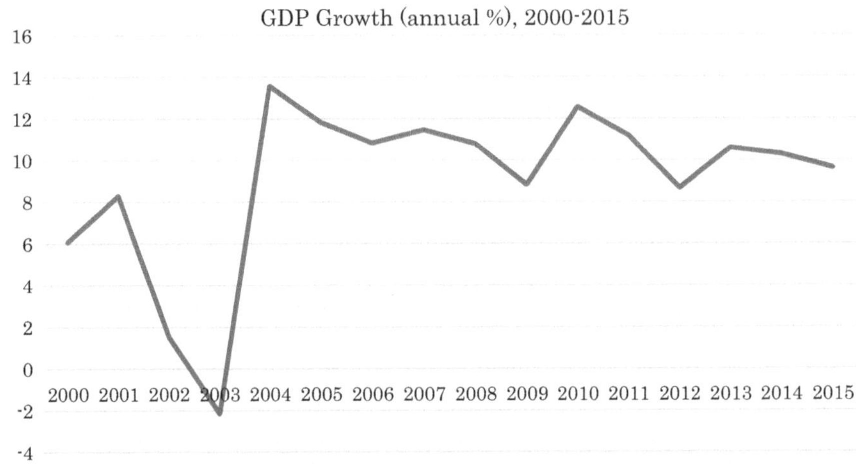

Fig. 5.1 Economic growth of Ethiopia, 2000–2015. *Data from database* World Development Indicators (Last Updated: 04/27/2017)

(Markakis 2011, 273). In the election in 2000, the EPRDF won 481 out of 546 seats at the House of People's Representative (Markakis 2011, 272).

Not the entire leadership of the TPLF, however, agreed to the cessation. Hardliners within the EPRDF condemned Prime Minister Meles of yielding pressure from the U.S. calling for truce (Markakis 2011, 273). Meles did not listen to their voices instead, he expelled twelve members from the TPLF central committee and then removed actual and potential dissidents within the EPRDF (Markakis 2011, 273–274). He labelled those who were expelled hard core radicals or the left wing which did not understand changing world, while he exploited the expertise of technocrats to lead a nation in an age of globalization (Markakis 2011, 274; Lefort 2012, 682).

After the turmoil, the EPRDF geared toward economic development with the Sustainable Development and Poverty Reduction Program (SDPRP) for the years from 2002 to 2005, which triggered a decade long high economic growth as we can see in Fig. 5.1 (Arkebe 2015, 80).

The policymakers carried out institutional reform to promote export, foreign direct export, and manufacturing sector. Regarding the export promotion, Prime Minister Meles created the National Export Coordination Committee in 2003. The NECC, following the example of South Korean counterpart, held a monthly meeting chaired by Prime Minister Meles from 2003 to 2012. The committee reviewed the performance of export products, discussed bottle necks and made decision to improve the performance (Arkebe 2015, 99).

In terms of foreign direct investment, the government restructured the Ethiopian Investment Authority into the Federal Investment Commission in 2002 and once again reformed it into the Federal Investment Agency in 2006 (Arkebe 2015, 90). In 2004, the government targeted Turkey, India and China as the sources of the

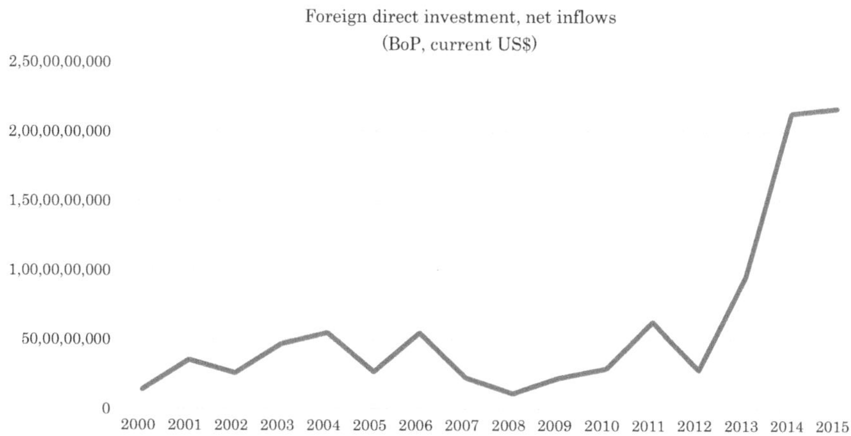

Fig. 5.2 FDI Inflow, 2000–2015. *Data from database* World Development Indicators (Last Updated: 04/27/2017)

investment as well as Netherlands in various fields. For instance, the Netherlands government provided incentives to the firms investing floriculture industry in Ethiopia (Arkebe 2015, 88).

Among the targeted economies, however, China played an impressive role. The Ethiopian government cultivated the tie with China in the 1990s (Adem 2012, 146). The Ethiopian government made an agreement with China to create special economic zone in the suburb of Addis Ababa. Ethiopia became the fourth largest recipient of Chinese FDI in the field of infrastructure in Africa following Angola, Sudan and Nigeria, which are all resource-rich countries unlike Ethiopia (Adem 2012, 147). The following Fig. 5.2 shows inflow of FDI from 2000 to 2015.

It is clear that the Ethiopian government is very much interested in its economic relations with China, though Fig. 5.2 counts the FDI from all countries. The Ministry of Finance and Economic Cooperation established a special branch called Ethio-China Developmental Cooperation Office independent of the Bilateral Cooperation Directorate.[3]

The government also worked for nurturing manufacturing sector. As the following Fig. 5.3 shows, manufacturing sector increased its share in GDP, though its growth was not that impressive as general growth of Ethiopian economy shown in Fig. 5.1. Arkebe Oqubay, former mayor of Addis Ababa and a special advisor to prime minister, worked for industrial policy making and has studied the impact by himself in his Ph.D. dissertation, which is later published from Oxford University Press with the title of *Made in Africa: Industrial Policy in Ethiopia* (Arkebe 2015). In his study, Arkebe picks up cement industry, flower cutting industry, and leather industry. According to his study, both import substitution strategy for the cement industry

[3]MoFEC Homepage (http://www.mofed.gov.et/web/guest/ethio-china-development-co-operation-office) accessed on June 15, 2017.

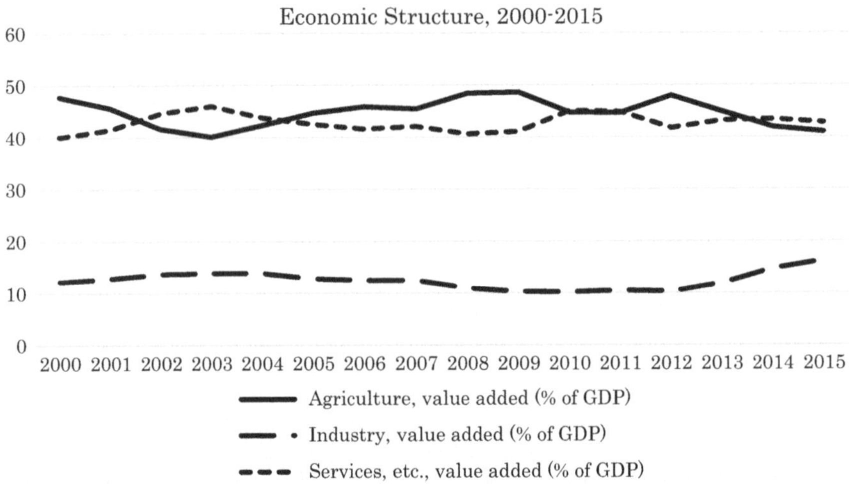

Fig. 5.3 Economic structure, 2000–2015. *Data from database* World Development Indicators (Last Updated: 04/27/2017)

and export-led industrialization strategy for the flower cutting industry worked well, while industrial policy for leather industry failed to achieve impressive economic performance partly because of the existing interests opposing any changes.

Considering the impressive record of economic growth, it might be a surprise to know the fact that the EPRDF failed to achieve a land slide victory in the 2005 elections. The opponents of the EPRDF, such as the Rainbow Ethiopia, mobilized themselves into a Coalition for Unity and Democracy (CUD) before the elections. The CUD supported the idea of liberalism and free market, while it opposed ethnic federalism and land ownership by the state (Markakis 2011, 275). Berhanu Nega, who led the Rainbow Ethiopia, was once a head of a think tank which had a deep connection with business sectors being critical of economic policy of the government (Nishi 2009, 53). Mobilizing the moral and financial supports from the urban middle class within the country and Ethiopian diaspora, the CUD-led opposition won at least one third of the seats of the lower house including the entire 23 seats in capital city, Addis Ababa (Nishi 2009, 53; Markakis 2011, 275). The CUD leaders were, however, not satisfied with the announced result of the elections and their supporters organized rallies which resulted into a violent crush with 193 casualties, more than 700 injured person, and more than 1000 roundup including opposition leaders (Markakis 2011, 276).

One year after this bloodshed and suppression of the opposition party, Meles prepared the paper, "African Development: Dead Ends and Beginnings and criticized those who supported the free market economy in Africa" (Meles 2012a). We should remember the voice of CUD supporting free market when we read Meles' critique on free market economy. The EPRDF did not entirely reject the policy proposals by the opposition in 2005. The EPRDF, for instance, shifted its focus from small-scale subsistence farmers to the large scale commercial farming in its agricultural development-led industrialization reflecting the campaign agenda of the CUD during the 2005 election (Nishi 2013, 8–9).

When it comes to politics, however, the EPRDF has never allowed opposition to play a significant role. In the 2010 election, the EPRDF won all the seats except one for "token opposition" (Markakis 2011, 277). Most of keen observers on Ethiopian politics have argued that Meles consolidated his dominant power since 2001 (Vaughan 2011). As we have mentioned earlier, Meles contributed his chapter to the edited volume, *Good growth and governance in Africa: Rethinking development strategies* (Meles 2012b). In his chapter, instead of explaining the strategy of his government, he spent so much pages to criticize neo-liberal economics with a night watchman state model and rent seeking behavior. It is actually confusing because Meles linked the night watchman state with neo-liberal economics instead of liberal economics. Meles in a different occasion argued that he should be careful about hasty democratization in Africa where rent-seeking activity is rampant (De Waal 2012, 153).

Meles and policymakers in the ruling coalition continuously addressed national agenda in their policy making. They were neither parochial rent seekers nor blind followers of capricious pundits in international community. They were nationalist policymakers considering national agenda and made decision to address it. The political turmoil after the 2000s, however, reveals the fact that the government faced a tension generated by its own change or contradiction in policy making. The government had once promoted liberalization in the 1990s, while the opposition party advocated in the 2000s. Meanwhile, the government promoted a developmental state building with which it could differentiate its policy orientation from the opposition. The developmental state building is, however, not a complete solution, especially in the context of the making of ethnic federalism. This is because, the former expects local governments to abide by the central government's decision, while the latter allows them to be autonomous (Fana 2014). The central government promoting development from the center faces repercussion from the people in the federal states, who had been encouraged to unite under the name of their ethnicity. The ruling coalition is now expected to address the challenge generated by its own policy innovation.

5.5 Conclusion

The both cases reveal significance of nationalist leadership in developmental state building. Mahathir bluntly declined the IMF's policy prescription in the midst of financial crisis and Meles defended national flag career against the IMF's austerity measure. They were, however, not at all isolationists. Mahathir indeed maximized his relations with Japan to mitigate the pressure from the IMF, while Meles cultivated a tie with the World Bank to reconstruct the relations with the IMF. Furthermore, both Malaysia and Ethiopia promoted foreign direct investment to nurture manufacturing sectors. While Mahathir found Japan a partner through his Look East policy, Meles institutionalized the ties with China through economic bureaucracy. They were nationalists in the sense they thought about development of national economy, took a necessary position against international organization, if necessary, and were open to policy options maximizing the opportunity given by globalization.

No leaders could, however, impose their state building project on a clean slate. While Mahathir gradually shifted from the politics of ethnicity to the politics of developmental state building, Meles had institutionalized the politics of ethnicity and once promoted liberalization before he began to advocate developmental state building.

The political leaders nurtured their strategy seeking for their own survival. Mahathir and Meles did not simply crack down the opposition but to expand its mass base by committing economic growth. Rather they found the way to accommodate the voice of the opposition either through elections and/or governance of the dominant coalition, though they never allowed the opposition to gain the power. In this sense, the political leaders of developmental state might end up being simple predators once they stop listening the voices of those who oppose them. They can be the leaders of the developmental states as long as they continuously learn the way to develop in the midst of power struggle.

References

Adem S (2012) China in Ethiopia: diplomacy and economics of sino-optimism. Afr Stud Rev 55(1):143–160

Arkebe O (2015) Made in Africa: industrial policy in Ethiopia. Oxford University Press, Oxford

Amsden A (1992) Asia's next giant: South Korea and late industrialization. Oxford University Press, Oxford

BNM AR (Bank Negara Malaysia Annual Report) (1998) Kuala Lumpur

Clapham C (2018) The Ethiopian developmental state. Third World Q 39(6):1151–1165

De Waal A (2012) Review article: the theory and practice of Meles Zenawi. Afr Aff 112(446):148–155

Evans P (1995) Embedded autonomy: states and industrial transformation. Princeton University Press, Princeton

Fana G (2014) Securitisation of development in Ethiopia: the discourse and politics of developmentalism. Rev Afr Polit Econ 41(1):64–74

Getachew R (2003) Privatization in Ethiopia: process and Performance of Privatized manufacturing firms. Master thesis, School of Graduate Studies, Addis Ababa University

Johnson C (1982) MITI and the Japanese miracle: the growth of industrial policy, 1925–1975. Stanford University Press, Stanford

Khoo BT (1995) Paradoxes of Mahathirism: an intellectual biography of Mahathir Mohamad. Oxford University Press, Kuala Lumpur

Khoo BT (2003) Beyond Mahathir: Malaysian politics and its discontents. Zed Books, London and New York

Khoo BT (2005) Mahathirism after the Asian crisis Beyond Mahathir. In: Shiraishi T, Abinales PN (eds) After the crisis: hegemony, technocracy and governance in Southeast Asia. Kyoto University Press, Kyoto, pp 156–178

Khoo BT (ed) (2012) Policy regimes and the political economy of poverty reduction in Malaysia. Palgrave Macmillan, UK

Khoo BT, Khoo KJ (2012) The political economy of poverty eradication in Malaysia: an overview. In: Khoo BT (ed) Policy regimes and the political economy of poverty reduction in Malaysia. Palgrave Macmillan, UK
Lefort R (2012) Free market economy, 'developmental state' and party-state hegemony in Ethiopia: the case of the 'model farmers'. J Mod Afr Stud 50(4):681–706
Markakis J (2011) Ethiopia: the last two frontiers. James Currey, Oxford
Meles Z (2012a) African development: dead ends and new beginnings; Preliminary draft. Downloaded from http://www.meleszenawi.com/african-development-dead-ends-and-new-biginnings-by-meles-zenawi/african_developmentdead_ends_and_new_beginnings_ by_meles_zenawi/. Accessed 1 July 2016
Meles Z (2012b) States and markets: neoliberal limitations and the case for a developmental state. In: Noman et al (eds) Good growth and governance in Africa: rethinking development strategies. Oxford University Press, Oxford, pp 140–174
Mine Y (1996) Minami Afurika: "Niji no kuni" no ayumi. (South Africa: a footpath of a "Rainbow Country"). Iwanami Shoten, Tokyo
Nishi M (2009) Gendai Afurika no kokyosei: Echiopia shakai ni miru komyuniti, kaihatsu, seiji jissen. (The public of modern Africa: community, development, and political practice in Ethiopia). Showado, Kyoto
Nishi M (2013) Problems and possibilities of democratic developmentalism in Ethiopia. Paper presented at the 56th annual meeting of the African Studies Association, Baltimore Marriott Waterfront Hotel, Baltimore, 21–24 Nov 2013
Noman A, Botchwey K, Stein H, Stiglitz JE (eds) (2012) Good growth and governance in Africa: rethinking development strategies. Oxford University Press, Oxford
Ohno K (2013) Sangyo seisaku no tsukuri kata: Ajia no besuto purakutisu ni manabu. (How to make industrial policy: learning from Asian best practices). Yuhikaku, Tokyo
Radelet S (2010) Emerging Africa: how 17 countries are leading the way. Brookings Institution Press, Baltimore
Suehiro A (1998) Hatten tojo koku no kaihatsu shugi. (Developmentalism in developing economies). In Tokyo Daigaku Shakai Kagaku Kenkyujyo. (Institute of Social Science, The University of Tokyo) (ed) 20 seiki shisutemu 4: Kaihatsu shugi. (The 20th century global system 4: Developmentalism). Tokyo University Press, Tokyo, pp 13–46
Stiglitz JE (2002) Globalization and its discontents. W.W. Norton & Company, New York
Taylor I (2005) The developmental state in Africa: the case of Botswana. In: Mbabazi P, Taylor I (eds) The potentiality of 'developmental states' in Africa: Botswana and Uganda compared. Council for the development of social science research in Africa, Dakar, pp 44–56
Vaughan S (2011) Revolutionary democratic state-building: party, state and people in the EPRDF's Ethiopia. J Eastern Afr Stud 5(4):619–640
Wade R (1990) Governing the market: economic theory and the role of government in East Asian industrialization. Princeton University Press, Princeton
Wade R (2001) Capital and revenge: the IMF and Ethiopia. Challenge 44(5):67–75
Wheelwright EL (1965) Industrialization in Malaysia. Melbourne University Press, Melbourne
World Bank (1993) The East Asian miracle: economic growth and public policy. Oxford University Press, Washington
Young J (1997) Peasant revolution in Ethiopia: the tigray people's liberation front, 1975–1991. Cambridge University Press, Cambridge

Chapter 6
Development and Developmentalism in Post-genocide Rwanda

Shinichi Takeuchi

6.1 Introduction

The concepts of "developmentalism" and "developmental state" have attracted attention in Africa, which has recently experienced rapid economic growth. Although the successful growth may be largely attributable to favorable prices of primary goods, particularly oil, some of less resource-dependent countries achieved considerable growth, which may be comparable to the rapid economic growth that Asian countries experienced earlier. It seems important to investigate the similarities and differences in the growth factors, mechanisms, and sustainability between Asia and Africa.

Rwanda has seen continuous economic growth after its civil war and genocide at the beginning of the 1990s. Although the country is not abundantly endowed with oil and other resources, its real gross domestic product (GDP) per capita has more than doubled from 333 to 690 US dollars between 2000 and 2015.[1] The concept of developmental state may be applied to post-genocide Rwanda,[2] because of its leaders' emphasis on development ideology, their preferences for social engineering, and the country's high economic performance. However, it is true that Rwanda has adopted different strategies for development from those of typical Asian developmental states, as we will see later.

[1] The data are in constant 2010 US dollars and taken from the World Development Indicators (WDI).

[2] Biedermann (2016). A workshop entitled "Rwanda—A Developmental State and/or Donor Darling" was held at German Development Institute on October 2016. See the following URL for detail. (https://www.die-gdi.de/en/events/rwanda-a-developmental-state-and-donor-darling/).

S. Takeuchi (✉)
African Studies Center, Tokyo University of Foreign Studies, Fuchu, Japan
e-mail: shinichi_takeuchi@tufs.ac.jp

Y. Takagi et al. (eds.), *Developmental State Building*, Emerging-Economy State and International Policy Studies, https://doi.org/10.1007/978-981-13-2904-3_6

Based on the idea of political settlement (Khan 2010), Whitfield et al. (2015) shed light on the roles of industrial policies in the economic development of Ghana, Uganda, Tanzania, and Mozambique, and argue that political power has had impacts on economic development. Thus, their research has bearing on the African developmental state debate. It, however, does not explore how the industrial policies or development policies of these countries have facilitated or delivered economic development. Instead its purpose is to demonstrate the relevance of their typology of ruling coalitions and policies in the four countries.

This chapter is an attempt at understanding the mechanism that has enabled the high economic growth in post-genocide Rwanda. It highlights political factors that have affected the economic growth since the civil war ended in 1994. During this period, the government has been led by the ruling Rwandan Patriotic Front (RPF), which won the civil war as rebels. This chapter analyzes the mechanism by which a highly concentrated political power realizes rapid economic development. Illuminating the mechanism will also contribute to the comparison the Rwandan experience with those of Asian experience as well as of other authoritarian countries in Africa, such as Ethiopia and Uganda.

The chapter is organized as follows. The next section briefly examines Rwanda's macro-level socio-economic performance characterized by the high economic growth and considerable improvements in social indicators. Section 6.3 examines industrial policies and their implementation in the post genocide era and confirms that contrasting policies that could be categorized as neo-liberalist policies and interventionist policies, have coexisted. While the Rwandan government has generally adopted neo-liberal economic policies, it has almost constantly intervened to promote some sectors, particularly agricultural and rural sectors. Section 6.4 analyzes three leading sectors that have contributed to the rapid economic growth, i.e., the agricultural, mining, and modern business sectors, and discusses the political influence on the growth of these sectors. Section 6.5 explores reasons why the country has adopted seemingly contradicting economic policies. It finds the most plausible reason is that such policies have been taken to satisfy two demands: one is to be consistent with Rwanda's concern with the international mainstreaming, and the other is to achieve internal goals of power consolidation and state building. In the final part, we review the nature of the Rwandan economic growth and discuss its implication for growth sustainability.

6.2 Macro Development Performance in Post Genocide Rwanda

According to the World Development Indicators[3], Rwanda's real GDP grew by 5.0 percent per year on average from 2000 to 2015. This is a remarkable growth performance in view of that of Africa as a whole. One of the main drivers of the rapid

[3]Statistical data in this section are based on the WDI when there is no particular indication.

growth has been a sharp increase in external trade, of which value grew more than 14 times in 20 years between 1995 and 2015, as the index (year 2000 = 100), which had been 97.9 in 1995, surged to 1404.5 in 2015.[4]

During the same period, the provision of educational services has considerably increased. The net rate of primary school enrollment was 80% at the end of the 1990s (even though the gross rate was already 100% by then), but it increased steadily and reached 98.5% in 2010. The gross rate of secondary school enrollment increased from less than 10% in 1999 to 40% in 2013. The gender parity index has exceeded 1.0 since 2011, meaning that the secondary school enrollment rate has been higher for girls than for boys. Not only the educational sector but also the public health sector has had considerable improvements. Infant and under-five-years mortality rates decreased dramatically from 129.6 and 268.3 in 1995 to 31.1 and 41.7 in 2015, respectively. As a result, life expectancy at birth doubled from 31.6 years in 1995 to 64.5 years in 2015.

During the period from 1995 to 2015, the country's real GDP increased roughly five times. Still it is too early to say that Rwanda has succeeded in economic transformation and take-off. The national income still remains low in its absolute level, and the rapid economic growth has not brought about a clear transformation of industrial structure. The agricultural share of GDP steadily decreased from 39 to 29%, while the service share increased from 51 to 57%, and the mining and construction share increased from 5 to 9%.[5] The manufacturing sector kept a constant share around 5 to 6%, meaning that although it kept pace with the growth of the aggregate economy, it could not grow as fast as the mining and construction sectors.

Another notable change is the worsening inequality. Despite the rapid economic growth, "poverty levels in Rwanda remain well above pre-war levels" (UNDP 2007a, p. 7). The Head Count Index under the national poverty line (about 0.44 dollars a day in nominal terms) was 47.5 in 1990 and 56.9 in 2006. The Gini coefficient has sharply increased from 0.289 in the mid-1980s to 0.468 in 2000 and further to 0.510 in 2006 (UNDP 2007b; Republic of Rwanda 2007). It has remained high around 0.50 in the 2010s and is comparable to the Gini coefficient in Brazil (0.515 in 2014).

Rwanda's socio-economic performance in the post genocide period can be characterized by four points. First, its economy has grown rapidly, and service delivery in its social sector has been clearly ameliorated. Second, its industrial structure has not changed significantly, and industrial upgrading has not been observed clearly. Third, poverty reduction remains high on the agenda because the absolute income level has been low and economic inequality has been worsening since the end of the civil war.

[4]We need to be cautious about the reliability of macro-level statistics in Africa (Jerven 2013). Particularly, in case of Rwanda, it is said that official statistics of production volume and value might be systematically exaggerated under the system of the performance contact (*imihigo*), in which local officers set goals of developmental performance and the achievement is monitored by their superiors. See Ingelaere (2010) and Chemouni (2014) for details.

[5]The manufacturing sector refers to industries belonging to the International Standard Industrial Classification (ISIC) divisions 15–37.

Fourth, the rapid economic growth in the period has been achieved under the authoritarian rule. Practices of the authoritarian rule include the oppression of dissidents, human rights violations, the monopoly of power by the Rwandan Patriotic Front (RPF) elites (particularly, former military officers), and the technology of disinformation (e.g., Beswick 2010; Dorsey 2000; Ingelaere 2010; Pottier 2002; Reyntjens 2004, 2011, 2013; Silva-Lender 2008). In fact, the country has had poor rating in the indices of political rights and civil liberties, human rights, democracy, and democratic governance.[6] Assessment is divided when it comes to different aspects in governance. For example, the World Governance Indicators (WDI) includes six ratings; i.e., voice and accountability, political stability, government effectiveness, regulatory quality, rule of law, and control of corruption.[7] Rwanda has fared increasingly well over time in terms of the five ratings other than "voice and accountability," particularly in terms of "control of corruption," but its score on "voice and accountability" remains low.

Rwanda's politics in the post genocide period has been dominated by the RPF. The former rebel group was originally organized in Uganda in the 1980s by Rwandan Tutsi refugees (Prunier 1998). Most of them were children of Tutsi refugees who had fled their home country at the political uprisings that occurred at the time of the independence.[8] With the assistance of the Ugandan Museveni regime, the RPF invaded Rwanda and won a military victory in 1994 after a bloody guerrilla war and the genocide (Prunier 1995; Reyntjens 1994). As the war was a total victory for the RPF, all main opponents were pushed out of the territory by the end of the war. In addition, the RPF has made full efforts to consolidate and concentrate political power ever since, including repression against dissidents. Although the constitution adopted in 2003 stipulates a democratic political system, anti-government movements have been harshly suppressed.[9] The facts that even the non-RPF parties in the parliament have always supported the president Kagame at the presidential elections suggests that there is no room in Rwanda's political space for substantial opposition parties (Reyntjens 2013).

---

[6]These indices are provided by Freedom House, CIRI (Cingranelli and Richards), Economic Intelligence Unit (EIU), and Polity IV.

[7]The indices are available at http://info.worldbank.org/governance/WGI/#home.

[8]The political uprising, or the social revolution, caused a drastic change in political power in Rwanda. The Tutsi, who were politically dominant, were expelled to abroad and the Hutu elite took power through their party, the Parti du Mouvement de l'Emancipation Hutu—Parmehutu, just before the independence. However, it should be emphasized that the Tutsi-Hutu divide and the Tutsi's political dominance had been strengthened under the colonial rule. See Lemarchand (1970) for detail.

[9]The most well-known case was the ban of the then biggest opposition party, the Mouvement Démocratique Républicain (MDR), just before the legislative election in 2003.

6.3 Policies and Strategies for Development

What kind of policies has been taken to realize the rapid economic growth? This section examines development policies adopted by the Rwandan government, so as to understand the underlying thought and strategy. At first, the four policy papers are analyzed for this purpose: (1) *Rwanda Vision 2020* (Republic of Rwanda 2000), (2) *Poverty Reduction Strategy Paper* (Government of Rwanda 2002), (3) *Economic Development and Poverty Reduction Strategy, 2008–2012* (Republic of Rwanda 2007), and (4) *Economic Development and Poverty Reduction Strategy II, 2013–2018* (Republic of Rwanda 2013).

Although the four policy papers were published in different periods of time between 2000 and 2013, their focuses and promoted policies were rather consistent. There are two contrasting components in the policies. At first glance, their economic policies in general are characterized by the idea of laissez-faire and neo-liberalism. The major pillar of the development strategy is the promotion of the private sector development through improvement in business environments. In this context, the importance of good governance, human resource development, and infrastructure development is strongly emphasized.

"Good governance" is one of the keywords that Rwandan government has emphasized repeatedly.[10] While one of its official papers defines good governance "as accountability, transparency and efficiency in deploying scarce resources" (Republic of Rwanda 2000, 14), efficiency in bureaucracy has been, in practice, the central tenet of this concept. The government's argument that "we need a small but effective, flexible public sector" (Republic of Rwanda 2000, 14) has been repeatedly stated its policy papers. "Good governance" is therefore targeted mainly for the improvement of the business environment, which is in turn needed to promote the private sector development.

Human resource development has been another area of priority in this country. It is also considered to be crucial for making business environments competitive. The budget allocation to the education sector and the healthcare sector has been made possible largely by donors' contribution, and it seems to be effective as shown in their performance. In addition, the development of infrastructure and connectivity has been ardently advocated for overcoming the disadvantages of being landlocked. Its eagerness to develop Information and Communication Technologies has the same root.

Thus, the policy papers stress the imperatives for business environment improvement and propose concrete measures, but they do not indicate any particular sector to be prioritized for promotion. The only exception is that the policy papers propose to strengthen the competitiveness of the four exporting sectors (i.e., coffee, tea, tourism, and mining) (Republic of Rwanda 2007, 56). The fact that the promotion of new industries has not been attempted or considered suggests that the policy papers are tinged with the idea of laissez-faire and neo-liberalism.

[10] See, for example, the official website of Republic of Rwanda, Governance and Home-grown solutions. (http://www.gov.rw/about-the-government/governance-home-grown-solutions/).

However, the appearance of laissez-faire is quite contrasting with interventionist policies and practices in the rural and agricultural sectors. The most outstanding one that can be found in the abovementioned policy papers is the Vision 2020 Umurenge Program (Republic of Rwanda 2007, 75–80), which can be considered a countrywide program for rural development. Aiming to eradicate extreme poverty by 2020, the program is intended to increase jobs and export in rural areas. This is not, however, the only case of interventionistic policy in the sectors.

Since the seizure of power in 1994, the RPF-led government has implemented a series of interventionist policies in the rural sector to change the country's economic structure radically. Three policies are particularly noteworthy (Takeuchi and Marara 2014). First, "land-sharing" was implemented between Tutsi returnees and Hutu residents. Immediately after the RPF's victory in the civil war, hundreds of thousand Tutsi refugees began to return to Rwanda, from where they had been expelled for two to three decades. As their original family lands had been in many cases occupied by neighbors, the government instructed Hutu residents in the Eastern part of the country, where lands were relatively abundant, to "share their properties" (or more precisely, "give the half of their properties") with Tutsi returnees. As a result, the latter could obtain lands for their resettlement to the detriment of the former.

Second, the family law of 1999 stipulated equal rights for males and female to inherit land. Although Rwanda in tradition was a patrilineal society, in which women basically had no inheritance rights of land. Although the implementation of the new family law created considerable confusion and a number of conflicts, it has been rather effective thus far as both administration and judiciary have protected women's rights following the governmental decision. In other words, the successful implementation of the new family law has been ensured by the RPF's complete control over the local governing system.[11]

Third, the land registration was actively carried out following the stipulation in the Organic Land Law in 2005, and it was almost completed as of 2013. Despite the fact that a number of challenges regarding the process of land registration exist (Takeuchi and Marara 2014, 94–95), it is quite remarkable that the land certificate has been distributed all over the country.

In addition to these policies, Rwanda's rural sector has been the target of a series of interventionist policies in the post-genocide era, including the land consolidation, the land use planning (see below), and ban on thatched roofs.[12] Thus, in post-genocide Rwanda, the laissez-faire and neo-liberal approach was applied to macro-economy

[11] Such full control has been possible not only due to the RPF's capability but also due to the Rwandan social structure. The latter is characterized by the absence of autonomous local power. Traditional chiefs, who had had such power, were exterminated by the "social revolution" at the end of the colonial period (Lemarchand 1970). The local administration is capable of social mobilization in rural areas, as the 1994 genocide showed (Human Rights Watch 1999). Since the RPF's seizure of state power, the ruling party has controlled the nation's local administration.

[12] Around 2011, the local administration launched a massive campaign against thatched roofs, which were blamed for hygienic problems. Local officers ordered the destruction of a number of huts with thatched roofs. Although they promised to provide residents with tin roofs, the provisions were often delayed, and victims had to wait several months without roofs.

management and industrial sector management whereas an interventionist approach was applied to the rural sector management.

6.4 Assessment of the Contributing Sector

To understand the mechanism of the rapid growth of the Rwandan economy, this section reviews the experiences of the agriculture, mining, and modern business sectors, which grew particularly rapidly, and links the rapid growth of these three sectors with political factors.

Agricultural production has significantly increased in Rwanda for the last two decades, even though the GDP share of agriculture has declined. For example, food production in 2013 was 1.72 times as great as that in 2004–2006, whereas the corresponding ratio was just 1.30 for the average among the countries in Sub-Saharan Africa. The favorable performance of the agricultural sector in Rwanda seems to be attributable to government interventions. In addition to the measures explained in the previous sections, the government implemented a number of projects for marshland development, such as soil improvement and irrigation projects. The government also set up the Organic Land Law in 2005 that included land consolidation, i.e., "a procedure of putting together small lots of land in order to manage the land and use it in an efficient uniform manner so that the land may be more productive," and the provision of fertilizers and improved seeds for farmers.[13] These measures, implemented under the framework of the Crop Intensification Program, have been considered to contribute to the rapid agricultural production growth.[14]

The mining sector has marked even more remarkable growth. Before the civil war, coffee and tea accounted for a large part of the country's export. The mining sector, which has a long history, had ceased its production in the mid-1980s, mainly due to its bad management. Since the second war in the Democratic Republic of the Congo (1998–2002), however, mineral export increased rapidly, which was partly attributed to the massive smuggling of mineral resources from the Congolese territory, into which the Rwandan military invaded, to Rwanda (Marysse and André 2001).[15] The

[13]Organic Law No. 08/2005 of 14/07/2005 determining the use and management of land in Rwanda, article 2.

[14]Although it tended to induce farmers to specialize in the production of those crops for which improved seeds were available, farmers might be faced with greater risk as a result of specialization. Rwanda's recent agricultural reforms including the land consolidation and the land registration have stirred vigorous debates. Some researchers are critical of the reform because of several reasons including limited access to the improved seeds and the fertilizer, widening gap effects among farmers, as well as high-handed and top-down approaches (Pritchard 2013; Cioffo, Ansoms and Murison 2016; Dawson et al. 2016), but others defend such policies as no alternative would be viable considering disadvantageous conditions in Rwanda (Harrison 2016).

[15]It has been pointed out that Rwandan army systematically pillaged mineral resources in the Eastern DR Congo. The amount that the Rwandan army gained from the Congo in 1999 was attained to around 80% of its budget in the same year (United Nations 2002, par. 71).

rapid increase in mineral export in recent years has been also partly attributed to the restart of domestic production, even though the exact volume is unknown.

In the 2000s, facing serious criticisms from the international community, the Rwandan government began to take a series of policy measures for modernizing the mining sector and ensuring the traceability of the mineral it exports (MINIRENA 2010). It liberalized the sector and recognized activities of foreign capitals (Behuria 2015). The number of mining licenses issued by the government to mineral producers rapidly increased from less than 50 in 2008 to nearly 800 in 2014 (MINIRENA n.d., 6). The sector has been characterized by domination of foreign companies as "two large foreign firms export around 75% of Rwanda's minerals" (cited in Behuria 2015, 436), and the overwhelming majority of producers seem to be small and artisanal. Thus far, the growth of the mining sector has been driven largely by a small number of foreign companies and an increase in the number of non-mechanized small producers without any technological upgrading. Thus, Rwanda's mining sector development has had a close link with the external policies, which began with the war in the Democratic Republic of the Congo (DRC), followed by the massive pillage carried out by the army and the response to the criticism from the international community. Unlike the modern business sector (see below), the RPF-led government did not rely on its business group in the mining sector, aiming at "cleaning its image of involvement in conflict minerals" (Behuria 2015, 443).

Even if the ratio to the total GDP has not remarkably increased, it is undeniable that the business sector has also had rapid growth during the post genocide period. Both production and export of manufacture goods have significantly increased (Balchin et al. 2016, 8). What is unique to Rwanda is that the ruling party, RPF, and the national army (Rwandan Defense Force: RDF) have played the central role in the growth of modern business sector. RPF owns the whole equity of Rwanda's biggest investment holding company (Cristal Ventures Limited: CVL), the owner of a number of Rwanda's leading companies.[16] The whole CVL group was estimated to represent over 3 percent of the country's GDP in 2009 and to pay taxes which amounted to around 9 percent of all direct tax revenues in the fiscal year 2009/10 (Booth and Golooba-Mutebi 2012, 389). Another important business group, Horizon Group, received its initial capital from a fully military-owned enterprise, Military Micro Finance Cooperative Society (ZIGAMA-CSS) (Gökgür 2012, 20). In addition, state-owned enterprises, such as Rwanda Air, are active in the modern business sector (Gökgür 2012, 38). In short, the growth in modern business sector has been dependent on the initiatives of the RPF, the military, and the state.[17]

---

[16] CVL was formerly called as Tri-Star. Its 100% subsidiaries include Real Contractors (construction), Inyange Industries (food processing and beverages), and Bourbon Coffee Shops (coffee marketing). It partially owns MTN Rwanda Cell (mobile telephone). See Gökgür (2012, 39) for detail.

[17] Weis (2016) argues that the same mechanism has worked in Ethiopia. The ruling party (Ethiopian People's Revolutionary Democratic Front: EPRDF) as owner of companies has played a leading role in economic growth.

6.5 Political Factors Affecting Economic Performance

To understand the co-existence of two contrasting ideas—lasses-faire and interventionist—in Rwanda's development strategy, it is important to take into account the nature of its external relations and that of internal control. The RPF-led Rwanda has solidified its position in the international community, which the previous regime could not do. Two factors have contributed to this remarkable change.

First, the international community, particularly main donors tended to hold the RPF-led Rwanda in high regard as a country managing to overcome deep scars of the genocide. The flip side of this admiration was the sense of guilty coming from the inability of the major international players to prevent the genocide (Reyntjens 2013; Pottier 2002). In this context, the RPF gained a moral or psychological advantage by claiming that it had succeeded in stopping the genocide when the international community had completely failed. This advantage that the RPF gained has been called as the "genocide credit" and has been one of major factors contributing to Rwanda's position as a "donor darling" (Marysse et al. 2006), while keeping donors' conditionality from having democratizing effects (Hayman 2008).

Rwanda's diplomatic position has been further strengthened due to the fact that the United Kingdom (UK) and United States (US) have become its strong supporters. Although the reasons for the approach between Rwanda, on the one side, and the UK and US, on the other, are multiple and complex, it is clear that the RPF was considered a good game changer for the two great powers in the 1990s, when France had a close connection with Rwanda's Habyarimana and Zaïre's Mobutu (see Prunier 1995; Reyntjens 2009). UK Prime Minister Tony Blair approached Rwanda to pursue an "ethical foreign policy" (Porteous 2008). US President Bill Clinton visited Kigali, the capital of Rwanda, in March 1998 to apologize for not having acted to prevent the genocide. Ample examples point to how the two countries have strongly backed Rwanda, but the most conspicuous one is their pressure to dismiss Carla del Ponte, the prosecutor of the International Tribunal Court for Rwanda, in 2003 when she declared her intention to try war crimes that the RPF had committed (Peskin 2008, Ch. 9).

Another factor has been Rwanda's active diplomacy. Since the establishment of its government, the RPF has made systematic efforts to put Rwandan persons in strategic positions at African Union, African Development Bank, and other international organizations.[18] The country has been a big contributor to the United Nations Peace Keeping Operations as well.[19] In addition to these systematic efforts, President Kagame himself has been eager to express his ideas and opinions in international

[18]Patick Mazimpaka, who had once been a vice-chairman of the RPF, assumed the Deputy Chairperson of the African Union Commission during 2003 and 2008. Donald Kaberuka run for the president of African Development Bank between 2005 and 2015, after serving as Minister of Finance and Economic Planning between 1997 and 2005.

[19]As of April 2018, Rwanda is the fourth biggest contributor to the UN PKO in providing 6264 persons including police, UN military experts on mission, staff officers and troops. Information retrieved on 16th June 2018 (https://peacekeeping.un.org/sites/default/files/2_country_ranking_0.pdf).

conferences.[20] In total, the Rwandan government has made considerable efforts for putting their country in the mainstream of international diplomacy.

The country, however, has made no concession with regard to international requirements that might affect the RPF's internal political dominance.[21] Such attitude suggests that Rwanda's main concern with the international mainstreaming have aimed to establish political environments that would protect the current RPF-centered internal political order.[22] In this context, the country's laissez-faire policy expressed in its policy papers is quite understandable. On the one hand, the RPF-led government has kept its macroeconomic policy, which is visible to the international community, consistent with the economic liberalism, as it has been the de facto international standard since the 1980s, and as the UK and the US have been its strongest supporters. On the other hand, the government has applied an approach of active interventionism to rural and agricultural policies, which were the areas of particular importance in terms of internal politics.

The stated purpose of this interventionism has been the rational land use. The government has recognized a wide range of serious land issues including land scarcity, fragmentation of land, degradation of soil, and reiterated the strong need for rational and effective land uses (Republic of Rwanda 2004, Ch. 3). Since the vast majority of Rwandan nationals are farmers relying on small parcels of land, problems like poverty reduction and food shortage have been also associated with this objective.

In addition to the land consolidation policy, which was mentioned earlier, the policy of villagization (*umudugudu*) is another good example of the interventionism. The villagization policy originally launched to provide houses for Tutsi returnees coming back to Rwanda after decades of their absence. Recently, it has transformed into a kind of rural land use planning. Claiming that the villagization is indispensable for building infrastructure such as paved roads, electricity, and drinkable water supply, the policy makers have promoted the zoning in rural areas and urged people to move into the "residential" zone. Considering the fact that Rwandans traditionally did not reside in gathering but lived scattered over a thousand hills, the current change in rural landscapes is enormous. The policy of efficient land use has been thus pursued through various interventionist measures (Newbury 2012).

Pursuit of the rational land use may not be the only reason for the interventionism. Ansoms (2009) argues that the RPF political elites tend to embrace social engineering, which can be explained by their elitist perception that farmers lack knowledge necessary to improve agriculture. Besides the ideological reasons, the interventionist measures have been closely linked with the demand for political control of rural

[20] For instance, Kagame actively attends international conferences, and is a regular participant of the World Economic Forum (Davos conference). In addition, he has accepted many requests of an interview and expressed widely his views and opinions.

[21] Besides the above-mentioned response to donors' requirements for democratization, Rwanda has no substantial concession to the international criticism about human rights violations and mineral exploitations that its soldiers had alleged to commit in the Democratic Republic of the Congo.

[22] We can recall the fact that when United Nations published the Mapping report on human violation in the DR Congo (OHCHR 2010), Rwanda threatened to withdraw its troops from UN Peace Keeping Mission in Darfur.

areas. The clearest one was the policy of land sharing. As we have discussed in the previous section, the provision of land for Tutsi returnees, the core supporters of the RPF, had a direct bearing on consolidating the RPF's political base. It is important to point out that the land registration has had the same effects. Through the registration, pieces of land acquired via land sharing have become official and legitimate, equipped with certificates, thus solidifying the land rights of returnees. Considering that the Tutsi returnees are the RPF's core supporters, it is natural to understand that the series of policy measures over land had the clear objective of supporting them and consolidating its own power base in rural areas.

In other words, territorial control has been the center of interest in agricultural and rural policies in Rwanda. The central objective of the land sharing policy was to establish supporters' base for the ruling party in distributing land resources. Other policies, including land consolidation, villagization, and land registration, have also contributed to strengthening administrative capabilities for the control of rural areas.

These interventionist policy measures have been designed and implemented in advocating goals with universal values, such as poverty reduction, rural (or agricultural) development, and good governance. Although it is undeniable that the Rwandan government has made an effort to pursue these goals, it is also clear that it has been fully conscious of the political effects of these measures. In Rwanda, where the rural population still accounts for more than 70% of the total population,[23] rural areas are crucial for territorial control. Active interventionism in the agriculture and rural sectors in post-genocide Rwanda has been closely linked to the RPF's political motivation. The interventionist policy measures can be considered the central piece of Rwanda's state building in the post-genocide period.

6.6 Discussion and Conclusion

This chapter has analyzed the mechanism of economic growth in Rwanda and indicated that contrasting economic policies have been adopted; that is, laissez-faire policies in the modern business and mining sectors and interventionist policies in the agricultural and rural sectors. Whereas these sectors have witnessed rapid growth in their activities, the biggest beneficiaries have been those who have close connections with the ruling party, the RPF.

The contrasting economic policies have coexisted due to political factors. Taking a diplomatic stance to reinforce its relationship with the international community, particularly the US and UK, the country has had practically no other option but to accept the basic line of neo-liberal economic policy, which has been the de facto standard for African countries for a couple of decades. The RPF-led government, however, has made no compromise when it comes to its own power consolidation.

[23]Rwanda used to be one of the most rural-centered country in Africa, as more than 94% of the population lived in rural area in 1990. Although the proportion has continued to decrease since then, it still accounted for 70% in 2016 (Data from World Development Indicators).

Strong interventionist policies have been taken to agricultural and rural sectors, which have been critical for the political control in rural areas of the country.

The examination of Rwanda's three growth drivers has illustrated their close connection with politics. First, the interventionist policies towards agricultural and rural sectors have been intimately connected with the objectives of the RPF's territorial control. The main beneficiaries of these policies have been the core supporters of the party. Second, Rwanda's policies regarding mineral production cannot be separated with its intervention into the Congo war (1998–2002). Although their majority seemed to come from the DRC during and right after the Congo War, it seems that internal production has steadily increased, as the government has actively admitted exploitation. The increase in internal production has been imperative for Rwanda not only for its economic growth but also for deflecting the criticism of smuggling from itself. Third, Rwanda's modern business sector has experienced in the post-genocide period the considerable growth of business groups owned by the RPF and the military. Although the policy used for this sector has been laissez-faire, it is quite clear that these business groups could benefit from the country's political environment, namely RPF-led authoritarianism.

These findings about the mechanism of the rapid growth suggest that sustainability is a challenge for the country. For example, the policy of land consolidation, which prohibits peasants from engaging in risk-hedge behavior in planting a wide range of agricultural products, would cause enormous damage due to unpredictable weather. It would be inevitable for the business sector, in which main companies closely connected to the RPF and/or to the army dominate, to suffer from the negative effects of oligopoly in the near future. The most fundamental question is whether this growth model, established on the premise of the RPF's rule, would be sustainable when the party lost power. The factors enabling the nation's rapid economic growth may hinder it if the political conditions change. Strength and vulnerability of Rwanda's development can be considered two sides of the same coin.

References

Ansoms A (2009) Re-engineering rural society: the visions and ambitions of the Rwandan elite. Afr Aff 108(431):289–309

Balchin N, Gelb S, Kennan J, Hope M, te Velde DW, Williams C (2016) Developing export-based manufacturing in Sub-Saharan Africa. https://www.odi.org/publications/10395-developing-export-based-manufacturing-sub-saharan-africa. Accessed 18 June 2017

Behuria P (2015) Between party capitalism and market reforms: understanding sector differences in Rwanda. J Mod Afr Stud 53(3):415–450

Beswick D (2010) Managing dissent in a post-genocide environment: the challenge of political space in Rwanda. Dev Change 41(2):225–251

Biedermann Z (2016) The case of Rwanda as a developmental state. In: Achtenhagen L, Brundin E (eds) Entrepreneurship and SME management across Africa. Springer, Singapore, pp 139–157

Booth D, Golooba-Mutebi F (2012) Developmental patrimonialism? The case of Rwanda. Afr Aff 111(444):379–403

Cioffo GD, Ansoms A, Murison J (2016) Modernising agriculture through a 'new' green revolution: the limits of the crop intensification programme in Rwanda. Rev Afr Polit Econ 43(148):277–293
Chemouni B (2014) Explaining the design of the Rwandan decentralization: elite vulnerability and the territorial repartition of power. J Eastern Afr Stud 8(2):246–262
Dawson N, Marin A, Sikor T (2016) Green revolution in Sub-Saharan Africa: implications of imposed innovation for the wellbeing of rural smallholders. World Dev 78:204–218
Dorsey M (2000) Violence and power-building in post-genocide Rwanda. In: Doom R, Gorus J (eds) Politics of identity and economics of conflict in the great lakes region. VUB University Press, Brussels, pp 311–348
Gökgür N (2012) Rwanda's ruling party-owned enterprises: do they enhance or impede development. Discussion paper, Institute of Development Policy and Management, University of Antwerp
Government of Rwanda (2002) Poverty reduction strategy paper. Kigali
Harrison G (2016) Rwanda: an agrarian developmental state? Third World Q 37(2):354–370
Hayman R (2008) Rwanda: Milking the cow: creating policy space in spite of aid dependence. In: Whitfield L (ed) The politics of aid: African strategies for dealing with donors. Oxford University Press, Oxford, pp p165–184
Human Rights Watch (1999) Leave none to tell the story: Genocide in Rwanda. New York
Ingelaere B (2010) Peasants, power and ethnicity: a bottom-up perspective on Rwanda's political transition. Afr Aff 109(435):273–292
Jerven M (2013) Poor numbers: how we are misled by African development statistics and what to do about it. Cornel University Press, Ithaca
Khan M (2010) Political settlements and the governance of growth-enhancing institution. Draft paper in research paper series on 'Growth-Enhancing Governance', SOAS Research Online. http://eprints.soas.ac.uk/9968/
Lemarchand R (1970) Rwanda and Burundi. Pall Mall Press, London
Marysse S, Ansoms A, Cassimon D (2006) The aid 'darlings' and 'orphans' of the great lakes region in Africa. Discussion paper 2006.10, Institute of Development Policy and Management
Marysse S, André C (2001) Guerre et pillage économique en République Démocratique du Congo. In: Marysse S, Reyntjens F (eds) L'Afrique des grands lcs, Annuaire 2000–2001. L'Harmattan, Paris, pp 307–332
Ministry of Natural Resources (MINIRENA) (2010) Rwandan mining policy. Kigali
MINIRENA (n.d.) Newsletter: "Unfolding the Rwandan mining sector". Kigali
Newbury C (2012) High modernism at the ground level: the imidugudu policy in Rwanda. In: Straus S, Waldorf L (eds) Remaking Rwanda: state building and human rights after mass violence. University of Wisconsin Press, Madison, pp 223–239
OHCHR (United Nations Human Rights Office of the High Commissioner) (2010) Democratic Republic of the Congo, 1993–2003: Report of the mapping exercise documenting the most serious violations of human rights and international humanitarian law committed within the territory of the Democratic Republic of the Congo between March 1993 and June 2003. United Nations
Peskin V (2008) International justice in Rwanda and the Balkans: virtual trials and the struggle for state cooperation. Cambridge University Press, Cambridge
Porteous T (2008) Britain in Africa. Zed Books, London
Pottier J (2002) Re-imagining Rwanda: conflict, survival and disinformation in the late twentieth century. Cambridge University Press, Cambridge
Pritchard MF (2013) Land, power and peace: tenure formalization, agricultural reform, and livelihood insecurity in rural Rwanda. Land Use Policy 20:186–196
Prunier G (1998) The Rwandan patriotic front. In: Clapham C (ed) African guerrillas. James Curry, Oxford, pp 119–133
Prunier G (1995) The Rwanda crisis: history of a genocide: 1959–1994. Hurst & Company, London
Republic of Rwanda (2000) Rwanda vision 2020. Kigali
Republic of Rwanda (2004) National land policy. Kigali
Republic of Rwanda (2007) Economic development and poverty reduction strategy, 2008–2012. Kigali

Republic of Rwanda (2013) Economic development and poverty reduction strategy II, 2013–2018. Kigali
Reyntjens F (1994) L'Afrique des grands lacs en crise: Rwanda, Burundi, 1988–1994. Karthala, Paris
Reyntjens F (2004) Rwanda, ten years on: from genocide to dictatorship. Afr Aff 103:177–210
Reyntjens F (2009) The great African War: Congo and regional geopolitics, 1996–2006. Cambridge University Press, Cambridge
Reyntjens F (2011) Constructing the truth, dealing with dissent, domesticating the world: governance in post-genocide Rwanda. African Affairs 110(438):1–34
Reyntjens F (2013) Political governance in post-genocide Rwanda. Cambridge University Press, Cambridge
Silva-Leander S (2008) On the danger and necessity of democratisation: trade-offs between short-term stability and long-term peace in post-genocide Rwanda. Third World Q 29(8):1601–1620
Takeuchi S, Marara J (2014) Land tenure security in post-conflict Rwanda. In: Takeuchi S (ed) Confronting land and property problems for peace. Routledge, Oxon, pp 86–108
United Nations (2002) Final report of the panel of experts on the illegal exploitation of natural resources and other forms of wealth of the Democratic Republic of the Congo. (S/2002/1146) (8 Oct 2002)
UNDP (United Nations Development Program) (2007a) Turning vision 2020 into reality: from recovery to sustainable human development, national human development report Rwanda 2007. Kigali
UNDP (2007b) Human development report 2007/2008. New York
Weis T (2016) Ethiopia's vanguard capitalists: How the EPRDF mobilizes for economic development. Foreign Aff, 26 May 2016. https://www.foreignaffairs.com/articles/ethiopia/2016–05-26/ethiopias-vanguard-capitalists. Accessed 9 Aug 2018
Whitfield L, Therkildsen O, Buur L, Kjaer AM (2015) The politics of African industrial policy: a comparative perspective. Cambridge University Press, Cambridge

Chapter 7
Growth Policy and Regional Balance: Developmental State-Building in Myanmar

Toshihiro Kudo and Satoru Kumagai

7.1 Introduction

Until recently, the Myanmar economy was stagnant and poverty-stricken. The major cause was considered to be the military rule that had started in 1962. The economy, however, had grown even under the military government, slowly though. Such a growth had been facilitated by the development strategy made by the military and quasi-military government before the democratic government started in 2016. How could the belated economic development start under the military rule? Will economic development be sustained under the newborn democracy?

Myanmar seems to provide a window into a late-comer developmental state. Although it is unclear whether it is completely appropriate to call this country a developmental state, it is clear that at least the former leader of the military government, Than Shwe, was influenced by Indonesia's Suharto, Malaysia's Mahathir, and other Asian leaders who headed developmental state-building. Although Than Shwe's open-door strategy in the 1990s failed to boost foreign trade and foreign aid and investment flows, the subsequent leaders' policies have had continuity with his strategy. Since the end of the military rule in 2011, the country has experienced faster economic growth in real GDP per capita than Malaysia, Thailand, Indonesia, and India.

This chapter explores similarities and dissimilarities between the experiences of Myanmar and Southeast Asian emerging-economy states to learn about what kind of political and economic regime delivers economic growth and what drives changes in such regimes. It turns out that the economy of Myanmar has recently been grow-

T. Kudo (✉)
National Graduate Institute for Policy Studies (GRIPS), Tokyo, Japan
e-mail: t-kudo@grips.ac.jp

S. Kumagai
Institute of Developing Economies, Japan External Trade Organization (JETRO), Chiba, Japan

Y. Takagi et al. (eds.), *Developmental State Building*, Emerging-Economy State and International Policy Studies, https://doi.org/10.1007/978-981-13-2904-3_7

ing rapidly because of increasing foreign investments which have brought physical and financial capital, advanced technologies, and managerial resources, increasing foreign aids which have brought infrastructure and human resource development, and rapidly increasing import and export. The economy will grow further as its connectivity with the regional and global economies improves. It seems that openness has played an important role in economic development in almost all East Asian countries. These countries increased economic openness for varying reasons. In general, openness is not necessarily associated with democratization as some countries exhibit high levels of economic openness and low levels of democracy. We argue, however, that in the case of Myanmar, changes toward openness and democracy have been connected with each other probably because one of the major reasons for both changes was the economic sanctions imposed by the major Western countries.

Another purpose of this chapter is to explore a way to cope with regional inequality, which could emerge as a major challenge in the near future due to the country's geographic and ethnic diversity. This country has as many as 135 distinct ethnic groups in the country.[1] The largest group, Bamar, accounts for about 70% of the total population, speaks the country's official language, and dominates the government and military.[2] The second largest group is called Shan people, who account for about 10 of the Myanmar population and live mostly in the Shan State occupying a quarter of the Myanmar territory. Some ethnic groups demanded full autonomy or secession from the Union of Myanmar. The ethnic diversity would keep policy makers sensitive to economic inequality among ethnic groups, which would be closely associated with regional inequality or income gap between center and periphery.

The economic center of Myanmar is Yangon, a port city in the southern part of the country, which was developed by British colonialists as the administrative, military, and commercial center. Although it is no longer the capital city, it remains the largest city of the country today. The capital was relocated in November 2005 from Yangon to a newly developed city, Nay Pyi Taw, about 360 km north of Yangon and 270 km south of the second largest city, Mandalay. The relocation was criticized as the military government's economically irrational action. We argue, however, that the relocation may help the country achieve growth with equity to the extent that it contributes to the development of a two-polar economic system with Yangon and Mandalay being economic centers. To explore this possibility, we conduct simulations by using a general-equilibrium, geographic model. The results of simulation analysis indicate that the two-polar system leads to higher growth and less regional inequality than both the unipolar system with Yangon being the single center and the multipolar system with many cities as regional centers.

The rest of this chapter is organized as follows. Section 7.2 describes the features of Myanmar's political and economic regime, its economic geography, and its economic

[1]The Myanmar government officially recognized 135 ethnic groups in the country, although their classification is academically controversial. See the website of Ministry of Hotels and Tourism (http://www.myanmar.gov.mm/ministry/hotel/fact/race.htm, accessed July 29, 2018).

[2]The 2014 Myanmar Population and Housing Census (2014 Myanmar Census) was conducted in March-April 2014 after the thirty-one year interval. However, the ethnic population data is not yet released.

policies in more detail. It highlights particularly the geographical distribution of economic activities and trade and investment policies. Section 7.3 reviews some theories on economic growth and regional balance, together with some examples from abroad. Section 7.4 discusses the strategy for future economic development that pays attention to the coordination of regional interests. Section 7.5 concludes the chapter.

7.2 Development Policies Under Military Rule (1962–2011)

7.2.1 Socialist Regime (1962–1988)

Myanmar shares a long border of 1357 mile with China, 1314 mile with Thailand, 857 mile with India, 152 mile with Bangladesh, and 128 mile with Laos. It also shares coastal waters with Malaysia and Singapore. The eastern borders with China, Laos, and Thailand and the northwestern border with India are mountainous. In the middle part of the country between the mountainous areas, there is a stretch of flatland along the Ayeyarwady (or Irrawaddy) River. The south and north ends of this stretch are Yangon and Mandalay, respectively. They are about 630 km apart. Mandalay is the former royal capital and the second largest city today with the country's highest density of 1880 people per kilometer. The second highest population density is Yangon's 740 people per kilometer. The new capital city, Nay Pyi Taw, is located halfway between Yangon and Mandalay as shown in Fig. 7.1. This figure also shows the distribution of district-level population density. In contrast to the flatland, the mountainous areas have considerably low densities. In Puta-O, Hpapun, and Bawlake districts, there are less than 10 people per kilometer.

While every part of the country accommodates multiple ethnic groups, minority groups tend to inhabit the mountainous areas near the national borders. Some ethnic groups live across the international borders, and some are armed requesting full autonomy. The military rule began in 1962. The military government adopted a socialist regime seeking the "Burmese Way to Socialism." It restricted foreign trade and investment. The national borders were essentially closed for 25 years. The socialist government nationalized major industries and controlled agriculture. State-owned enterprises led industrialization to some extent, but the impact of industrialization was limited because the vast majority of the population was farmers in rural areas.

7.2.2 The SLORC/SPDC Era (1988–2011)

The closed-door policy impoverished the country. In 1988, protests and demonstrations escalated into an anti-government uprising, and the military government responded to it brutally. During the uprising in 1988, the State Law and Order Restora-

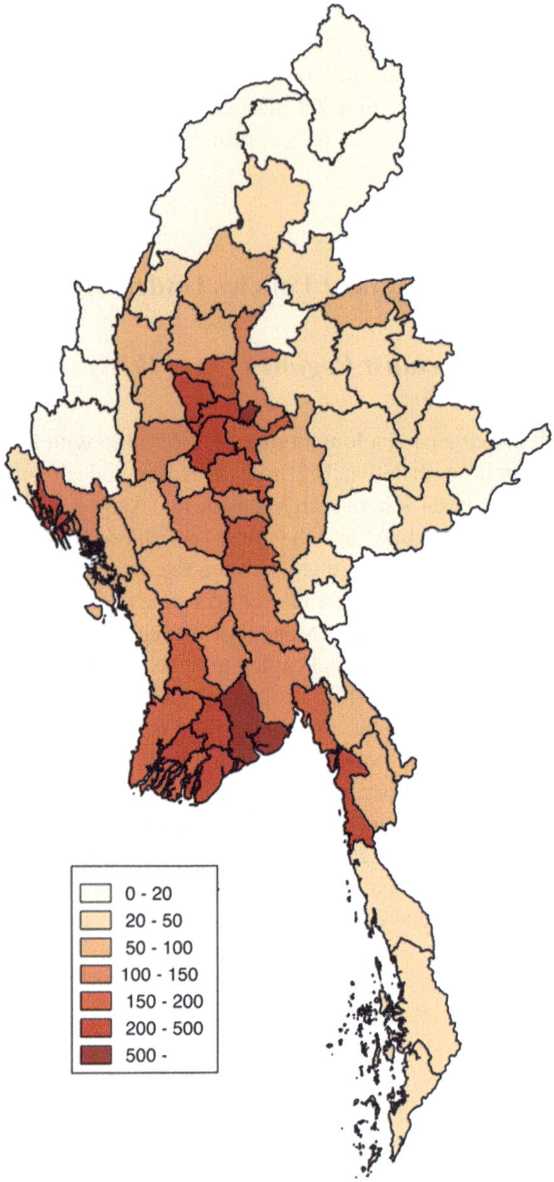

Fig. 7.1 Estimated population density by district (2014, people per square kilometer). *Source* Population and Housing Census of Myanmar (2014)

tion Council (SLORC) came into power and declared martial law. It abolished the socialist regime together with the closed-door and self-sufficiency policy. In 1990, Myanmar had a multiparty election. Although the result was a landslide victory of the National League for Democracy (NLD), it was ignored by the military government, which instead cracked down the democratic force and placed democracy icon

Aung San Suu Kyi under house arrest. These appallingly vicious actions triggered increasingly severe economic sanctions by the Western countries against Myanmar.

From 1992 to 2011, Senior General Than Shwe stayed in power as the head of state and the chairman of SLORC, which was reorganized into the State Peace and Development Council (SPDC) in 1997. Although he was a strong dictator suppressing the free press and abusing human rights, he was also a reformist. He relaxed state control over the economy, privatized state-owned enterprises, legalized cross-border trade with neighboring countries, and started to accept foreign investment. He also promoted the country's participation in the Association of South East Asian Nations (ASEAN).

At least three reasons are conceivable as to why Than Shwe shaped the open door policy and a market-oriented economy. First, it became evident that the closed-door socialist regime would deliver neither economic development nor political stability. Instead it brought poverty, ethnic conflicts, and people's uprising. In other words, learning from failure could be a part of the reason why the military government changed the policy drastically in the early 1990s. Other East Asian countries also learned from failure of adopting the import substitution industrialization strategy before switching to the export-oriented development strategy. Thus, learning from failure seems a common cause for policy change.

Second, Myanmar observed successful economic growth of developmental states of East Asia including South Korea, Taiwan, Singapore and Malaysia. All of them adopted export oriented economic development strategy under authoritarian regime. The Myanmar military must have thought why not they could not do the same thing. It is natural for Myanmar to imitate the same growth strategy as late comer.

Third, while the Western countries imposed economic sanction against Myanmar, Asian countries did not participate in the sanction.[3] On the contrary, open-door policy adopted by Myanmar was welcomed by neighboring countries, China and Thailand in particular. Following the end of the Cold War, China ceased its dual-track foreign policy toward Myanmar in which it endorsed party-to-party relations between the China Communist Party (CCP) and Burma Communist Party (BCP) in addition to state-to-state relations (Than 2003: 194). Beijing established its good and direct relations with Yangon. Thailand also abandoned its secret strategy of using the Karen and other ethnic insurgents deployed alongside the border areas as a buffer against the Myanmar army and the Burma Communist Party (BCP). Chatichai Choonhavan, the Thai Prime Minister from 1988 to 1991, coined the famous phrase: "Change Indochina from a battlefield to a commercial field." The military government in Myanmar then initiated a ceasefire policy with ethnic insurgents, most of whom occupied the border areas, in 1989. Thus, peace was realized in these areas for the first time since the independence of Myanmar. These political and diplomatic changes paved a way for opening and legalizing Myanmar's border trades wits its neighboring countries.

Myanmar joined the Greater Mekong Sub-region (GMS) of economic cooperation in 1992. This was a significant departure from its traditional isolationist foreign

[3]See Kudo (2009) for details.

policy. Following this, Myanmar joined the ASEAN and the Bay of Bengal Initiative for Multi-Sectoral Technical and Economic Cooperation (BIMSTEC) in 1997. It joined the Mekong-Ganga Cooperation in 2000 and the Ayeyarwady-Chao Phraya-Mekong Economic Cooperation Strategy (ACMECS) in 2003.

Nevertheless, the sanctions imposed by the Western countries must have significantly retarded Myanmar's growth. As mentioned earlier, the economic sanctions started as a result of SLORC's anti-democratic actions. It might have been clear to SLORC/SPDC that if the country had been democratized, the Western countries would not have had a reason for continuing the sanctions. Still SLORC/SPDC was reluctant to democratize the country. Former Prime Minister General Khin Nyunt announced the Roadmap to Discipline-flourishing Democracy of seven step processes in 2003. However, he was abruptly overthrown from his position and arrested by the military authorities in 2004.

Than Shwe dreamed "leapfrogging industrialization", but it was never achieved under the international sanctions regime with little FDI and ODA inflow. Moreover, the industrial policy in this era was crude or even irrational. Than Shwe started to establish new state-owned factories and pushed his regional commanders to take initiative in the industrial development of their own regions. As a result, 18 industrial zones in nine Regions and States were established by Myanmar Industrial Development Committee (MIDC). Many of them, however, lacked basic infrastructure, such as sufficient power supply, access to ports, airports, trunk roads, communication facilities, and sewage system. They also lacked skilled labor, large markets, and raw materials. Some of small- and medium-sized factories located in city center were forced by the authorities to move to newly established industrial zones in suburbs where above-mentioned infrastructure and human resources were totally missing.

For example, motorcycle manufacturing was assigned to two industrial zones in Magway Region, a poor region far from both product markets and sources of material supply, because of a regional commander's insistence. All materials were imported from Yunnan Province of China and then transported by land through Mandalay. After motorcycles were "assembled" in Pakokku and/or Yay Nan Chaung Industrial Zones and shipped to Mandalay, the biggest market for motorcycles in Myanmar. Transportation between these industrial zones and Mandalay was redundant and costly, making it impossible for locally made motorcycles to compete with motorcycles smuggled from China. The motorcycle assembly industry might be viable if it had been assigned to the Mandalay Industrial Zone, where skilled workers and machine processing services and parts makers were available. Thus, the crude industrial policy in the Than Shwe era was doomed to failure due to inadequate locational choices and the lack of infrastructure, human resources, and adequate technology.

The relocation of the capital city was implemented also during the Than Shwe era. It was suddenly announced by the government in the middle of 2005. Even the neighboring countries did not know the plan. For example, Thailand was constructing a new embassy building in Yangon. Before the relocation, Pyinmana, or today's Nay Pyi Taw, was a small town along the road connecting Yangon and the old royal city, Mandalay, with poor infrastructure for communication and transportation. It took eight hours by car from Yangon at that time. Government buildings and residential buildings and lifeline facilities for government employees as well as a highway to Yangon were constructed from scratch. The military had already shifted its headquarters to near the new capital, which might be strategically important from the viewpoint of maintaining domestic security as it is a geographic node of the regions. Economically, however, the relocation was criticized as an irrational move. We will return to this point in Sect. 7.4.

7.3 Development Policies in the Liberalization and Democratization Era (2011–2015)

7.3.1 End of Economic Sanctions

Many reforms in both political and economic arenas started in 2011 under the quasi-military government led by President Thein Sein, who was a retired general and former prime minister of Than Shwe's military government. His administration started wide-ranging reforms in both economic and political areas. The international community positively responded to his reforms and lifted or relaxed the economic sanctions against Myanmar. As a result, Myanmar's export increased by 1.6 times from 2010 to 2015, and its import increased by 4.1 times for the same period, turning trade balance into red. FDI's inflow also increased drastically from 1.42 billion US$ in Fiscal Year (FY) 2012 to 9.5 billion US$ in FY 2015. ODA came back to build both physical infrastructures and legal and institutional infrastructures, too (ADB 2012, p 1).

In March 2016, the NLD that was elected by the people in the general elections of November 2015 established a democratic government. The Union Solidarity and Development Party (USDP) headed by Thein Sein transferred its power to NLD in a peaceful and smooth manner. The newly established government is facing many challenges, and we have not yet know how they promote their reforms.

7.3.2 Industrial Policy

Thein Sein's government restructured the industrial policy under the previous regime. For example, the trade liberalization led to increases in motorcycle imports and the termination of the operation of the inefficient motorcycle factories in Magway Region. Recently, a special economic zone (SEZ) began operation on a full scale successfully in Thilawa, only 25 km away from the downtown of Yangon. In early 2011, the Myanmar government and the Japanese government agreed on the development of this special economic zone by intensively constructing the international standard infrastructure such as electricity, water, road and port, in and around Thilawa SEZ by utilizing Japanese ODA. It has successfully attracted substantial FDI and become a leading industrial estate in Myanmar. One successful factor is its proximity to Yangon. Foreign business persons and engineers prefer to live in Yangon. Foreign investors can employ Myanmar management staff and engineers from Yangon. They can utilize Yangon ports and airport for their logistics. Yangon also offers the biggest market in the country. In the future, foreign investors will be able to find and nurture their sub-contractors nearby, since Yangon has the largest industrial cluster in Myanmar.

7.3.3 Economic Development Strategy

In June 2012, President Thein Sein declared that his reform strategy had entered into its second phase with focus on economic development (NLM dated 20 June, 2012).[4] The new strategy consists of four major policies:

(1) sustaining agriculture development toward industrialization and all-round development;
(2) balanced and proportionate development among states and regions in terms of budget and taxation, foreign aid, and foreign and local investment[5];
(3) inclusive growth for entire population, and
(4) compilation of quality and accurate statistics.

Even after the government was replaced by the NLD government headed by State Counsellor, Aung San Suu Kyi, in March 2016, these policies seem to remain high priority. Prioritizing agriculture was reasonable as agriculture accounted for 36% of GDP, a majority of labor, and 25–30% of export earnings. Even in manufacturing production, the food processing industry and other natural-resource-based industries accounted for large shares. It is natural to view agriculture as a source of broad-based development and poverty reduction. Inclusive growth for entire population was a new word for Myanmar, and no one disagreed with the concept. Myanmar's official statistics was obsolete and narrowly covered the country's economic and industrial situations. It was critically important for policy makers to have timely and accurate statistics.

However, these policies are not easy to materialize. In particular, achieving a regional balanced development is a challenge. In reality, this policy objective was inherited to the present government from the earlier regimes. It is considered to be critically important for nationwide peace in a country with ethnic minority insurgencies mostly in mountainous states (not in the proper regions) along the borders with

[4]The government submitted a five-year short-term National Plan (FY2011–FY2015) to the parliament. The Myanmar government set a bold target of raising GDP per capita by 1.7 times in five years, which critics considered to be unrealistic.

[5]Myanmar is administratively composed of seven Regions and seven States. Seven Regions are mainly inhabited by Burmese, the major ethnic group, and seven States are mainly inhabited various ethnic minorities such as Shan, Karen, Kachin, Rakhine, Chin, Mon and so forth. Population density of seven Regions are generally higher than that of seven States.

neighboring countries. The pursuit of economic equality, however, could harm economic growth (Brülhart and Sbergami 2009). As Sonobe (2018) argues in Chap. 7 of the first volume of this series, sustainable economic growth is driven by technological and institutional innovations in a broad sense, including borrowing ideas and practices from abroad, and innovations take place in economic agglomerations (i.e., places where economic activities are concentrated) rather than peripheries and inevitably create winners and losers. It is hard to achieve growth with equity without a special strategy or favorable condition. We discuss such a strategy and a condition in the next section.

7.4 Geography of Industrial Development

7.4.1 Estimated Population and GDP by District

Myanmar has geographical and climatic diversity. At the national level, Myanmar's population density is about 80 people per square kilometer. It is lower than Vietnam (290 people per square kilometer, year 2010) and Thailand (130 people per square kilometer, year 2010). These two countries have population sizes and territory sizes comparable to those of Myanmar. The regional variation in population density, however, is so great in Myanmar that national average does not mean much to the effort to understand the economic geography of this country.

Figure 7.1 shows the distribution of population by district. The central regions along the Ayeyarwady River have generally high population density. Mandalay has the highest density of 1880 people per square kilometer, which is followed by that of Yangon, 740 people per square kilometer. These two areas are the center of population agglomeration. On the other hand, the population of mountainous districts is very low. Some areas, including Puta-O, Hpapun, and Bawlake, have less than 10 people per square kilometer.

The availability of regional GDP data is limited in developing countries. It is possible to estimate the regional distribution of economic activities by using the distribution of nighttime lights because it is well known that the two distributions are closely correlated. Taking the national GDP as given, we estimated the regional distribution of GDP by applying the standard methodology (e.g., Ghosh et al. 2010) to the nighttime light data and land-use data.[6] The results are shown in Fig. 7.2, which compares the distribution of GDP density (that is, GDP per km^2) in Myanmar to those in Thailand and Vietnam.

Thailand has a unipolar or mono-centric spatial distribution of economic activities whereas Vietnam is a two-polar country. The single center of Thailand's economic activities is Bangkok. In Vietnam, Hanoi is the center of the northern part of the country and Ho Chi Minh City is the center of the southern part. In Myanmar,

[6] See also Keola et al (2015).

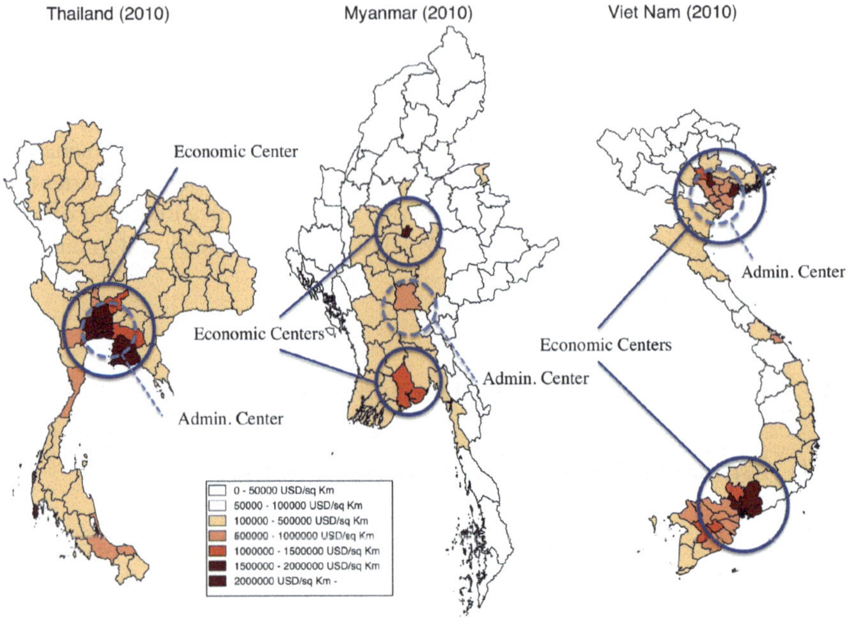

Fig. 7.2 GDP density of Thailand, Myanmar and Vietnam. *Source* Authors based on IDE-GSM dataset

Table 7.1 The primary-to-secondary-city ratios of population and GDP (2010)

	Primary and secondary cities	Population	GDP
Thailand	Bangkok:Chaing Mai	5.3:1	25.4:1
Myanmar	Yangon:Mandalay	4.3:1	4.1:1
Viet Nam	Ho Chi Minh:Hanoi	2.0:1	3.4:1

Source Authors calculation based on IDE-GSM dataset

Yangon, Nay Pyi Taw, and Mandalay have high levels of GDP per capita. Table 7.1 illustrates the extent of the primary-city concentration in Thailand in comparison with Vietnam and Myanmar. Bangkok is five times as large as Chaing Mai, the second largest city, in terms of population but it is 25 times as large in terms of GDP. Thus, Bangkok is nearly five times as rich as Chaing Mai in terms of GDP per capita. The income gap between the primary and secondary cities is much smaller in Vietnam and non-existent in Myanmar according to this table.

Table 7.2 shows the spatial Gini coefficients of selected countries. The spatial Gini coefficient takes a value of 1 if all the activities are concentrated in one region and 0 if n regions have an equal share of economic activities.[7]

[7]Note that it is not proper to compare the spatial gini coefficients for different countries because it is affected by the definition of region. However, in the simulation by IDE-GSM, one tendency is that coefficients increase for all the countries in 2030 compared with 2005, while the coefficient

Table 7.2 Spatial Gini coefficients, 2005

Country	Spatial Gini
Myanmar	0.280
Thailand	0.471
Vietnam	0.402
Cambodia	0.399
Laos	0.266
Malaysia	0.249
Indonesia	0.507
Philippines	0.592
China	0.412
Japan	0.095
Korea	0.068
Taiwan	0.416
India	0.349
Bangladesh	0.150

Source Authors' calculation based on IDE-GSM simulation results

7.4.2 Locations of Industries

Figure 7.3 shows the number of plants by five major industries and by five major industrial areas as of April 1997.[8] The five major industries are food products, textiles, wood, wood products, metal products, motor vehicles and trailers. They accounted for 88% of the total private registered industrial enterprises in the country. The five major industrial areas are Yangon, Mandalay, Bago, Ayeyarwady, and Sagaing. They accounted for about 70% of privately owned plants registered at the Directorate of Industrial Supervision and Inspection (DISI).

From Fig. 7.3, there are several noteworthy findings. First, the food processing industry accounts for 63% of all enterprises in the country. Even among the five major industries, the food processing industry is by far the most dominant industry in terms of the number of enterprises. Second, however, the situation is different in Yangon and Mandalay. For these economic centers, the food processing industry is not as important as in other regions, and other industries are active. Mandalay and its vicinity account for nearly 80% of the nation's textile manufacturers, whose main products are in many cases traditional clothing such as "longyi" (sarongs) and cotton blankets.

for East Asia as a region decreases during the same period. This means that economic activities are expected to agglomerate intra-nationally but disperse inter-nationally.

[8]The data source for this figure is the Directorate of Industrial Supervision and Inspection (DISI) of Ministry of Industry (1), now the Ministry of Industry. The data is outdated, but the industrial structure had changed little in the last decade, and the picture presented here is still relevant to around Year 2010.

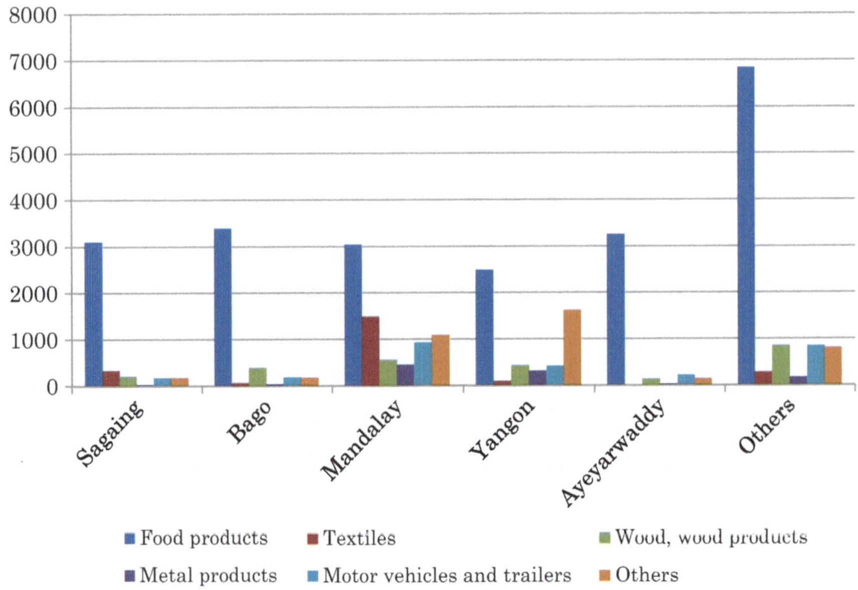

Fig. 7.3 Number of private industries in major regions by business categories, as of April 1997. *Source* DISI, Ministry of Industry (1)

Third, Mandalay has an industrial zone which is a cluster of automobile-related businesses. The majority of automobiles in the country are second-hand models made more than ten years ago. The demand for repair services and spare parts are naturally high. The Mandalay industrial zone satisfies a large part of these demands and also accommodates a number of plants producing electric appliances, agricultural machines and equipment, and other types of machinery. Fourth, Yangon is a more diversified industrial center and has a number of plants in miscellaneous or "other" industries, which include rubber and plastic products, publishing and printing, chemical products, and paper manufacturing.

In this country, enterprises are predominantly small-scale, even though even large-scale enterprises by the standard of Myanmar can be medium- or small-scale by the standard in developed countries.[9] Small-scale enterprises account for 57% of employment in the country, 37% of investment, and 36% of production output. Large-scale enterprises are more capital-intensive than medium- and small-scale enterprises. They account for 24% of employment, 40% of investment, and 37% of output (Kudo 2012). Of large-scale private plants, 43% were located in Yangon and 21% were in

[9]In Myanmar, a plant is considered to be large-scale either (1) if the amount of investment is in excess of 5 million Kyat (about 6250 US dollars), (2) if yearly production output exceeds 10 million Kyat (about 12,500 US dollars), (3) power equipment of 50 horsepower or higher, or (4) if the number of employees exceeds 100.

Mandalay, and 20% in Sagaing, Bago, and Ayeyarwady combined in 2009. In other areas, there were virtually no large-scale plants.

7.4.3 Economic Agglomeration and Growth

Inevitably, economic growth is geographically uneven because some regions have more advantage in doing business than other regions. Workers and firms tend to be attracted to developed regions where they seek higher wages and larger markets. The key word is economic agglomeration, which is either the geographic concentration, as a phenomenon, of economic activities or the place where economic activities agglomerate.

In economic agglomerations, skilled workers are more available, and jobs requiring special skills are more available to workers with such skills than in remote, separated areas; the division of labor among firms is more developed because of large scales of production; and new ideas and useful knowledge are more available because of the scale and diversity of industries, occupations, and expertise. Thus, economic agglomerations tend to have faster economic growth, which would in turn reinforce the advantages of the agglomerations to the extent limited by the negative effect of agglomeration; that is congestion.

Among the enormous literature on economic agglomeration, two studies are particularly noteworthy for the purpose of this chapter. Henderson (2003) examines growth enhancing effects of urban concentration for some 70-80 countries for the period 1960–1990 in 5 year intervals and argues that (1) economic concentration in the country's primary city has pro-growth effects at the beginning, but this effect peaks out once the effect of congestion outweighs the benefits of agglomeration, (2) the extent of urban concentration corresponding to the highest economic growth declines as output per worker increases. Thus, richer economies should have less congested cities. Brülhart and Sbergami (2009) find supportive evidence that the agglomeration of economic activity boosts economic growth until the per capital income of the country reaches about 10,000 US dollars (2006 prices).

These studies suggest that there is a trade-off between economic growth and regional equality in countries with income below a certain threshold level. It is probably not a good idea to emphasize regional equality too strongly when a country is in its early stage of economic development. Fujita and Thiesse (2002, p 391) argue that "even those who stay in the periphery are better off than under dispersion provided that the growth effect triggered by the agglomeration is strong enough." Even residents in the economic periphery benefit from the economic growth of the center as the growth increases the variety of products and services available to them and the demand for migrant labor from the periphery. According to Henderson's (2003) model, a 0.1 standard-deviation increase or decrease (that is, over- or under-concentration) in the share of economic activities in the primary city from the optimal share would reduce the annual per capita GDP growth rate by 0.6%.

An implication of the literature reviewed above for the economic development of Myanmar is that the concentration of productive activities in Yangon is costly not only from the viewpoint of state building and domestic security but also from the congestion viewpoint. The question of what the appropriate level of concentration in Yangon is may translate into a question of whether Myanmar should have unipolar, two-polar, or multipolar economic geography. To address this question, we use a geographical simulation model.

7.4.4 Poverty Situation

Before embarking on, it seems useful to review the poverty situation in the country. Figure 7.4 shows the poverty situation by state or region. The horizontal axis measures the poverty share; that is, the percentage of the national poverty population belonging to the state or region in question. The vertical axis measures the poverty incidence; that is, the percentage of the poor in the population of the state or region in question. The state/region with highest poverty share is Ayeyarwady (18.6%) followed by Mandalay (15.0%) and Rakhine (12.2%). The state/region with highest poverty incidence is Chin (73.3%) followed by Shan East (46.4%) and Rakhine (43.5%).

Different strategies of poverty eradication must be set for states/regions where the poverty incidence is not too high but the poverty share is high (locates lower-right), and for the states/regions the poverty incidence is high while the poverty share is low (locates upper-left). The former case includes Ayeyarwady, Mandalay and Magway, and the latter includes Chin and Shan East. For the former case, industrial development in and around these states to absorb surplus labor force is a possible strategy. For the latter case, re-distribution of income may be a better solution because it is difficult to develop industries in the place where the population is very small or the population density is very low. A specific policy is needed for Rakhine, the state with both high poverty share and high poverty incidence with a complex ethnic situation.

Yangon has a poverty share of 8.1%. If combined with neighboring Ayeyarwady, their poverty share becomes 26.7%. If Yangon takes care of the poverty population in Mandalay and Magway, part of populated and poor Central Dry Zone (CDZ), the share reaches 50.6%, just above half of the national poverty population. This is clearly too much for Yangon alone. A poverty eradication strategy depending on mono-centric economic agglomeration in Yangon has some risk. Considering that Mandalay already has relatively high economic agglomeration, it is more reasonable for Mandalay to take care of its own poverty population as well as the poverty population of neighboring Magway (and Sagaing). For Myanmar, it seems to be desirable to have a two-polar economic structure like Vietnam.

Fortunately, Myanmar is surrounded by more developed economies with high economic growth such as China, Thailand, India, Bangladesh, and Lao PDR. Figure 7.5 shows that some of the eastern border cities of Myanmar have higher levels of income,

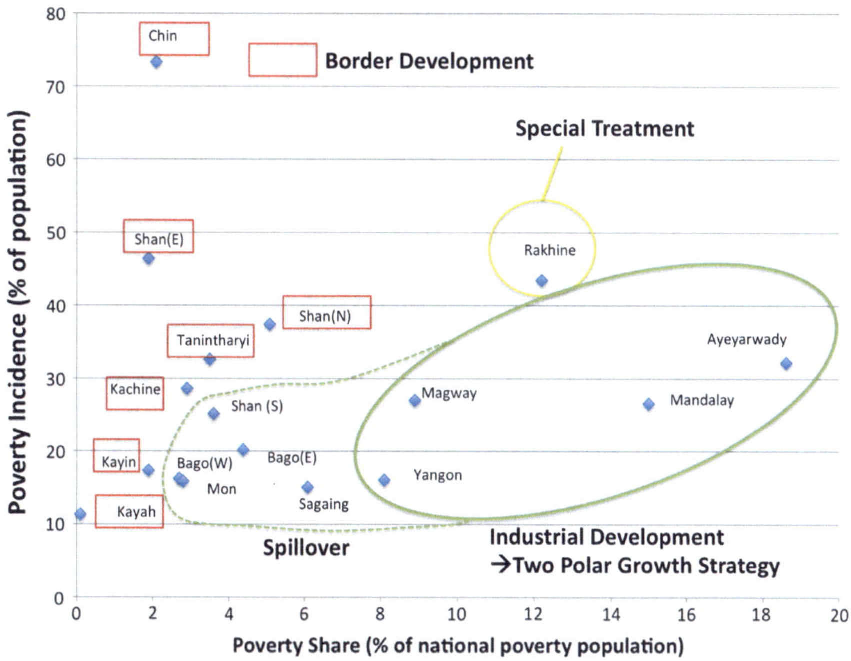

Fig. 7.4 Poverty situation and development strategy by state/region (2010). *Source* Authors based on UNDP (2011)

and this is probably due to closer links with its emerging neighbors like China and Thailand. Conversely, western border cities have thus far failed to develop through links with their neighbors India and Bangladesh. Given experiences of border cities with China and Thailand, there are ways for western border cities to develop via enhanced connectivity with India and Bangladesh.

7.4.5 A Simulation Analysis

The geographical simulation model that we use below is the one developed by the Institute of Developing Economies (IDE-GSM). For details of this simulation model, see Kumagai et al. (2012a, b). We assume that the unipolar development strategy is to double the productivity in Yangon in 2013 exogenously. Similarly, the two-polar development strategy and the multipolar development strategy are respectively assumed to double the productivity in both Yangon and Mandalay and that in 13 regions in 2013 exogenously. The resulting increases in GDP of the country and changes in the geographical distribution of income over time from 2005 to 2030 are compared with those increases and changes under the baseline case, in which productivity grows at a rate projected based on the past data.

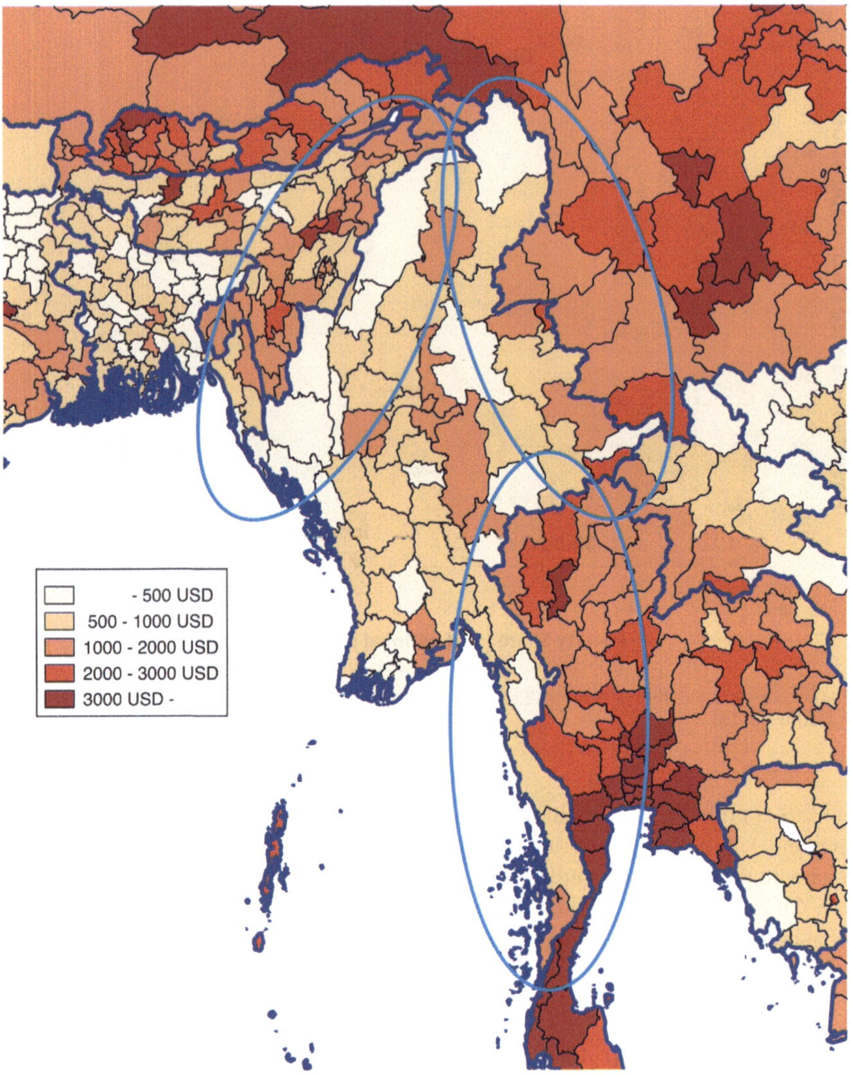

Fig. 7.5 GDP per capita for Myanmar and its neighbors (2010). *Source* Authors based on IDE-GSM dataset

The results of simulations are summarized in Tables 7.3 and 7.4. In the baseline case, the national GDP will be 3.51 in 2030 where GDP in 2005 is normalized to 1 (Table 7.3); Yangon's share of the national GDP, which is 19% in 2005, will increase to 26% in 2030 (Table 7.4); and Mandalay's GDP share, which is 5% in 2005, will also increase to 11%. Under the unipolar strategy, GDP per capita in 2030 will be 4.93 (Table 7.3); Yangon's GDP share will be 55% (Table 7.4); Mandalay's share will be 6%.

Table 7.3 Projected GDP per capita in 2030 by development strategy (National GDP per capita in 2005 = 1)

	(1) National	(2) Seven regions	(3) Seven states	(4) Ratio (2)/(3)
Actual GDP per capita in 2005	1.00	1.03	0.92	1.12
Projected GDP per capita in 2030				
No strategy (simple projection)	3.51	3.63	3.15	1.15
Unipolar strategy	4.93	5.47	3.14	1.74
Two-polar strategy	5.06	5.64	3.15	1.79
Multipolar strategy	4.10	4.35	3.33	1.30
Two-polar + connectivity strategy	5.17	5.75	3.26	1.76

Source Authors' calculation based on IDE-GSM simulation results

Table 7.4 GDP share of Yangon and Mandalay by development strategy

	GDP share of Yangon	GDP share of Mandalay
Actual GDP share in 2005	0.19	0.05
Projected GDP share in 2030		
No strategy (simple projection)	0.26	0.11
Unipolar strategy	0.55	0.06
Two-polar strategy	0.43	0.19
Multipolar strategy	0.30	0.13
Two-polar + connectivity strategy	0.42	0.19

Source Authors' calculation based on IDE-GSM simulation results

In the two-polar and multipolar cases, we assume that the costs of increasing the productivity parameter in a region are proportional to its population. The costs of doubling the productivity of a city with a population of five million are assumed to be five times larger than that of a city with a population of one million. We also assume that available public development expenditure is fixed and that if the number of development poles in increased, the expenditure would be shared by all growth pole regions proportional to their population. The increase in productivity of each region is assumed to be proportional to the development expenditure per capita. Suppose, for example, that there is a budget to double the productivity of the first polar region with a population of four million. If this budget is shared with the second polar region that has a population of one million, then the per capita development expenditure under the two-polar strategy becomes 4 million/(4 million + 1 million) = 0.8 compared with that under the unipolar strategy, and the resulting increase in productivity would be 80%.

Under this set of assumptions, the two-polar strategy would decrease Yangon's GDP share in 2030 from 55 to 43% and increase Mandalay's share from 6 to 19%, compared with the unipolar case, as shown in Table 7.4. The growth performance is slightly higher under the two-polar strategy than under the unipolar strategy, as shown in Table 7.3, which is consistent with the theoretical prediction based on the consideration of congestion diseconomies. The impact of the two-polar strategy in comparison with the unipolar strategy varies across regions and states. The two-polar strategy is also superior to the multipolar strategy in terms of GDP per capita growth in the country as a whole, which is consistent with both the theoretical prediction based on the agglomeration economy consideration and the intuition that scarce development resources should not be spread over too many regions.

Table 7.3 shows not only the national GDP but also the GDP per capita gap between the seven regions and seven states in Myanmar by development strategy. As mentioned earlier, seven regions are located near to the urban center and they are richer than seven states, although there were no big gap between them as of 2005. The gap considerably widens with a uni-polar and two-polar, while it a little bit widens with a multipolar strategy. The policy objective of growth with equity and inclusive growth will not be achieved with these strategies, particularly a uni- and two-polar ones

Here, we examine a complementary strategy, that is, improvement of connectivity in the border regions. In the improved connectivity scenario, we combined: (a) the customs facilitation measures at some national borders in 2015 and 2020, (b) upgrading the roads connecting these borders through major cities in Myanmar in 2015 and 2020, and (c) connecting Dawei and Kyaukphyu Ports with India and Europe in 2020. To incorporate (a) into the model, the time and money costs are reduced to the half at the following national borders: Tachileik-Mae Sai, Mongla-Daluo, Tamu-Moreh Kanchanaburi-Dawei, Kawthoung-Ranong, Myawaddy-Mae Sot, and Muse-Ruilli.

For (b), we assume the seven routes are assumed to be upgraded.[10] All of these routes can be developed as economic corridors in Myanmar. For (c), Dawei and Kyaukphyu ports are assumed to be connected with Kolkata, Chennai, and Rotterdam in 2020, and the so-called transit trade through Myanmar is assumed to become possible for Thailand and China.

As shown in Table 7.3, the simulation predicts that improvement in connectivity will increase GDP per capita of the country. Compared with the two-polar case without improved connectivity, the two-polar plus improved connectivity will raise GDP per capita in the seven regions without reducing GDP per capita in the seven states, thus narrowing the income gap between center and periphery. Table 7.4 shows the GDP share of Yangon is slightly reduced by enhancement of connectivity.

[10]The seven routes are (1) Yangon-Mandalay (2015); (2) Muse-Mandalay-Kyaukphyu (2015, then upgrading the route to Sittwe in 2020); (3) Myawaddy-Paan-Yangon (2015, then upgrading the route to Pathein in 2020); (4) Yangon-Mandalay second link on the western side of Bago Yoma (2020), (5) Mandalay-Monywa-Tamu (2020); (6) Mongla-Kyinetone-Tachileik (2020); and (7) Yangon-Mawlamyine-Dawei-Myeik-Kawthoung.

7.4.6 Possible Industrial Development in Periphery

Another important component of inclusive development is industrial development in periphery. Because of the limitation of space, we do not discuss industries in the periphery in general, but we focus on border industry, which is defined as industry located in border areas of two or more countries (Kudo and Kuroiwa 2009).

The development of border industries is influenced by two major factors: complementary resource endowment and cross-border infrastructure. In the Greater Mekong Sub-region (GMS), Thailand and China are relatively advanced economies. Vietnam is entering the advanced stage of economic development. Cambodia, Lao PDR and Myanmar (CLM) are still in their rudimentary development stage. Border areas between relatively advanced and less developed economies offer their respective complementary location advantages. CLM economies provide migrant labor, while Thailand offers major inputs (materials, parts, and components), technology, and capital. In border areas, complementary resources which exist side by side across borders are combined to produce cost-competitive products. Of course, some of these resources must be transported across the border to be utilized for production in border towns. Thus, a certain degree of cross-border mobility of productive inputs is required for the birth and growth of a border industry.

The second factor is cross-border infrastructure. In East Asia, service link costs, or the cost of connecting remotely located production blocks, have been reduced substantially. This has made it possible for multinational corporations (MNCs) to aggressively exploit wage differences between developed and less developed economies in East Asia and to develop extensive production and distribution networks in the region. Myanmar, however, has yet to be integrated into such networks in spite of its abundant, reasonably well-educated, and low-waged labor force. Underdeveloped infrastructure, notably in transportation and electricity, hinders the country from participating in production and distribution networks. In labor-intensive export sectors, high transport costs could easily wipe out the labor cost advantage.

Border industries could offer a solution to such problems. The required infrastructure investment to connect its border areas with the existing infrastructure in neighboring countries may be far smaller than that for developing a nationwide infrastructure system. For example, firms in Myanmar-Thai border areas could gain access to the well-developed Laemg Chabang Port via well-connected road networks in Thailand. In border areas, firms would also have better access to utility services such as electricity, water, and telecommunications that are provided by more advanced neighboring countries. Thus, firms located in border areas can enjoy all the benefits of lower service link costs (lower transport and communication costs) and more reliable and cheaper utility services (especially electricity) as well as lower labor costs.

In this way, border industry could grow and complement the two-polar growth strategy. The border areas in Myanmar could have industrial development and become frontiers and conduits that absorb the dynamism of emerging countries in the neighborhood, such as Thailand and China at present and India and Bangladesh.

7.5 Concluding Remarks

The Myanmar armed forces headed by Senior General Than Shwe enjoyed perhaps the longest stretch of military rule for 1988–2011 in the modern world. This authoritarian regime obviously sought socio-economic development of the country. Against the image of being a strong and merciless dictator, Than Shwe was actually the introducer of open-door and market-oriented economy to Myanmar after the quarter-century-long "Burmese Way to Socialism". He knew that many Asian countries had long been under authoritarian regime and still developed their economies rapidly. He apparently aimed to establish a so-called developmental state, following some Asian examples of Indonesia's Suharto, Malaysia's Mahathir and so forth.

However, he failed to realize a meaningful economic growth for another quarter-century under the international sanctions, and was finally replaced by a democratic government headed by Nobel Peace Laurate Aung San Suu Kyi after a five-year transition period of quasi-military government headed by President Thein Sein, Retired General. Than Shwe failed to attract Foreign Direct Investment (FDI) and Official Development Assistance (ODA), which was definitely necessary for the Myanmar economy to join global and regional production and distribution networks, mainly due to international sanctions. All his efforts to establish a developmental state made the military politically survive, but failed to realize economic growth. Myanmar was gradually impoverished, and the military government could not stop the exodus of people to the neighboring countries.

Having faced a prolonged stagnation, Than Shwe reverted to a planning-oriented economic policy in order to achieve so-called "leapfrogging industrialization". He started to construct new state-owned factories. At the same time, Than Shwe pushed his regional commanders, de facto powerful lords, to develop their own regions. Under the military rule, it was imperative for regional commanders to show "development" in their regions to climb up ranks in the military. Then, they established industrial estates all over the country regardless location disadvantages and high transaction costs.

After the quarter-century military rule, President Thein Sein assumed power in March 2011, and inaugurated wide-ranging reforms in both economic and political areas. The international community positively responded to his reforms and lifted and/or relaxed sanctions against the Myanmar economy. FDI started to inflow to Myanmar and ODA was resumed to build physical, legal, and institutional infrastructures. Given its rich endowment of resources including a diligent and literate population of fifty one million and rich investment opportunities in a range of sectors, the prospects for Myanmar's high growth is bright.

Entering a democratic era, regional balance has become not only an economic objective but also a political agenda. It is politically imperative for the Myanmar government to reduce the income gap among regions and states and between urban and rural areas. It is also necessary for the government to reduce the incidence of poverty that varies substantially by regions and states. More importantly, this political agenda was again put at the top priority by the NLD government.

Nevertheless, how to achieve "high" and "balanced" growth is a challenge when we try to see long-term development in Myanmar. We proposed a two-polar growth strategy with border development, an idea that solves two issues with one approach. This strategy would help Myanmar strike a good balance between high growth and low regional inequality by avoiding the excessive dispersion and concentration of economic activities. The World Bank (2009, p 1) conducted an across-the-board study on spatial aspects of economic development, and the main message of the study was that "Economic growth will be unbalanced, but development still can be inclusive". The same can be applied to Myanmar.

References

Asian Development Bank (ADB) (2012) Myanmar in transition: opportunities and challenges, Aug 2012. Available at https://www.adb.org/sites/default/files/publication/29942/myanmar-transition.pdf. Accessed on 21 Oct 2012

Brülhart M, Sbergami F (2009) Agglomeration and growth: cross-country evidence. J Urban Econ 65:48–63

Population and Housing Census of Myanmar (2014) The 2014 Myanmar population and housing census, The Union Report: Census Report, vol 2

Fujita M, Thiesse JF (2002) Economics of agglomeration: cities, industrial location, and regional growth. Cambridge University Press, Cambridge

Ghosh T, Powell RL, Elvidge CD, Baugh KE, Sutton PC, Sharolyn A (2010) Shedding light on the global distribution of economic activity. Open Geogr J 3:148–161

Henderson V (2003) The urbanization process and economic growth: the so-what question. J Econ Growth 8(1):47–71

Keola S, Andersson M, Hall O (2015) Monitoring economic development from space: using night-time light and land cover data to measure economic growth. World Dev 66:322–334

Kudo T (2009) Border area development in the GMS: turning the periphery into the centre of growth. ERIA Discussion Paper Series, Jakarta

Kudo T (2012) Explanatory note on data sources 4: Myanmar. In: Kuroiwa I (ed) Economic integration and the location of industries: the case of less developed East Asian countries. Palgrave Macmillan, London

Kudo T, Kuroiwa I (2009) Border industry in Myanmar: plugging into production networks through border industry. In: Kuroiwa (ed) Plugging into production networks: industrialization strategy in less developed Southeast Asian countries. Institute of Southeast Asian Studies, Singapore

Kumagai S, Hayakawa K, Isono I, Keola S, Tsubota K (2012a) Geographical simulation analysis for logistics enhancement in Asia. IDE Discussion Paper No. 369

Kumagai S, Keola S, Kudo T (2012b) Myanmar economy viewed at night. Policy Rev Myanmar Econ (4) IDE-JETRO

New Light of Myanmar (NLM) English newspaper in Myanmar

Sonobe T (2018) Middle-Income trap in emerging states. In T Shiraishi and T Sonobe (eds) Emerging states and economies: their origins, drivers, and challenges ahead. Springer

Than TMM (2003) Myanmar and China: a special relationship? Southeast Asian Aff 2003(1):189–210

UNDP (2011) Integrated household living conditions survey in Myanmar (2009–2010): poverty profile. UNDP, Yangon

World Bank (2009) Reshaping economic geography. World Development Report. World Bank, Washington

Chapter 8
Devolution and Local Development in Emerging States: The Case of Kenya

Tomoya Matsumoto

8.1 Introduction

It is often the case that top-down approaches for public policy decisions by the central government for local development do not satisfy local needs because of differences in local preference and endowment, combined with the limited knowledge of central planners about local needs (Easterly 2008). Also, due to multiple administrative layers and low motivation of public officers, implementation of such policies is inefficient in their delivery and unsatisfactory in quality and often ends up wasting resources. Moreover, public funds are often used by leaders to attract political support from local residents in exchange for public investment in their locality. This tendency has been observed by some existing studies in countries with a powerful authoritarian government and poorly educated citizens (Hodler and Raschky 2014).

It seems natural for local residents to demand devolution, which brings political decision-making and funds for public services closer to residents in a country with multiple groups of people with different interests. Moreover, devolution movements are often seen more in emerging economies where regional gaps are expanding and more people are politically enlightened and raising their voices. Consequently, local residents and firms demand improvement of public services more aggressively in emerging countries than in poorer countries (Bahl and Ichimura 2008).

In Kenya, the president had been having strong political influence in public resource allocation since its independence (Burgess et al. 2015; Briggs 2014). Since the 1992 election, the multiparty political system has been embraced in this country, and the president's influence has weakened, at least in the case of allocation of road infrastructure investment funds (Burgess et al. 2015). There have also been two significant changes, toward devolution, in Kenyan politics in the last two decades. First, Kenya established the Constituency Development Fund (CDF) in 2003, which is an

T. Matsumoto (✉)
Otaru University of Commerce, 3-5-21 Midori, Otaru 047-8501, Japan
e-mail: tmatsumoto@res.otaru-uc.ac.jp

Y. Takagi et al. (eds.), *Developmental State Building*, Emerging-Economy State and International Policy Studies, https://doi.org/10.1007/978-981-13-2904-3_8

annual budgetary allocation by the central government to each of the constituencies of the Members of Parliament (MP) and whose distribution is exclusively rule-based, so that political powers would not distort the allocation. Whereas the CDF is an innovative tool to bring funds and their expenditure decisions to people at the grassroots level to maximize their welfare, there are also concerns regarding the utilization of the funds because the constituencies largely vary in physical or geographic characteristics, as well as the degree of residents' solidarity and capacity (Kimenyi 2005). We do not know much about its welfare impact since there is no study that systematically examines the bottom-up policies, planned and implemented by different localities, although there are several case studies targeting a specific constituency to examine the role of the CDF projects and their consequences (Auya and Oino 2013; Simiyu et al. 2014; Katamei et al. 2015; Ngiri and Nyaribo 2016).

Second, a new constitution, promulgated in 2010, aimed at division of political power and established a system of devolved government with 47 lower-level county governments. For the implementation, the 47 new county governors were elected in 2013 and became responsible for the provision of some public services, such as pre-primary education, healthcare service delivery, and local road infrastructure. At the same time, county governments gained the right to collect some types of taxes by themselves, such as property and entertainment taxes as county revenue, in addition to the equitable share allocated by the national government. County governments have enhanced discretion to utilize public funds for their local residents. Its impact on subnational economic performance has not been systematically analyzed.

With devolution in Kenya, the question arises as to which change enhances local economic development and improves the use of public funds by local authorities. Because of the paucity of accurate measurements of economic performance at the subnational level, it has been difficult to examine the effect of political and financial devolution on regional economic development and consequently no study addresses this issue.

Nonetheless, progress of remote sensing techniques, in the last decade, using image information from outer space via satellites enables us to accurately measure an indicator that represents subnational economic activities. Since seminal works (Henderson et al. 2012; Chen and Nordhaus 2011; Doll et al. 2006) show high correlation between nighttime light intensities, extracted from satellite images of earth, and the GDP of corresponding regions or countries, more and more studies have been using satellite nighttime light images to analyze various socioeconomic issues with subnational economic indicators (Amavilah 2017; Alesina et al. 2016; Asher and Novosad 2017; Mellander et al. 2015; Hodler and Raschky 2014).

Given the availability of a long-term (1992–2016) subnational economic performance indicator based on nighttime light intensity, Kenya provides a unique quasi-experimental environment to make a comparison in economic performance across regions, before and after a political system change and/or a change in leadership. To our best knowledge, there are no rigorous empirical studies on local development examining its determinants during the devolution era of an emerging state in Africa. This chapter is an attempt to fill the gap.

Using satellite image information on nighttime light intensity as a measurement of subnational economic performance, we investigate factors affecting the economic development at the subnational level in Kenya from 1992 to 2016. We find that (i) ethnicities of counties are not correlated with their average annual growth rate of nighttime light intensity from 1992 to 2012. However, (ii) during the recent 5-year period from 2012 to 2016 that largely overlapped with the ruling period of President Uhuru Kenyatta, whose ethnicity is Kikuyu, the Kikuyu dominant counties, which have more than a 50% share of the Kikuyu population, show much higher growth rates of nighttime light intensity than other counties; (iii) county governors' characteristics, such as their educational attainment or experiences as a member of parliament, are not associated with the county growth rates; (iv) proportions of secondary school graduates and urban population of counties are positively associated with the county growth rate of nighttime light intensity.

The remainder of this chapter is organized as follows. Section 8.2 briefly describes the background of Kenyan politics since its independence and the current devolution process. The data used in this chapter and their descriptive statistics are presented in Sect. 8.3. Section 8.4 presents the empirical strategies and the regression results. Section 8.5 interprets and discusses the empirical findings, followed by the conclusion in Sect. 8.6.

8.2 Kenya's Political Background

Kenya has experienced significant political system reforms from a highly centralized autocracy to a decentralized democracy. The national assembly and presidential elections under the multiparty system were first held in 1992, responding to local and foreign pressures to introduce democracy. Until then, the government of Kenya was organized under the one-party system and the president had monopolized the authority of personnel matters to hire and dismiss government administrators, as well as cabinet ministers, and hence, exerted a tremendous influence on the allocation of public resources (Burgess et al. 2015). During the last 15 years since Mwai Kibaki won the presidential election in 2002, after the 24-year rule of Daniel Arap Moi, significant policy reforms toward decentralization have been implemented.

First, the Constituency Development Fund (CDF) was established through the Constituency Development Fund Act of 2003, which is an annual budgetary allocation by the central government to each of the constituencies of the Members of Parliament (MP) and whose distribution is exclusively rule-based, so that political powers would not distort the allocation. Moreover, utilization of the fund is largely at the discretion of the constituents, although there are some restrictions in its use to ensure transparency and accountability (Kimenyi 2005). The CDF is a devolved fund involving redistribution of resources and authority through legislation, although it currently accounts for only 2.5% of the national government budget.

Second, the new constitution was promulgated in 2010 and altered the division of political power and established a system of a devolved government and 47 lower-level county governments. The new president and 47 new county governors were elected under the new constitution in March 2013. The county governments became responsible for the provision of certain types of public services, such as pre-primary education, health service delivery, and the construction and maintenance of local roads on behalf of the national government. At the same time, counties had rights to impose several types of taxes, such as property and entertainment taxes to earn their revenue, in addition to the equitable share allocated by the national government. Kenya's Commission on Revenue Allocation (CRA) recommends to the National Assembly the basis for equitable division of the revenue of the national government among the county governments, as well as the amount of money that each county government receives. Currently, 15% of the national government revenue is allocated as the equitable share. Since the political system reform, the county governments have had enhanced discretion to utilize public funds for their local residents through the devolution movement. Thus, it is expected that the decentralized system enhances the role of local leaders and also strengthens the influence of local residents on regional development.

8.3 Data

We examine economic performance indicators at the subnational level and their relationships with ethnic composition, population size of the regions, and local political leaders' and residents' characteristics to see the influence of those factors on local economic development. Table 8.1 shows summary statistics of the variables used in the analyses. The sources and constructions are described in the following subsections.

8.3.1 Nighttime Luminosity

We need longitudinal subnational-level indicators, representing economic performance of each area, to examine the difference in economic development across areas within a country. As the unit of subnational area of Kenya, we choose counties that are new administrative units, envisioned by the 2010 Constitution of Kenya and organized by the general election in 2013 as the units of devolved government. There are 47 counties whose boundaries are based on the legal districts as on 1992. We utilize satellite image data on nighttime luminosity and construct the nighttime light intensity, by county, to represent economic performance of the area from 1992 to 2016, based on areas surrounded by the current county borders as the county units.

The nighttime luminosity has been increasingly used by researchers who need subnational economic performance data, in particular, for developing countries like Sub-Saharan African countries where there are no accurate economic performance data at the subnational level (Jerven 2013).

Table 8.1 Summary statistics

Variables	(1)	(2)
	Mean	Std. dev.
Annual growth rate of nighttime light intensity		
From 1992 to 2016	0.030	0.015
From 1992 to 2002	0.014	0.044
From 2002 to 2012	0.053	0.032
From 2012 to 2016	0.016	0.025
Ethnic diversity (1 − Herfindahl index)	0.299	0.220
Major ethnicity dummy		
1 if Kikuyu county	0.149	0.360
1 if Kalenjin county	0.149	0.360
1 if Kamba county	0.064	0.247
1 if Luhya county	0.085	0.282
1 if Luo county	0.085	0.282
Annual growth rate of population size		
From 1990 to 2015	0.029	0.013
From 1990 to 2000	0.027	0.009
From 2000 to 2010	0.031	0.016
From 2010 to 2015	0.015	0.008
Characteristics of county residents from 2009 census		
Proportion of urban residents	0.258	0.203
Proportion of university graduates	0.010	0.011
Proportion of residents with tertiary level education	0.036	0.029
Proportion of residents with secondary level education	0.188	0.098
Characteristics of county governors elected in the 2013 election		
Years of experience as a MP	1.851	3.323
Age of the county governor	47.725	8.426
1 if the county governor has a Ph.D.	0.128	0.337
Observations	47	

Following existing studies (Alesina et al. 2016; Asher and Novosad 2017), we use satellite image data on nighttime light as a proxy for subnational economic performance. We use the geo-referenced nighttime luminosity images processed by NASA, the National Oceanic and Atmospheric Administration (NOAA), and the Department of Defense of the U.S. More precisely, we use (i) data from 1992, 2002, and 2012 of Version 4 DMSP-OLS Nighttime Lights Time Series, which compile annual average luminosity of cloud-free nighttime light[1] and (ii) the nighttime light luminosity images, which are similar but more recent, provided by the Suomi National Polar-orbiting Partnership (NPP) satellite, equipped with the Visible Infrared Imaging Radiometer Suite (VIIRS), a new sensor that collects imagery and radiometric measurements with a higher resolution of both spatial units and lighting levels than the satellites used to construct Version 4 DMSP-OLS Nighttime Lights Time Series. We used the processed, cloud-free, and moonlight-free data for year 2012 and 2016, released by NASA scientists.[2]

The selected years for the analyses: 1992, 2002, 2012, and 2016, are close to the general election years and, in particular, 2002 and 2012 are the years when political regimes changed.[3] In the analyses, the annual growth rates of the average nighttime luminosity index over grids surrounded by a county border are defined as the county's growth rates of nighttime light intensity and used as the dependent variable. Figure 8.1 shows the spatial distribution of nighttime light luminosity by grid in different time periods. Lighter yellow cells correspond to much brighter areas. The thresholds of color changes are set at 0, 5, 10, 15, ..., and 95th percentile values of the 2012 nighttime luminosity data.

8.3.2 *Ethnic Groups and Settlement Patterns*

Kenya has more than forty ethnic groups. The largest ethnic group is Kikuyu and accounts for 17% of the total population, according to the Population and Housing Census of Kenya, conducted in 2009. It is followed by Luhya, Kalenjin, Luo, and Kamba, whose population shares are 14, 13, 12, and 10%, respectively. The ethnic composition has been more or less stable since the independence of the country in 1963 (Burgess et al. 2015) and the settlement patterns have been maintained without any significant change, except in highly populated towns and cities. Figure 8.2 shows the spatial settlement patterns of major ethnic groups.[4] We use the 1989 Population Census information on ethnic composition by district to construct ethnicity-related variables at the county level, namely, major ethnicity dummies, and the Herfindahl

[1]These data are downloaded from the following URL. https://ngdc.noaa.gov/eog/dmsp/downloadV4composites.html.

[2]NASA Earth Observatory images by Joshua Stevens, using Suomi NPP VIIRS data from Miguel Román, NASA's Goddard Space Flight Center are downloaded from the following URL. https://www.nasa.gov/feature/goddard/2017/new-night-lights-maps-open-up-possible-real-timeapplications.

[3]It was not in 2012 but in 2013 that the general election was held and selected President Uhuru Kenyatta. Since the nighttime luminosity data with high resolution are consistently available in 2012 and 2016 but not in 2013, we use the 2012 data, instead.

[4]The data source of the geo-referenced settlement patterns is the GeoEPR 2014 (Vogt et al. 2015).

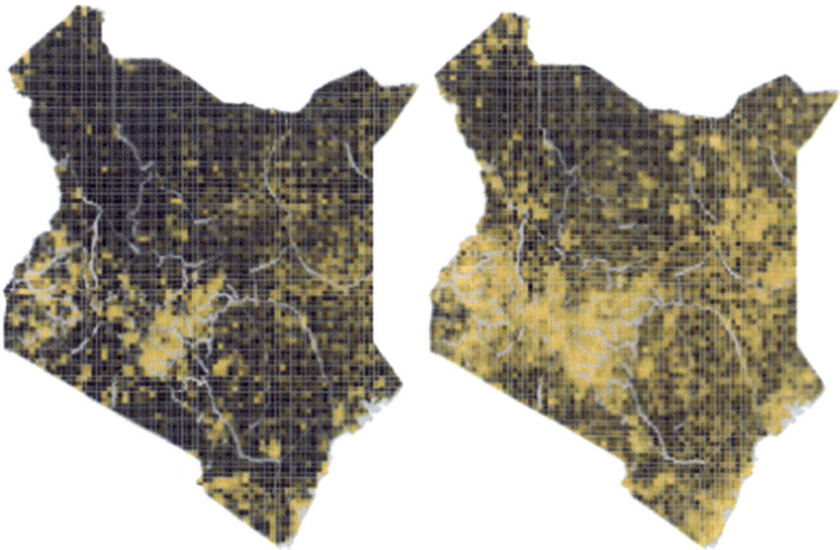

Fig. 8.1 Nighttime light intensity at grid level. *Note* Lighter yellow cells correspond to brighter areas at night. The thresholds of color changes are set at 0, 5, 10, …, and 95 percentile values at the grid level in the 2012 nighttime luminosity data

index of ethnic composition, indicating the degree of concentration of ethnicity in counties.[5]

Five major ethnicity dummies, Kikuyu, Luhya, Kalenjin, Kamba, and Luo, are constructed, each of which takes the value of 1 if the corresponding ethnic group's population share in 1989 at the county level is more than 50% and 0 otherwise. There are 7 Kikuyu counties whose corresponding ethnicity dummy takes 1, 7 Kalenjin counties, 3 Kamba counties, 4 Luhya counties, and 4 Luo counties. There are 22 counties that do not have a dominant ethnic group or another minor ethnic group is dominant.

8.3.3 Population Data

We use Gridded Population of World (GPW) series to obtain the sub-national level of population for the relevant years (GPWv3, GPWv4). Version 3 of GPW covers the population estimates at the grid

[5]There are 41 districts in the 1989 Population Census and 6 of them are subdivided, which correspond to the current 47 counties. We assign the same values of those ethnicity-related variables constructed from the 1989 census data to the counties that were a part of the subdivided former districts. In the analyses, we use (1 − Herfindahl index) as the measurement of ethnic diversity.

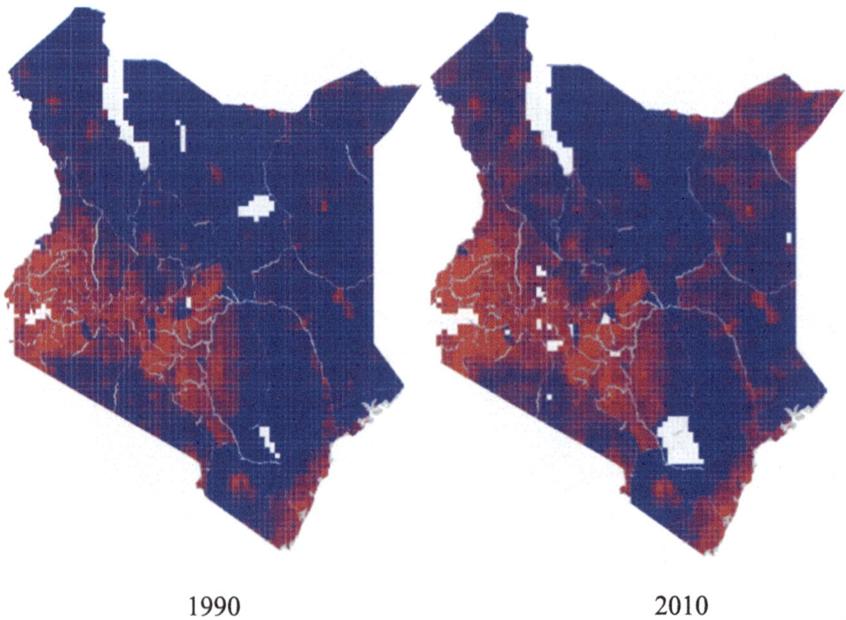

Fig. 8.2 Population density at grid level. *Note* Deeper red cells correspond to more populated areas. The thresholds of color changes are set at 0, 10, 20, …, and 90 percentile values at the grid level in the 2010 population data

cell resolution of 2.5 arc-minutes (about 5 km at equator) for the years 1990, 1995, and 2000, and version 4 covers those at the grid cell resolution of 30 arc-seconds (about 1 km at equator) for the period after 2000, 2005, 2010, and 2015. Since we use the nighttime luminosity data in 1992, 2002, 2012, and 2016 and there is no population estimates for the corresponding years, we interpolate the population estimates for the relevant years by assuming constant growth rates between the 5-year periods for which the GPW estimates are available. We use this data to control for the population size of counties in the regressions. Figure 8.3 shows the spatial distribution of population over grid cells. Deeper red cells correspond to more populated areas. The thresholds of color changes are at 0, 10, 20, …, and 90th percentile values of the 2015 population data.

8.3.4 *Characteristics of Governors and Residents of Counties*

The governors elected in the general election in 2013 under the devolved government have had greater authority on use of public funds for county residents than local leaders in the past. It is interesting to see the association between the governors' characteristics and the growth rates of counties. We collected, online, the attributes

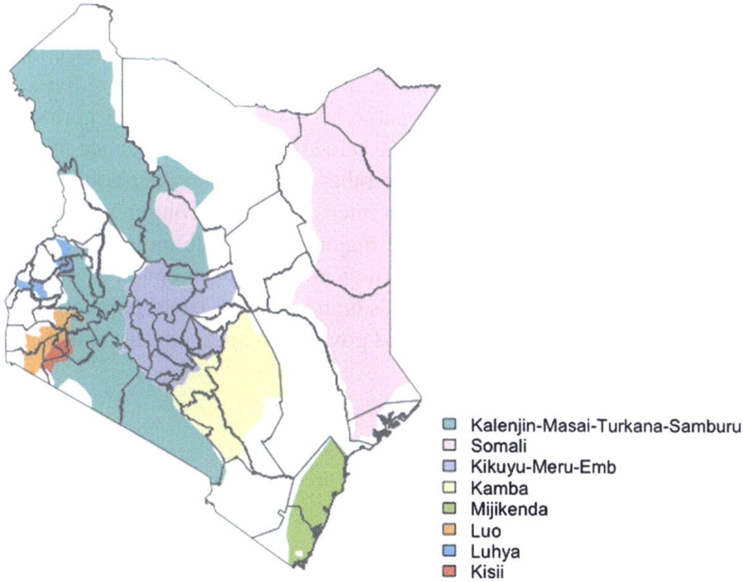

Fig. 8.3 Spatial settlement patterns of ethnic groups

of the elected governors in 2013, such as age, number of years of experience as a Member of Parliament (MP), whether the governor was born and brought up in the same county, whether he/she is M.A. or Ph.D. holder, whether he/she studied abroad, rates of votes obtained in the election, political party, and coalition to which the party belongs.

In addition to the governors' attributes, under the decentralized democracy, local residents' voices may have a stronger influence on the usage of public resources than those under the centralized system. Thus, there is a possibility that the human capital of the county could affect the usage of public resources and, hence, regional development. We use proportion of secondary school, tertiary school, or university graduates among adult residents in a county as its human capital indicator. This information on educational attainment of county residents is taken from the Population and Housing Census of 2009.

8.4 Empirical Specification

In order to examine factors affecting the economic growth rates at the subnational level, we run simple growth regressions of nighttime light intensity, as follows:

$$GR_{i,t} \equiv \frac{\ln y_{i,t+\tau} - \ln y_{i,t}}{\tau} = \alpha \ln y_{i,t} + x'_{i,t}\beta + \varepsilon_{i,t},$$

where $GR_{i,t}$ is the average annual growth rate of nighttime light intensity (NLI) at the i-th county from year t to $t + \tau$, which is calculated as the difference in natural log of nighttime light intensity indicator y_i between year t and $t + \tau$ divided by τ. As explanatory variables, we use the natural log of y at the initial period, whose coefficient α is expected to take a negative value if there is convergence in the nighttime light intensity across counties or, in other words, if brighter counties at night show lower growth rate of nighttime light intensity; $x_{i,t}$ is a column vector of county characteristics, including a series of the major ethnicity dummies, one minus the Herfindahl index of ethnic composition (indicating a measurement of ethnic diversity), whether the county is the president's home county, size of population, human capital indicators of county residents, and governors' ages, educational attainment, and years of experience as an MP.[6]

8.5 Results

8.5.1 Growth of Nighttime Light Intensity and Ethnicity

Table 8.2 presents the regression results of average annual growth rates of nighttime light intensity of 47 counties on 5 major ethnicity dummies in order to examine the difference in the growth rates across counties with specific major ethnic groups. Among 47 counties, there are 7 Kikuyu, 7 Kalenjin, 3 Kamba, 4 Luhya, and 4 Luo dominant counties. The other 22 counties, where there is no single ethnic group whose share is more than 50%, are considered as the reference group in the regression. Column 1 shows the regression result using the average growth rates of the entire sample period (1992–2016) as the dependent variable. It suggests that the average annual growth rates of Kikuyu dominant counties are higher by 1.4 percentage points than the other 22 counties, which do not have a dominant ethnic group, while those of counties with another major ethnic group show insignificant difference.

Column 2 presents the results of the same regression using the limited sample period corresponding to President Moi's era under the multiparty system (December 1992–December 2002). There seem to be no major ethnicity dummies that are significantly associated with the growth rates. Similarly, Column 3 presents the results using the sample period largely overlapping with President Kibaki's era (December 2002–April 2013) and shows no significant effects of ethnicity dummies either. The coefficient of the constant term indicates the average annual growth rate of nighttime light intensity in the reference group, comprising the 22 counties with no dominant ethnic group, and shows low (or almost zero) growth rate in the Moi period (Column 2) and high (or about 5%) annual growth rate in the Kibaki period (Column 3), which is consistent with the national level GDP trend between the eras of these two pres-

[6]We also used the governor's political affiliation, the rate of votes obtained in the election, a dummy indicating whether he/she was originally from the county or not as covariates in the regression analyses. But none of them are statistically significant.

Table 8.2 Average annual growth rate of nighttime light intensity and major ethnicity of county

Variables	(1)	(2)	(3)	(4)
	Whole sample period	Moi (Kalenjin) period	Kibaki (Kikuyu) period	Kenyatta (Kikuyu) period
	1992–2016	1992–2002	2002–2012	2012–2016
1 if Kikuyu county [7]	0.0140**	0.00261	0.0165	0.0361***
	(0.00640)	(0.0195)	(0.0141)	(0.00951)
1 if Kalenjin county [7]	0.00854	0.0253	−0.00482	−2.94e-05
	(0.00640)	(0.0195)	(0.0141)	(0.00951)
1 if Kamba county [3]	0.0136	0.00969	0.0218	0.00315
	(0.00907)	(0.0277)	(0.0200)	(0.0135)
1 if Luhya county [4]	0.00254	0.0222	−0.0134	−0.00669
	(0.00801)	(0.0245)	(0.0177)	(0.0119)
1 if Luo county [4]	−0.00730	−0.0113	−0.00869	0.00617
	(0.00801)	(0.0245)	(0.0177)	(0.0119)
Constant	0.0266***	0.00807	0.0517***	0.0101**
	(0.00314)	(0.00960)	(0.00693)	(0.00467)
Observations	47	47	47	47
R-squared	0.182	0.065	0.093	0.29

Standard errors in parentheses. $^{***}p < 0.01$, $^{**}p < 0.05$, $^{*}p < 0.1$
Coefficients are obtained by running simple OLS of the average annual growth rate of nighttime light intensity at county level on a set of major ethnicity dummies. A major ethnicity dummy (Kikuyu, Kalenjin, Kamba, Luhya, or Luo) takes 1 if the corresponding ethnic group's population share in 1989 at the county is more than 50% and 0 otherwise. Numbers in brackets indicate the number of counties which take 1 for the corresponding major ethnicity dummy

idents. Column 4 presents the result using the sample period that largely overlaps with President Uhuru Kenyatta's era and shows significantly higher average growth rates in Kikuyu dominant counties by 3.6 percentage points than those in reference group counties, which have no dominant ethnic groups. To summarize, there is no systematic correlation between the growth rate of nighttime light intensity and major ethnicity of counties until 2012, while Kikuyu dominant counties show higher growth rates since then. It is well-known that President Kenyatta (April 2013–) is from one of the Kikuyu dominant counties, namely, Kiambu and served as the Member of Parliament for the Gatundu South constituency in the county from 2002 to 2013, until he became the President.

Table 8.3 shows the results of the regressions, like those given in Table 8.1, with some additional controls. The initial level of the nighttime light intensity is controlled for and the presidents' home county dummies are included. The results reconfirm that there is no correlation between the growth rate and ethnicity until 2012, while Kikuyu dominant counties show higher growth rates since 2012. Interestingly, Kiambu county, which is the home county of President Uhuru Kenyatta shows the highest annual average growth rate of nighttime light intensity from 2012 to 2016, among all the 47 counties. In addition, the coefficient of the natural log of the NLI in the initial period is positive and significant in this period (2012–2016), which indicates divergence rather than convergence in the nighttime light intensity across counties or, in other words, higher growth rate in the counties where the initial level of the nighttime light intensity is higher. This suggests that the inequality across counties may increase during the period.

We add two more explanatory variables, a measurement of ethnic diversity of counties and the natural log of population size of counties during the initial period in the regressions in Table 8.4. The coefficient estimates of the major ethnicity dummies and the home county dummies of presidents are similar to those in the previous regressions that excluded the two variables. The initial population size is positively associated with NLI growth in the latest 5-year period. Populated counties became brighter than less populated counties in this period. This finding also suggests the divergence in nighttime light intensity and escalation of inequality across counties under the process of devolution. The coefficient estimate of the measurement of ethnic diversity of counties is positive and significant in the regression of the NLI growth during the Moi period (1992–2002), indicating that higher growth rate of the nighttime light intensity during this period is observed in more ethnically diversified counties. As comprehensively reviewed in Alesina and La Ferrara (2005), ethnic diversity can have both positive and negative effects on the economic performance of societies. On the one hand, ethnic diversity can bring about a variety of ideas, abilities, experiences, and cultures, which can be a source of innovation and creativity and lead to higher economic performance. On the other hand, it can make collective actions among residents difficult due to differences in preferences, leading to high costs of provision and maintenance of public goods, and can also create tension between ethnic groups due to conflict of interests and lower economic performance. Although it seems interesting to explore the reason for the positive coefficient of the ethnic diversity index on NLI growth during President Moi's period, further investigation is required for the identification of factors.

8.5.2 Growth of Nighttime Light Intensity Under the New Constitution

The new constitution, promulgated in 2010, established a system of a devolved government with 47 lower-level county governments and, subsequently, new county governors were elected in 2013 who were responsible for the county's governance and development. Expecting stronger influence of local governments and residents on local economic development after the dramatic political system change in Kenya, we examine county-level factors associated with the growth of nighttime light intensity. For this period, some additional information, such as the proportion of urban residents, and several indicators of the educational level of county residents, namely, proportions of university graduates, residents with tertiary level education, and resi-

Table 8.3 Average annual growth rate of nighttime light intensity (NLI) and major ethnicity of county

Variables	(1)	(2)	(3)	(4)
	Whole sample period	Moi (Kalenjin) period	Kibaki (Kikuyu) period	Kenyatta (Kikuyu) period
	1992–2016	1992–2002	2002–2012	2012–2016
ln (NLI in the initial year)	−0.00182	−0.00855	−0.00881	0.00669**
	(0.00260)	(0.00786)	(0.00539)	(0.00278)
1 if Kikuyu county	0.0115	0.00584	0.00969	0.0210**
	(0.00766)	(0.0232)	(0.0163)	(0.00814)
1 if Kalenjin county	0.00704	0.0162	−0.0133	0.00822
	(0.00773)	(0.0234)	(0.0160)	(0.00805)
1 if Kamba county	0.0133	0.00794	0.0208	0.00241
	(0.00946)	(0.0286)	(0.0202)	(0.0101)
1 if Luhya county	5.68e-05	0.0105	−0.0235	0.00185
	(0.00906)	(0.0274)	(0.0189)	(0.00960)
1 if Luo county	−0.00897	−0.0191	−0.0178	0.0136
	(0.00867)	(0.0262)	(0.0187)	(0.00944)
1 if Balingo (Moi's home county)	−0.00424	−0.00542	0.00350	−0.0130
	(0.0166)	(0.0502)	(0.0355)	(0.0177)
1 if Nyeri (Kibaki's home county)	0.00437	−0.0199	0.0257	0.0130
	(0.0168)	(0.0509)	(0.0360)	(0.0180)
1 if Kiambu (Kenyatta's home county)	0.0123	−0.00622	0.0198	0.0865***
	(0.0176)	(0.0532)	(0.0372)	(0.0186)
Constant	0.0402**	0.0724	0.119***	−0.0441*
	(0.0198)	(0.0599)	(0.0415)	(0.0228)
Observations	47	47	47	47
R-squared	0.201	0.102	0.165	0.641

Standard errors in parentheses. ***$p < 0.01$, **$p < 0.05$, *$p < 0.1$

Coefficients are obtained by running simple OLS of the average annual growth rate of nighttime light intensity at county level on the log of the initial level of the NLI level, a set of major ethnicity dummies and the president's home county dummies. A major ethnicity dummy (Kikuyu, Kalenjin, Kamba, Luhya, or Luo) takes 1 if the corresponding ethnic group's population share in 1989 at the county is more than 50% and 0 otherwise

Table 8.4 Average annual growth rate of nighttime light intensity (NLI) and major ethnicity of county

Variables	(1)	(2)	(3)	(4)
	Whole sample period	Moi (Kalenjin) period	Kibaki (Kikuyu) period	Kenyatta (Kikuyu) period
	1992–2016	1992–2002	2002–2012	2012–2016
ln (NLI in the initial year)	−0.00312	−0.0136*	−0.00623	0.00289
	(0.00268)	(0.00780)	(0.00598)	(0.00279)
1 if Kikuyu county	0.00817	−0.00434	0.0120	0.0167**
	(0.00784)	(0.0229)	(0.0168)	(0.00751)
1 if Kalenjin county	0.00291	−0.00266	−0.00543	0.000449
	(0.00809)	(0.0236)	(0.0172)	(0.00784)
1 if Kamba county	0.0108	0.0101	0.0147	−0.00137
	(0.0101)	(0.0293)	(0.0214)	(0.00951)
1 if Luhya county	−0.00495	−0.00139	−0.0224	−0.00895
	(0.00963)	(0.0281)	(0.0204)	(0.00938)
1 if Luo county	−0.0128	−0.0242	−0.0195	0.00451
	(0.00928)	(0.0270)	(0.0202)	(0.00916)
1 if Balingo (Moi's home county)	−0.000278	0.0133	−0.00437	−0.00671
	(0.0166)	(0.0484)	(0.0360)	(0.0163)
1 if Nyeri (Kibaki's home county)	0.00842	0.00453	0.0139	0.0198
	(0.0170)	(0.0496)	(0.0368)	(0.0167)
1 if Kiambu (Kenyatta's home county)	0.0136	0.0143	0.00436	0.0880***
	(0.0180)	(0.0525)	(0.0387)	(0.0174)
Ethnic diversity (1 − Herfindahl index)	0.0132	0.0756**	−0.0369	0.0164
	(0.0114)	(0.0332)	(0.0257)	(0.0112)
ln (population in the initial year)	0.00435	0.00632	0.00317	0.0107***
	(0.00394)	(0.0115)	(0.00864)	(0.00393)
Constant	−0.00940	0.00770	0.0684	−0.162***
	(0.0506)	(0.148)	(0.110)	(0.0495)
Observations	47	47	47	47
R-squared	0.263	0.232	0.212	0.721

Standard errors in parentheses. ***$p < 0.01$, **$p < 0.05$, *$p < 0.1$

Coefficients are obtained by running simple OLS of the average annual growth rate of nighttime light intensity at county level on the log of the initial level of the NLI level, a set of major ethnicity dummies and the president's home county dummies. A major ethnicity dummy (Kikuyu, Kalenjin, Kamba, Luhya, or Luo) takes 1 if the corresponding ethnic group's population share in 1989 at the county is more than 50% and 0 otherwise dents with secondary level education, were taken from the Census in 2009, conducted by the Kenya National Bureau of Statistics.

Table 8.5 shows the results of the regressions of the NLI growth from 2012 to 2016 on the county-level factors. We reconfirm that there is no sign of convergence of nighttime light intensity across counties during this period in the regressions with the additional controls. If there is a sign of convergence, the coefficient of initial level of nighttime intensity should be negative. The coefficient in Column 1, however, is positive and significant. Although the coefficients are insignificant in Columns 2–4, controls that are highly and positively correlated with nighttime light intensity at the initial level, such as proportion of urban residents in 2009, are included in the regressions. Moreover, the proportion of urban residents in 2009 is positively associated with the growth rate of nighttime light intensity between 2012 and 2016. These results imply that brighter counties at night in the initial year (or 2012) became even much brighter over the years.

The variables representing residents' average educational level above secondary school are all positive and significant, indicating strong positive correlation between conventional human capital indicators and economic development of counties. Although this finding is interesting, these simple regressions do not reveal the mechanism. There seem to be many different scenarios, which can account for the positive correlation. For instance, as often shown in studies of cross-country growth regression, human capital can be an important source of innovation and, hence, high economic growth can be realized in places with educated residents. It is also possible that residents' education may be a good proxy of competence or capacity of local government officers and those in areas with more educated residents may be able to implement government projects more successfully and use public resources more efficiently, which may lead to higher economic growth. Alternatively, educated residents may show different preferences for usage of public resources and have significant influence under a decentralized political system, which indirectly affects the economic performance of the areas. Further investigation is necessary to identify the mechanism behind this.

Table 8.6 shows the results of similar regressions with additional controls on the ethnic diversity indicator, the natural log of population size during the initial period (2012), and the governors' characteristics. The coefficients of the variables used in the previous regressions, presented in Table 8.5, have the same signs and suggest the robustness of the correlations of those variables with the NLI growth, although some of them change their statistical significance slightly. The changes in the significance levels are possibly due to multicollinearity of the initial population size with the educational variables, since they are strongly and positively correlated. In terms of the coefficients of the newly added governors' attributes, none of them are statistically significant, although we expected that governors' leadership, motivation, and capability would influence the economic performance of counties under the decentralized system. This may reflect the inability of the governors' attributes, used in these analyses, to capture their leadership, motivation, and capability or may indicate very weak influence of the governors on local development, even under the new constitution.

Table 8.5 Average annual growth rate of nighttime light intensity from 2012 to 2016

Variables	(1)	(2)	(3)	(4)
	Model 1	Model 2	Model 3	Model 4
ln (NLI in 2012)	0.00525**	−0.000568	9.61e-05	0.00280
	(0.00233)	(0.00194)	(0.00197)	(0.00217)
1 if Kikuyu county	0.0208***	0.0216***	0.0198***	0.0135**
	(0.00700)	(0.00509)	(0.00527)	(0.00580)
1 if Kiambu (Kenyatta's home county)	0.0868***	0.0740***	0.0705***	0.0715***
	(0.0177)	(0.0129)	(0.0131)	(0.0125)
Proportion of urban residents		0.0333**	0.0297*	0.0229
		(0.0146)	(0.0161)	(0.0153)
Proportion of university graduates		0.613**		
		(0.251)		
Proportion of residents with tertiary level education			0.253**	
			(0.107)	
Proportion of residents with secondary level education				0.0904***
				(0.0295)
Constant	−0.0302	0.000747	−0.00638	−0.0326*
	(0.0181)	(0.0140)	(0.0143)	(0.0172)
Observations	47	47	47	47
R-squared	0.608	0.806	0.804	0.819

Standard errors in parentheses. ***$p < 0.01$, **$p < 0.05$, *$p < 0.1$
Proportions of urban residents, university graduates, residents with tertiary level education, residents with secondary level education are constructed based on Census in 2009

8.6 Conclusions

Kenya has experienced a significant change in its political system from a highly centralized autocracy to decentralized democracy during the last twenty years. This chapter examines local economic development and its determinants during the period of devolution. Using satellite images of nighttime light intensity as a measurement of subnational economic performance, we investigate factors affecting the economic development in Kenya from 1992 to 2016.

First, we find that there is no systematic relationship between major ethnicity of counties and their growth rates of nighttime light intensity until 2012. This seems consistent with the finding from the analysis of public resource allocation from 1963

Table 8.6 Average annual growth rate of nighttime light intensity from 2012 to 2016

Variables	(1)	(2)	(3)	(4)
	Model 1	Model 2	Model 3	Model 4
ln (NLI in 2012)	0.00390	−0.000799	−0.000365	0.00171
	(0.00239)	(0.00205)	(0.00205)	(0.00230)
1 if Kikuyu county	0.0198***	0.0214***	0.0197***	0.0148**
	(0.00673)	(0.00521)	(0.00534)	(0.00610)
1 if Kiambu (Kenyatta's home county)	0.0859***	0.0688***	0.0666***	0.0684***
	(0.0173)	(0.0138)	(0.0139)	(0.0135)
Proportion of urban residents		0.0410**	0.0374**	0.0315*
		(0.0152)	(0.0165)	(0.0167)
Proportion of university graduates		0.465		
		(0.286)		
Proportion of residents with tertiary level education			0.200	
			(0.120)	
Proportion of residents with secondary level education				0.0736**
				(0.0355)
Ethnic diversity (1 − Herfindahl Index)	0.0125	−0.0103	−0.0104	−0.00961
	(0.0103)	(0.00909)	(0.00908)	(0.00874)
ln (population in 2012)	0.0102***	0.00547*	0.00585*	0.00503
	(0.00372)	(0.00314)	(0.00305)	(0.00307)
Years of experience of the county governor as a MP	−0.000415	−0.000114	−0.000220	−0.000255
	(0.000718)	(0.000561)	(0.000554)	(0.000543)
Age of the county governor	0.000142	8.69e-05	7.15e-05	1.72e-07
	(0.000283)	(0.000223)	(0.000225)	(0.000227)
1 if the county governor has Ph.D.	0.00136	−0.000420	−0.00120	−0.00113
	(0.00671)	(0.00522)	(0.00519)	(0.00509)
Constant	−0.169***	−0.0732	−0.0822*	−0.0884**
	(0.0488)	(0.0440)	(0.0418)	(0.0397)
Observations	47	47	47	47
R-squared	0.700	0.831	0.832	0.838

Standard errors in parentheses. $^{***}p < 0.01$, $^{**}p < 0.05$, $^{*}p < 0.1$
Proportions of urban residents, university graduates, residents with tertiary level education, residents with secondary level education are constructed based on Census in 2009

to 2011 in Kenya by Burgess et al. (2015), which argues that ethnic favoritism disappears after the country has embraced a multiparty democratic system. The second finding of this paper, however, shows a somewhat different scenario during the latest five-year period (2012–2016) that overlaps with the ruling period of President Uhuru Kenyatta (whose ethnicity is Kikuyu). Kikuyu counties show much higher growth rates than other counties, and moreover Kiambu county, which is the home county of the president, shows the highest growth rate among 47 counties. We do not claim that this is the evidence of revival of ethnic favoritism, since the result shows only correlation rather than causation, and there are many possible confounding factors that create spurious correlation between ethnicity and economic performance.

Third, personal characteristics of county governors, such as their educational attainment and past experiences as an MP, are not associated with the growth rate. Fourth, human capital indicators of the counties, measured by proportions of secondary school graduates or university graduates, are positively associated with the growth rate of nighttime light intensity in recent periods.

This study simply shows empirical findings regarding factors associated with subnational economic growth by examining, as a case study, an emerging country in Africa that has experienced high economic growth and a significant change in its political system over the last two decades. Although the findings seem interesting, it does not analyze the mechanisms behind the results, which remains for future research.

References

Alesina A, Michalopoulos S, Papaioannou E (2016) Ethnic inequality. J Polit Econ 124(2):428–488

Alesina A, La Ferrara E (2005) Ethnic diversity and economic performance. J Econ Lit 43(3):762–800

Amavilah VH (2017) Artificial nighttime lights and the "real" well-being of nations: 'measuring economic growth from outer space' and welfare from right here on Earth. MPRA Paper 79744, University Library of Munich, Germany, June 2017

Asher S, Novosad P (2017) Politics and local economic growth: evidence from India. Am Econ J: Appl Econ 9(1):229–273

Auya S, Oino P (2013) The role of constituency development fund in rural development: experiences from North Mugirango constituency, Kenya. Int J Sci Res 2(6):306–312

Bahl RW, Ichimura S (2008) Decentralization policies in Asian development. World Scientific, Singapore

Briggs RC (2014) Aiding and abetting: project aid and ethnic politics in Kenya. World Dev 64:194–205

Burgess R, Jedwab R, Miguel E, Morjaria A (2015) The value of democracy: evidence from road building in Kenya. Am Econ Rev 105(6):1817–1851

Center for International Earth Science Information Network CIESIN Columbia University and Centro Internacional de Agricultura Tropical CIAT (2005) Gridded population of the world, version 3 (GPWV3): population density grid. http://dx.doi.org/10.7927/H4ST7MRB. Accessed 25 May 2017

Center for International Earth Science Information Network CIESIN Columbia University and Centro Internacional de Agricultura Tropical CIAT (2016) Gridded population of the world, version 4 (GPWV4): population density grid. https://doi.org/10.7927/H4X63JVC. Accessed 2 June 2017

Chen X, Nordhaus WD (2011) Using luminosity data as a proxy for economic statistics. Proc Natl Acad Sci 108(21):8589–8594

Doll CNH, Muller JP, Morley JG (2006) Mapping regional economic activity from nighttime light satellite imagery. Ecol Econ 57(1):75–92

Easterly W (2008) Institutions: top down or bottom up? MPRA Paper 39137, University Library of Munich, Germany, May 2008

Henderson JV, Storeygard A, Weil DN (2012) Measuring economic growth from outer space. Am Econ Rev 102(2):994–1028

Hodler R, Raschky PA (2014) Regional favoritism. Quart J Econ 129(2):995–1033

Jerven M (2013) Poor numbers: how we are misled by African development statistics and what to do about it. Cornell University Press, Ithaca

Katamei JM, Omwono GA Sr, Wanza L (2015) Challenges of strategy implementation on performance of constituency development fund projects in Kenya: a case of Marakwet west constituency. Int J Bus Adm 6(3):48–62

Kimenyi MS (2005) Efficiency and efficacy of Kenya's constituency development fund: theory and evidence. Economics Working Papers

Mellander C, Jose L, Stolarick K, Matheson Z (2015) Night-time light data: a good proxy measure for economic activity? PLoS ONE 10(10):e0139779. https://doi.org/10.1371/journal.pone.0139779

Ngiri DM, Nyaribo WM (2016) Effect of constituency development fund on socio-economic development in Mbeere South constituency, Kenya. Int J Econ Finance Manag Sci 4(4):182–189

Simiyu RS, Mweru JN, Omete FI (2014) The effects of decentralized funding on socio-economic welfare of Kenyans: a case study of the constituency development fund in Kimilili (Kenya). Eur J Acc Auditing Finance Res 2(7):31–51

Vogt M, Bormann NC, Rüegger S, Cederman LE, Hunziker P, Girardin L (2015) Integrating data on ethnicity, geography, and conflict: the ethnic power relations data set family. J Conflict Resolut 59(7):1327–1342

Chapter 9
Conclusion

Tetsushi Sonobe

9.1 Introduction

The previous chapters created fascinating narratives of state building and economic development in Asia and Africa. As the editors promised in Chap. 1, this volume has accounted for important roles of human agency in developmental state building. It has also tried to avoid *post hoc ergo propter hoc* reasoning about success stories from East Asia by accounting for the ongoing processes of developmental state formation in three low-income countries, Myanmar, Ethiopia, and Rwanda. Paying attention to human agency in diverse cases has made the narratives more interesting than otherwise.

This short chapter aims to digest the major points of the narratives. The volume covers Japan, where Johnson (1982) framed the concept of developmental state, and the three tigers, namely, Korea, Taiwan, and Singapore. These countries are now high-income countries. The volume also includes cases of Malaysia and Indonesia, which are upper-middle-income developmental states, and the three low-income countries mentioned above. These case studies present considerable similarities and dissimilarities. I would like to advance hypotheses that explain them more or less coherently.

Chapter 1 argues that "the traditional developmental state approach suffers from its tendency to pay too much attention to political institutions and its relative neglect of the private sector." The chapter introduces the legendary pioneer of the Bangladesh garment industry which has grown into the world second largest producer in four decades after starting from scratch. The subsequent chapters, however, do not devote many pages to discuss the private sector. I would like to give due attention to the private sector in a discussion about how developmental state studies will develop in the future.

T. Sonobe (✉)
National Graduate Institute for Policy Studies (GRIPS), Tokyo, Japan
e-mail: sonobete@grips.ac.jp

Y. Takagi et al. (eds.), *Developmental State Building*, Emerging-Economy State and International Policy Studies, https://doi.org/10.1007/978-981-13-2904-3_9

9.2 What Have We Learned?

As Chap. 1 argues, "the development state should be defined in terms of the shared intentions among the leaders and policymakers" rather than "a specific set of policy instruments."[1] That is, a developmental state is a low- or middle-income country with leaders and policymakers sharing a strong will to deliver rapid economic growth so that the country catches up with high-income countries.

The narratives in the previous chapters indicate that this objective of the leaders and policymakers is associated with two major constraints. One is the world/regional order. A deviation from it might invite severe punishment from leading nations and other members of the international community, as Myanmar under military rule experienced (see Chap. 7). Protectionist trade policies and the use of foreign technologies without paying loyalties, not to mention the invasion of a foreign country and abuse of human rights, could be regarded as deviations. Another major constraint is the need to manage conflicts. As Chap. 3 emphasizes, economic development inevitably creates winners and losers, which is a source of conflict. Without managing conflict, rapid economic growth will cease before the dream of entering the ranks of high-income countries is realized.

Within the constraint of world/regional order, a developmental state has usually three ways to make its economy grow, even though it may exceptionally have four ways. The first is to increase its human capital through education and its physical capital through saving and investment. The second is to mitigate market failure problems arising from various types of transaction costs, external economies and diseconomies, and monopoly. The third is to obtain goods and services, technologies, and expertise at lower costs than producing and acquiring them domestically, that is, gains from trade and investment.

There are three implications induced from these ways to achieve economic growth. First, the success of a developmental state requires a rational and effective strategy for development. Hence, the degree of success depends much on the state capacity, which is the second implication. Third, the degree of success depends also on the managerial and technical capabilities of the private sector because the economy consists in large part of activities of private firms, farms, and individuals.

Exceptionally, there is a fourth way to boost the economy. It is the so-called infant industry protection. This is exceptional because most industries are not infant industries in the true sense, which will by definition grow into internationally competitive industries if temporarily protected from foreign competition. Most industries fail to grow even if they are protected for many years because they lack either technical expertise or proactive workers who are willing to acquire new skills.

The forth way worked in Japan in the 1950s when the Ministry of International Trade and Industry (MITI) used foreign exchange allocation extensively (see Chap. 2). This is because large-scale firms and their workers in Japan had already been able and willing to use new machines, to which new technologies were embodied, and to devise ways of using the machines efficiently.

[1] Policymakers here include technocrats and bureaucrats.

They had acquired such ability and attitude through the productivity movement that the US government allowed to transfer on a full scale from the United State to Japan soon after the outbreak of the Korean War in 1950, considering the strategical importance of Japan (Sonobe 2018). At least for some industries in Japan, the infant industry protection worked well (Komiya et al. 1988).

The concept of developmental states in its incipient period was associated with the infant industry protection policy because the seminal work by Johnson (1982) was based on the observation of the MITI's approach. This policy, however, was not used or did not work in the developing countries that became developmental states later than Japan. In these countries, productivity movement started actively only after Foreign Direct Investment (FDI) began to flow in massively. Until then, their industries were not infant industries in the true sense, and temporary protection, if provided, would not lead considerable productivity improvements. After the massive inflow of FDI began, infant industry protection became unnecessary. This is why we discard the definition of the concept in terms of a specific set of policies or policy instruments. Instead we expect that a developmental state will adopt any policies that are within the constraints and expected to lead its economy to a sustainable growth path.

Turning to the constraint of conflict management, two examples are particularly notable. One is the strategy of "growth first, distribution and stability later," which was pursued by the regime of General Park Chung Hee in Korea. While the strategy delivered surprisingly rapid economic growth, it created confrontation, making the regime increasingly authoritarian, and eventually led to the assassination of Park himself (see Chap. 3). To keep the economy growing, the successor had to make considerable efforts to mitigate confrontation and to increase social cohesion. Another notable example is the leadership of Prime Minister Mahatir of Malaysia. In this country, the "class structure that had crystallized along ethnic lines" before development started, and the leadership had to have "the imagination, resolve, and power to make stability a prerequisite for economic growth and equitably distributed growth a determinant of stability" (see Chap. 5).

Since economic development creates winners and losers, the coordination of conflict is imperative for developmental states to succeed. Political coordination must be more difficult in countries with a deeply divided society as an initial condition. In such countries, demand must be high for strong leadership of a charismatic political leader. Presumably that is why Park Chung Hee, Lee Kuan Yew (both appear in Chap. 3), Suharto (in Chap. 4), Mahatir, Meles (both in Chap. 5), and Kagame (in Chap. 6) among others emerged. Since economic development is intricately linked with conflicts, leadership, and coordination, the title of this volume includes "the Politics of Emerging Economies."

Japan was an exceptional developing country in this respect as well. Of course, political coordination of conflicting interests was important there. The favorable initial conditions, however, allowed it to succeed in high growth without relying on authoritarianism or a charismatic leader. It did not suffer from serious ethnic divide. Democratization, land reform, and fundamental rights for workers among other major changes were realized in the Allied occupation soon after the war. To the extent that the role played by political leaders was small, the role played by bureaucrats, especially those at the MITI, in planning and implementing the development strategy appeared large in this country. Its favorable initial conditions in terms of social cohesion and the ability to improve productivity must have a great bearing on the fact that Japan became the first developing country to enter the ranks of high-income countries.

9.3 What Should We Learn?

The above discussion of the constraints faced by a developmental state implies that it is a daunting task to lead a low- or middle-income country to chase the dream of catching up with high-income countries, unless the country has exceptionally favorable conditions. That is why leaders of developmental states must be nationalists who have a strong will and share it with capable policymakers (see especially Chap. 5). These are just necessary conditions, however. Even with a strong will to serve the country, leaders and policymakers may fail if the constraints are too severe. Even a brilliant, charismatic leader will give up being a developmentalist and instead turn into a predator capturing state resources if it becomes clear that firms are poorly managed, that political institutions are too inefficient, and that the people have only weak sense of social cohesion.

The accumulation of successful and unsuccessful experiences of the developmental states in the past will, however, help leaders of new developmental states draw lessons. Globalization is also creating an environment conducive to the growth of developing economies as discussed in Chap. 1. Increasing international labor mobility may increase remittance to developing countries. Global supply chains provide opportunities for developing countries to work with technologically and managerially advanced countries. Both official development assistances and non-government organizations' activities help human resource development, technology transfer, and finance needed for the growth of developing economies.

From these considerations, it seems natural to hypothesize that the proliferation of developmental state, which started very slowly in the 1970s and 1980s, will accelerate and turn a number of low- and middle-income countries into developmental states, even though it will then decelerate as remaining countries become few. As to the nature of newly emerged developmental states, we may advance a hypothesis that they will be more unfavorably conditioned with deeper ethnic divide, stronger regional rivalry sentiment, lower education attainment and achievement (or poorer quantity and quality of education), and so on.

Another hypothesis is that the public sector of a developmental economy will initially muster human resources to the economic policy department with a view to boosting economic growth and later increase resource allocation to the social policy department to address social equality and cohesion issues. A corollary to this hypothesis is that such a tendency of shifting resource allocation within the public sector will be clearer if the public sector abounds with high-quality human resources. If such resources are scarce, there will be only a few pockets of efficacy in the public sector and little reallocation of resources.

This volume has confirmed that there are several important factors relaxing and tightening the constraints other than the administrative capability of the public sector and managerial and technological capabilities of the private sector. Examples include economic geography and choice of industrial location as discussed in Chap. 7, devolution or decentralization discussed in Chaps. 4, 5, and 8, the availability of different types of technocrats or technologies as discussed in Chap. 4. We may be able to put forth hypotheses linking the nature or type of developmental state with a set of these factors.

There are several interesting and practical questions as to state capacity. For example, what is the effective way to increase the administrative capability of government offices substantially? How about the managerial capabilities of private firms? To what extent does advanced technology, such as artificial intelligence, help to improve the administrative capability? Will the applicability of advanced technology to public administration inevitably increase incentives of developmental states to build surveillance states? Will such application reduce the impetus toward democratization?

Developmental states are a major driver of world development and a cause of major uncertainties in the world. This is because becoming a developmental state is practically the only possible way for a low- or middle-income country to catch up with high-income countries in the presence of market failures, trade barriers, vested interests, and other obstacles. While a developmental state is built for the realization of an economic dream, it is built through political maneuver and coordination, as this volume has reiterated. Thus, we expect that there will be an increasing demand for developmental state studies in the future, and that trans-disciplinary dialogues like this volume will remain a useful approach.

References

Johnson C (1982) MITI and the Japanese miracle: the growth of industrial policy, 1925–1975. Stanford: Stanford UP

Komiya R, Okuno M, Suzumura K (eds) (1988) Industrial policy of Japan. Academic Press Japan, Tokyo

Sonobe T (2018) How Kaizen brightens Africa's future. In: Otsuka K, Jin K, Sonobe T (eds) Applying the kaizen in Africa: a new avenue for industrial development. Palgrave Macmillan, London

Correction to: Developmental State Building

Yusuke Takagi, Veerayooth Kanchoochat, and Tetsushi Sonobe

Correction to:
Y. Takagi et al. (eds.), *Developmental State Building*, Emerging-Economy State and International Policy Studies, https://doi.org/10.1007/978-981-13-2904-3

The original version of the book was inadvertently published with incorrect print ISSN in copyright page, which has now been updated. The book has been updated with the changes.

The updated original version of the book can be found at https://doi.org/10.1007/978-981-13-2904-3

Y. Takagi et al. (eds.), *Developmental State Building*, Emerging-Economy State and International Policy Studies, https://doi.org/10.1007/978-981-13-2904-3_10

Index

Y. Takagi et al. (eds.), *Developmental State Building*, Emerging-Economy State and International Policy Studies, https://doi.org/10.1007/978-981-13-2904-3

The manufacturer's authorised representative in the EU is Springer Nature Customer Service Centre GmbH, Europaplatz 3, 69115 Heidelberg, Germany. If you have any concerns regarding our products, please contact ProductSafety@springernature.com

Printed and bound by CPI Group (UK) Ltd, Croydon, CR0 4YY
25/09/2026
02222892-0002